Elvis
MEETS THE
Beatles

CHRIS HUTCHINS
AND PETER THOMPSON

Neville Ness House

Published in Great Britain in 2016 by
Neville Ness House Ltd

www.nevillenesshouse.com
www.chrishutchins.info
nevillenesshouse@sky.com

ISBN: 978-0993445736
A CIP catalogue record for this book is available from the British Library.

Cover Design by Ebooks by Design
Book Layout by Ebooks by Design www.ebooksbydesign.co

THE STORY

NO ONE LAUGHED more loudly than the King himself when the Beatles' manager Brian Epstein boasted, 'My boys are going to be bigger than Elvis Presley.' It was the early sixties, and Presley, a living legend, appeared unassailable. Yet, in 1964, John, Paul, George and Ringo suddenly topped the American charts – and Beatlemania rolled the King in the greatest rock coup of all time.

Chris Hutchins, then a music journalist in his early twenties, was at the eye of the hurricane as the Beatles swept all before them. No other writer grew as close to the Fab Four from Liverpool as they conquered the world.

As America turned on to the Beatles in a big way during their 1965 tour, Chris Hutchins used his extensive network of connections to master-mind the greatest rock summit meeting ever: a one-and-only rendezvous between the King and the pretenders who were seizing his throne.

With co-author Peter Thompson, Hutchins draws on his own exclusive sources and unpublished archives, as well as FBI files and explosive dossiers from the District Attorney's investigators in Memphis, to probe into the greatest rock story never told – one in which the lives of Elvis Presley and the Beatles became dramatically entwined. They reveal the passions and the powerplay, the corruption and the conspiracies, the vendettas and the vanity behind pop culture's greatest phenomena.

ABOUT THE AUTHOR

THE writer and broadcaster **Chris Hutchins** is an established author of highly acclaimed biographies of the rich, the famous and the royals. His first, *Fergie Confidential*, was an intimate biography of the Duchess of York and chronicled her troubled marriage to the Queen's favourite son, Prince Andrew. He followed this with a revelatory biography of the late Princess of Wales, *Diana's Nightmare: The Family*, a book which so established him as an authority on the royals that he was invited to cover Prince Charles' subsequent marriage for American television. Books that followed include *ATHINA: The Last Onassis*, which probed deeply into the world of the Onassis dynasty and *GOLDSMITH: Money, Women and Power*, the biography of the late billionaire entrepreneur, Sir James Goldsmith. More recently Hutchins turned his attention to matters Russian with fearless biographies of the country's leader, *PUTIN*, and best-known oligarch, *ABRAMOVICH: The billionaire from nowhere*. The author returned to the royal stage with a revealing book about Diana's son, *HARRY: The People's Prince*. Then it was back to rock 'n roll with *THE BEATLES: Messages from John, Paul George and Ringo* which featured on its cover one of the postcards John Lennon sent to the author during his travels and, more recently *ELVIS A Personal Memoir*.

As Prince Charles' former secretary Mark Bolland says of him: 'Chris Hutchins seems to have seen and done it all . . .'

Follow Chris Hutchins on Twitter. ChrisHutchinsFn

Peter Thompson, born in Melbourne, is the author of twenty books including biographies on the Princess of Wales, the Duchess of York, Athina Onassis and Jack Nicholson, all of which were written in collaboration with Chris Hutchins. He lives in London.

CONTENTS

FOREWORD

Chris Hutchins

I FIRST MET the Beatles in Hamburg as a reporter in November 1962. After Beatlemania broke out in Britain, I shared their adventures in the United States in 1964 and 1965.

I had also been a dedicated Elvis fan since boyhood, and had interviewed his manager, Colonel Tom Parker, on the telephone several times. I met him in Los Angeles in the summer of 1964, and the following year I met Elvis at the studios of Paramount Pictures in Hollywood. My purpose all along had been to arrange a meeting between Elvis and the Beatles. I did this by introducing Colonel Parker to Brian Epstein and pointing out the advantages to both camps. However, a reluctant Elvis kept ducking the issue because the Beatles were now so clearly on top. But in September 1964, I did manage to arrange a telephone conversation between him and Paul McCartney. When Elvis finally agreed to meet the Beatles the following summer, I was the only journalist present at that historic meeting at Elvis's Bel Air home on the night of 27 August 1965.

This story, like all my others at the time, appeared in the *New Musical Express*. As I was travelling and living with the Beatles on their tours, all of my reports were aimed at maintaining the group's image in the eyes of their fans. It was only after I had left the *NME* and worked for ten years as a press agent for Tom Jones, Engelbert Humperdinck, Gilbert O'Sullivan and such bands as the Bee Gees, the Moody Blues, Eric

Clapton's Cream, Procol Harum and Status Quo that I could begin to write the real stories I had uncovered in the world of show business.

I had many meetings with Elvis in Las Vegas in the Seventies, and came to know his wife Priscilla, who was by then separated from him and living in Los Angeles.

On the night of 16 August 1977, I heard from Memphis that Elvis was dead. I contacted Peter Thompson, who was editing the *Daily Mirror* that night, and the story caught the *Mirror's* first edition. Thompson cleared the entire front page, and ran my inside account of Elvis's life, 'The King Is Dead', across the centre pages of the next edition. In 1993 and 1994, Thompson and I went to the United States to uncover the real stories behind the events I had witnessed thirty years earlier, which is why this book is written as a first-person account.

Our thanks go to the many people who helped us, particularly Colonel Parker, who guided us as we retraced Elvis's steps from his birthplace in Tupelo, Mississippi, to Memphis, New York, Hollywood and Las Vegas, where the story begins . . . in the Imperial Suite of the Hilton Hotel in February 1973. It was quite a night.

CHAPTER ONE

Vendetta in Vegas

A SAVAGE electrical storm was raging across the Nevada desert when the hired limousine took us from Caesars Palace to the Hilton Hotel where Elvis was appearing. Lightning raked the sky and the neon signs along the Strip blinked moodily in the rain. The night was set for melodrama of a particular showbiz kind.

When the car pulled up, Joe Esposito was waiting to greet Tom Jones and conduct our small group to the Imperial Suite on the 30th floor. Elvis hadn't been expecting us to arrive in Las Vegas, but had been glad to get our phone call. Diamond Joe told us: 'The Boss would really appreciate the company of an old buddy tonight . . . But take it easy,' the head of the Memphis Mafia continued as the lift went up. 'He's got troubles.'

Elvis had been unwinding after his second show when someone had unwisely mentioned John Lennon. It was a bad move. Lennon's name was banned in the King's presence unless it was accompanied by words such as 'Commie' or 'junkie'.

'Lennon?' Elvis had snapped angrily, instantly flaring up. 'You oughta spell that L-e-n-i-n.'

Only those privy to his deepest thoughts knew at that time just how much Elvis hated the former Beatle or to what lengths he had gone to destroy him. If things had been bad for Elvis in 1963 when the Beatles first made their run at his title, they were infinitely worse now, even though the group had broken up. Paul, George and Ringo might not pose a threat any more, but John Lennon mattered more than ever.

To Elvis, he had become a symbol of anti-American activism, a mocking, unwashed, long-haired hero of a drug culture that was threatening the established order of things. In Elvis's eyes, he was a son of Satan, an anti-Christ who believed he was bigger than Jesus.

His judgment distorted by his own drug dependence, Elvis had waged an unrelenting campaign against John ever since they had first fallen out at their one and only meeting back in the Sixties. I remembered that occasion extremely well. I had been responsible for setting it up and had had a ringside seat at the events that took place. Priscilla had been there, too.

We now found Elvis in the suite's vast sunken living room with Charlie Hodge, Jerry Schilling and some of the other Guys. An assortment of party guests, hand-picked because they were either decorative or useful in some other way, were trying unsuccessfully to enliven proceedings. Rain pelted down on the penthouse roof, but the wraparound view of the encircling mountains was excluded by heavy drapes. Elvis was frightened of storms and the music was turned up loud to drown out the pyrotechnics.

We were received warmly enough, although a curtain of Welsh gloom descended on Tom the moment he gauged Elvis's mood. Tom sat down and ran his fingers through his big Afro mop of woolly black hair. He hated to see his friend in emotional pain. The reason was known to anyone with the ability to read or switch on a TV set.

The King's life had been torn apart when Priscilla, his wife of five years, had informed him of her decision to leave the marriage and live with her lover Mike Stone. There was to be no trial separation, no second chance. She had finally come to the conclusion that Elvis's addiction to drugs, prescribed and otherwise, had not only made him unwell but also extremely dangerous.

Priscilla had flown to Las Vegas in February 1972 to give Elvis the bad news. His reaction confirmed her worst fears. After an almost sexless marriage, he had forced her down on his bed and made angry love to her. Priscilla had fled back to Los Angeles, packed her bags and moved out of their Beverly Hills home, taking their daughter Lisa Marie with her. For the past twelve months, Elvis had been alternately suicidal and homicidal.

'Are you still trying to get her back?' asked Tom, settling into a glass of Dom Perignon. 'Do you still talk to her?'

'Every night, Tom. I call her every night. She just keeps on saying it's all over. The divorce is going ahead. This has been one helluva time.'

Elvis's calls to Priscilla had been anything but conciliatory. One night he had threatened to come for Mike Stone with an M-16 rifle, put him up against a wall and execute him. In deep distress, Elvis had stormed around the penthouse with the rifle, ignoring the pleas of his new girlfriend Linda Thompson. He had had to be sedated before someone got seriously hurt.

The way Elvis told it, however, he was the wronged party. Although his own extramarital romps with young girls were an open secret in showbiz circles, the thing that stuck in his craw was that Priscilla had dared to be unfaithful to him. Elvis felt shamed and betrayed. Even worse, she had chosen as her lover Mike Stone, the karate instructor Elvis and I had in common – and he possessed the physique of an Hawaiian Hercules. Her infidelity with this of all men threatened not only Elvis's public image but also his manhood.

Tom identified strongly with Elvis's sense of outrage, although no woman, neither his long-suffering wife Linda nor any of his numerous lovers, had ever left him. He had stayed with Linda and kissed all the others goodbye.

The irony was that, until Priscilla's defection, things had been going promisingly from Elvis's point of view. In January 1972, J. Edgar Hoover, the FBI director for whom Elvis worked as an undercover agent spying on 'subversive' entertainers, had succeeded in having a deportation order served on John Lennon and his second wife, Yoko Ono. Hoover, like Elvis, reasoned that the best way to deal with John's radical cheek was to deny him direct access to its protagonists in America.

'Kick him out and keep him out' was how Elvis put it to the Guys.

But John and Yoko had appealed against the order and, supported by artists, writers, actors and film-makers as well as high-powered attorneys, they were pressing to be granted permanent residence status.

'I think this has something to do with Yoko and me being so outspoken over the Vietnam war,' said John with typical understatement. 'We love it here. Like Mr Nixon in his broadcast on Vietnam, all we are saying is give peace a chance.' And in one bizarre manoeuvre, the Ono Lennons claimed diplomatic immunity on the grounds that they were ambassadors of the 'Cosmic Kingdom of Nutopia'.

Just as the battle had reached the courts, Hoover, the man whom Elvis misguidedly called 'the greatest living American', had died of a massive heart attack. With the chief motivator of the Lennon witch-hunt permanently off the scene, the FBI had started to lose interest. Moreover, the expense of spying on the Lennons, tapping their phones and keeping track of their eccentric movements twenty-four hours a day was simply too high to justify. Elvis had lost his greatest ally, ironically a man who had detested Elvis as much as he had despised John.

If he couldn't have his Cilia back, Elvis wanted two things more than anything else in life: he wanted Mike Stone out of the way, and he wanted John Lennon barred from the United States or, failing that, he wanted John dead. As the rain drummed down on the Imperial Suite beneath the giant red HILTON insignia on the roof, both objectives seemed to be slipping beyond his reach.

At this point, Elvis turned his attention to me. 'Chris,' he said, 'it was you who brought the Beatles to my house, wasn't it? What an asshole John Lennon turned out to be.'

'I had a run-in with him myself,' Tom cut in before I could reply. 'He made some smart-ass remark on a TV show we were doing back in England. I wanted to take him outside and see what sort of a hiding his intellect could stand.'

Tom's grudge brought a smile to Elvis's face, and he called Linda, an athletic Miss Tennessee beauty queen, to join the inner circle. To provide an antidote to Priscilla, his talent-spotter George Klein had introduced them at a private showing at the Memphian Theatre. Now a fully fledged member of the King's flying circus, Linda was aware that Elvis was now high and unpredictable.

'I would see him take as many as twenty or thirty pills during the course of an evening,' she related some time later. 'His behaviour was constantly erratic. His temperament was volatile and variable. He had a bad temper, and sometimes it would be the interaction of the drugs.

'It was basically the Marilyn Monroe/Judy Garland syndrome. He would take sleeping pills to knock himself out and then wake up groggy and take Dexedrine. The erratic behaviour – the bad temper, the shooting-out television sets, that kind of thing – resulted.'

But tonight the TV sets remained intact. There was no gun play, no karate exhibitions with the Guys, no singing competition with Tom Jones, certainly no drug-fuelled orgy. Elvis was in a space that Joe Esposito easily recognized and chose to play down.

'There was erratic behaviour, but it was the life we were leading,' he later explained. 'He had a lot of emotional problems. He'd get angry like anyone else. If he got mad, he might walk off stage. Sure, he did that. But it was down to the work, the emotional stress.' This refusal to see the real problem simply enabled Elvis to get away with even greater excesses.

Joe had met Elvis in the Army in 1959, and as overseer of the entire Presley operation, he had plenty of problems of his own. One of them was Elvis's valet, James Caughley.

'Joe was worried that stories about Elvis's erratic behaviour would get out,' said Caughley, known as Hamburger James or Fetchum Bill because of his menial duties. 'Shooting-out televisions when he didn't like what was on was just the half of it. I have watched Elvis, sitting at the breakfast table at the Hilton with a $22,000 gold engraved pistol in his hand, shooting at the chandelier. Now the Hilton didn't normally complain, but they made him stop that because it was causing a leak.

'One time after he and Linda had been rowing, he got up and started firing the pistol in the bedroom of the Hilton suite, firing at an ornament, a pot owl. Linda was in the bathroom and I was cleaning up the room when that god-damn gun went off. Linda screamed and I called out to her. Her bathroom backed on to the television area where the owl was positioned, and one of the bullets that had missed the owl went straight through the cheap wall and into Linda's bathroom, just missing her.

'Elvis did crazy things, but you can't blame it all on the drugs. He had a very emotional temper and could be riled sick. Nobody would stand up and tell him "No". He was like a little kid sometimes.'

One man who did stand up to Elvis was Henri J. Lewin, vice president of Hilton Hotels, in charge of its hotel/casino operations in Vegas. Lewin was a German Jew who had escaped from the Gestapo. Pop stars, even an armed one, held little terror for him. After he told Elvis to stop ventilating the ceiling, he gave him a few well-chosen words of advice.

'What the hell are you doing to yourself?' asked Lewin.

'You've got millions and all you want to do is lie on a couch, eat hamburgers and sleep. It isn't healthy. Get up and live a normal life.'

'You're a tough man, Mr Lewin,' Elvis replied defensively. 'You're much tougher than my father.'

'Yeah,' snapped Lewin, 'I tell you the truth.'

Henri Lewin told me that, after Priscilla left him, Elvis only lived and breathed for performances such as the one we had missed that night.

'When the band started playing the theme from *2001: A Space Odyssey*, my heart stopped beating and I entered a new dimension of excitement,' he recounted. 'Elvis jumped on stage and propelled himself like a spider to the front of his thirty-piece band. At the top of his voice, he sang, "I can't stop loving you" over the music. Then, to the surprise of 1800 people, he put down the microphone and sang the rest of the song. He had dropped the microphone, but you could still hear every word. Every chandelier in that big room was shaking.

'As I watched him closely, I had the feeling that he was actually under some kind of hypnotic trance during the whole performance, and his father Vernon Presley and the bodyguards were, in turn, under his spell. You could have poked a needle into any one of them and I doubt that they would have felt it.

'Elvis was walking on clouds on stage, but he died as soon as he came off. He was like a zombie.'

Elvis had recovered his equilibrium after a massive injection of a tranquillizer in his dressing room, though the man talking to us now was anything but calm or composed. When chef George Ziros wheeled his late-night meal into the livingroom on a large hot cart, Elvis waved it away. He wanted nothing to eat. What he wanted were solutions and none was forthcoming.

At one point, he retired to his bedroom. He returned even more wired than before. 'You oughta cut back on alcohol,' Elvis told Tom, noticing that his glass had been replenished during his absence. 'It can kill you.'

'I love you, Elvis,' Tom replied reasonably, 'but if you don't stop sticking that stuff up your nose, you won't be around to love much longer.'

He was the only man who could talk to Elvis like that and get away with it.

'It's all right, man,' said Elvis wildly, giving that famous smile. 'I tried everything before John Lennon even knew what a stimulant was.'

The Presleys had first met Tom at the Ilikai Hotel in Hawaii. After his performance one night, Priscilla had astonished the Welsh heart-throb by asking for his autograph. Tom and Elvis had been, in Priscilla's words, 'like a couple of schoolboys together'. When Tom had called on Elvis at his hotel, Priscilla, smiling broadly, had greeted him at the door. 'Elvis has just gone out to buy guitars for the two of you to goof around with,' she said. The three of them had gone to the beach where Elvis, despite the sticky heat, had kept his shirt on. He had been over dieting and was too embarrassed to reveal his scrawny torso in front of the well-muscled, hairy-chested Welshman.

After travelling to Vegas to watch Tom at the Flamingo in 1968, Elvis told him excitedly: 'Man, that was terrific. After seeing you, I want to get back up on stage myself.' This was the origin of Elvis's legendary comeback at the International Hotel (later bought by the Hilton chain), and he owed it to Tom Jones' example.

Off stage, Tom and Elvis put their friendship first, even exchanging rings. Elvis gave Tom a magnificent black sapphire (it later disappeared, along with a young lady, from his hotel bathroom), while Tom reciprocated with a tiger's-eye ring that Elvis had admired. Another Presley gift was a small Bible, on the flyleaf of which he had written a message: the words certainly looked sincere, but no one was ever able to decipher Elvis's handwriting.

There was to be no Bible-reading tonight. Elvis was starting to nod, his speech to slur. Sonny West, his friend and bodyguard, remembers Elvis being 'totally out of it on the couch in the living-room of his suite. I made a comment to a couple of the other guys that I wished we could film him to show him what he looked like,' he said later. 'He was sitting up and his eyes were closed and it seemed like they were lead weights. It made me think of Demerol because, when I had a back operation, I had Demerol. I had the doctor take me off it because I would lay there with my eyes closed in a euphoric twilight zone, but I also hallucinated. Elvis *looked* like I had *felt*:

At 4.00 am, we decided it was time to return to Caesars Palace, leaving the King to brood among the Guys until he passed out.

I was left to reflect on the unpleasant fact that the most celebrated rendezvous in the history of rock music had given rise to a highly dangerous feud between Elvis Presley and John Lennon, once the King's greatest fan. I had been aware of the bad feeling between them at the time, but the intensity of Elvis's rage was frightening. He seemed capable of just about anything.

Only after FBI files, which had been kept secret for twenty years, were finally opened was I able to find proof of his duplicity. Until then, it had just seemed like so much wild talk, despite the fact that Elvis had told Tom he had visited President Nixon in the White House and been appointed a special drug enforcement agent. When Tom had expressed disbelief, Elvis produced a badge from the Bureau of Narcotics and Dangerous Drugs and written credentials empowering him to identify himself as an agent of the Bureau. Elvis took it all very seriously. One of his greatest ambitions was to bust John Lennon, identified in another FBI memo as 'a heavy user of narcotics'. With Elvis's own drug use clearly out of control, Tom Jones told me: 'Elvis should have arrested himself.'

The FBI files reveal that, in a private conversation with Federal agents on New Year's Eve 1970, Elvis denounced the Beatles and directed J. Edgar Hoover's attention towards John Lennon in particular.

Presley indicated that he is of the opinion that the Beatles laid the groundwork for many of the problems we are having with young people by their filthy unkempt appearances and suggestive music while entertaining in this country during the early and middle 1960s.

Thus disclosed a confidential FBI memorandum obtained under the US Freedom of Information Act.

After Elvis's intervention, Hoover had ordered an immediate update of all files relating to John Lennon, and the surveillance operation against Lennon had moved into a higher gear.

So it was true. But why? In some ways, both men were unnervingly similar. Was it simply a case of like magnetic poles repelling one another? Or was John just a symptom of a deeper ailment inside Elvis?

Both men had been raised as the only children of weak fathers who lived, and influential mothers who were taken from them. Vernon Presley had served time in prison for forging a cheque, while Freddie Lennon had spent three months behind bars for stealing a bottle of vodka. When John's mother, Julia Stanley, a slim, vivacious redhead, had wed ship's steward Freddie in 1938, she had mischievously put down her occupation on the marriage certificate as 'cinema usherette'; it was to be an illusory marriage. Two years later, at 6.30 on the evening of 9 October 1940, John Winston Lennon was born at the Maternity Hospital, Liverpool, during a heavy German air raid. Torn between an adorable but inadequate mother and an appealing but footloose father, John was damaged for life.

Julia was knocked down and killed by a car on 15 July 1958, just a month before Gladys Presley was to die of her alcoholism in a Memphis hospital. John was 17, Elvis 23. Julia's death almost destroyed the Beatle, who had just been getting to know his mother again after years of estrangement. 'I was in a sort of blind rage for two years,' he said. 'I was either drunk or fighting.' His mother's rejection of him had driven John since childhood: 'The only reason I went for that goal [to be a star] is that I wanted to say, "Now, Mummy, will you love me?" '

Elvis tried to throw himself into Gladys's grave, sobbing: 'Oh God, everything I have is gone. I lived my whole life for you.' Later, he said: 'She was very close, more than a mother. She was a friend who would let me talk to her any hour of the day or night if I had a problem.'

The singer Patti Page recalls that, whenever she met Elvis in Las Vegas or Hawaii, her very presence would remind him of Gladys. 'I was his mother's favourite singer and I know he took her death extremely badly because that was his love,' she told me. 'Elvis used to ask me to sing her favourite songs for him, one of which was "Down the Trail of

Broken Hearts". I always thought he had a sad quality about him. You always noticed some sadness in him.'

After that, there were the aunts – Delta Mae for Elvis and Mimi for John – who doted on the two young men but never made up for the loss. Both men were plagued by a morbid fascination with death, Elvis taking his obsession to the extreme of visiting a Memphis morgue to look at the bodies of the departed.

Both men had been outsiders, shunned at school, who had turned to music as an outlet for pent-up emotions. Hearing 'Heartbreak Hotel' had changed John's life. 'Nothing really affected me until I heard Elvis,' he said. 'If there hadn't been Elvis, there would not have been the Beatles.' Both saw themselves as products of society's basement. Even when he was worth millions, Elvis still liked to describe himself as 'a poor country boy from Tennessee', while John, with all his riches, identified himself as a working-class hero opposed to wealth and privilege.

Both men had married young sweethearts – John to Cynthia Powell, Elvis to Priscilla Beaulieu – fathered a single child and seen their marriages end messily and unhappily in the divorce courts. Both men used hard drugs and sex as an escape from the unbearable reality of being. Hookers were frequently called in to give them a quick fix of erotic fantasy. Their attitude to any woman who couldn't be categorized as either a virgin or a mother was equally sick. Both became physically violent to women who upset them. 'I was a hitter,' confessed John. 'I fought men and I hit women.' Most telling of all, John's nickname for Yoko was 'Mother', while Elvis called Linda Thompson 'Mummy'.

John was extrovert yet mystical, a searcher for truth in strange places; Elvis secretive yet spiritual, an embracer of gospels and mystic texts. John the born leader, forceful, dominant, a master of words, some of his songs full of the violent outpourings of a disturbed mind; Elvis the loner surrounded by yes-men, polite, generous, a master of lyrics, his songs making even heartbreak sound exciting. It was indicative of their personalities that John should become the Walrus of Lewis Carroll's creations, while Elvis forever remained the Hound Dog of lowly esteem.

The motivating force the two shared in common, the well-spring that fed poison into their systems, came from deep down in their psyches. It stemmed from a self-centred fear that was more powerful than family, money or fame. Envious of each other and jealous of their own stardom, they had turned their mutual hostility into a contest of wills, an Olympian battle of the egos.

In Elvis's psychotic mind, his resentment was magnified into a war between ideologies: capitalism versus Communism, the forces of good fighting a diabolical evil. To John, it became a crusade for peace and justice in a troubled and unjust world in which Elvis was just another shop-soiled loser.

Even while he was fighting for his green card during 1972, John had gone into the studio and recorded *Some Time in New York City*, which was devoted to the highly explosive political causes he supported. He was incapable of compromise, only getting out of the ring when his lawyers advised him to exercise a little more restraint. 'I thought it was my duty to save the world,' he told me when we met up in Los Angeles in 1974.

Elvis and John achieved so much yet lost their lives in the process. Now, thirty years after they met, the sadness of it is that two men who could have been the greatest of friends ended up mortal enemies.

CHAPTER TWO

Memphis to The Mersey

INTERSTATE 55 follows the curve of the Mississippi through bare winter woods, thickets of billboards and acres of fuel storage tanks. It connects with US Highway 51 (now Elvis Presley Boulevard) near a drainage canal not far from Hernando's Hideaway, where a much younger Elvis had met the obliging blonde who had taken his virginity.

This is Memphis, Tennessee, the place Elvis called home. When he came back from his Army stint in Germany, somebody asked him what he had missed about Memphis and he had replied with one word: '*Everything!*' Memphis was his kind of town. 'He was one of us,' Memphian Mimi Phillips explained proudly. 'He never got too grand for his home town.'

Named after the ancient Egyptian city, the Memphis of the American Nile had survived fever, famine and floodtide. Originally built as a fort on the Fourth Chickasaw Bluff overlooking a grand sweep of the Mississippi, the fledgling outpost had been fought over by the Indians, the Spanish, the French and the English until, properly named by General James Winchester in 1819 and dignified by a town plan, it had dusted itself down, placed a shingle above the porch and declared itself open for business.

The Memphis of the Old South had the 'War between the States' and the Klan, a few heroes like Rhett Butler and even fewer heroines like Scarlett O'Hara. It had a flourishing Cotton Row, unspeakable Jim Crow laws and inevitable race riots. It had the corrupt 'Boss' Crump for mayor,

Davy Crockett as its one-time Congressman and an unenviable reputation as the murder capital of America.

Most important of all, especially as far as Elvis Presley was concerned, Memphis had Beale Street and the blues – the genuine, original W. C. Handy *Memphis* blues. 'Mr Crump don't 'low no easy-riders here,' the Father of the Blues had trumpeted in Pee-Wee's saloon. Easy-riders apart, Mr Crump allowed just about everything else in the way of pool halls, pawn shops, bordellos, honky-tonks and jive joints. Jazz and blues in one form or another – rhythm and blues – flowed into Memphis from St Louis in the north, New Orleans in the south and all points on the harmonic compass in between. R&B, the black sound waiting for a white voice to take it out of the ghetto, gave birth to rock 'n' roll and Elvis had been its liberator.

He had travelled a long, hard road from his birthplace, a two-room shotgun shack set in woodland on the dusty Old Saltillo Road on the east side of Tupelo, Mississippi. The rags-to-riches script was by Tennessee Williams out of Marvel Comics: Orpheus ascending like Captain Marvel Jr in a flash of lightning from the southern poverty trap. 'I identified with the hero in every comic book I ever read,' Elvis recalled. Captain Marvel Jr was his favourite. 'I could say we lived on the wrong side of the tracks, but in those days in Tupelo, there wasn't really a right side of the tracks. No one was eating too good. We never starved, but we were close to it at times.'

Elvis's mother had been born Gladys Love Smith on 25 April 1912, into a poor family in neighbouring Pontotoc County. Of the five surviving Smith sisters, Gladys was the most striking, a dark, slender beauty who loved flirting and dancing. Her father, Robert Lee Smith, made the best moonshine in the county, a talent that attracted the disapproval of the authorities. They ran him out of Pontotoc and he moved his family to a house in Lee County, four miles from Tupelo, where Gladys fell madly in love with a tall, fair-haired farm worker called Vernon Elvis Presley. It is an ironic truth that, if it hadn't been for 'white lightning', the couple would never have met when they did and Elvis Presley would never have existed.

When Gladys was 21 and Vernon had just turned 17, the couple eloped. They went to Pontotoc County to get a marriage licence because the groom was too young to marry legally in Lee County. Gladys claimed on the licence that she was only 19, the start of a deception about her real age that she maintained all her life. Vernon's age shot up to 22 for the sake of appearances, but no one seemed to care. The young lovers were married on 17 June 1933, at Verona, a few miles south of Tupelo. It was a very physical union.

Elvis was born at 4.35 am on 8 January 1935, half an hour after his twin brother, who had been delivered still-born. Elvis Aron (he later changed it to the biblical Aaron) was to say of Jesse Garon: 'They say that, when one twin dies, the other grows up with all the qualities of the other, too. If I did, I'm lucky.'

However, the main thing Elvis owed to his brother was not luck but fear about his own mortality and a deep sense of guilt that he had lived while the first-born had been chosen to die. To justify his own existence, Elvis knew from a very early age that he had to be the perfect child. Jesse might lie buried in a shoebox in an unmarked grave at Priceville cemetery, but Elvis and Gladys talked to him constantly. Jesse was always with them in spirit.

The early bonding of grieving mother, anguished son and celestial twin produced a form of co-dependence that crippled Elvis all his emotional life. As soon as he could speak, he started calling his mother 'Sattnin' and both his parents were 'My babies'.

Janelle McComb, a poet and neighbour who nursed the infant Elvis, remembers first encountering him during a visit to a Tupelo beauty parlour.

'Gladys was getting a perm under the hair-drier and Vernon was sitting on the steps holding Elvis,' she told me at her home in East Tupelo, which had since been elevated to 'Presley Heights'. 'Vernon's hair was really light and somebody came in and said, "There is some old white-haired man sitting outside holding a baby that's screaming his head off." Gladys jumped up and said, "That's Elvis!"

'I followed her out to take a look at the baby and that was my first introduction to Elvis Presley. The first time I met him he was looking up at me and crying, and the last time I saw him I was looking down at him and crying. It was forty-two years later, on the day of his funeral. All Elvis ever wanted was for somebody to love him.'

When Elvis was an impressionable 3-year-old, the relationship between mother and son became even more intense after Vernon was sentenced to three years' imprisonment at Parchman prison farm on the Mississippi Delta for altering the amount on a cheque from $4 to $40 to buy food.

'I used to go with Gladys and Elvis to see Vernon, and there were other people from here that went, too.' said Janelle McComb. 'We used to get on a yellow school bus and ride down to Parchman – it was a big outing. Let me tell you, we had a way of turning adversity into a fun thing in those days.'

As prisoners were granted conjugal rights, the physical side of the Presleys' marriage continued in the grim setting of a prison hut while Elvis played with the children of other inmates. Pleading family hardship, Vernon was paroled after serving only nine months, but the shame of his incarceration haunted the family. For the rest of their lives, Vernon, Gladys and Elvis feared that this terrible secret would become public and ruin his career. It never did. Tupelo kept its mouth loyally shut. Desperately poor, the Presleys found that the only reliable solution to life's problems was to be found in the Gospels, both written down and sung out loud.

Elvis had inherited a good singing voice from both his parents, a sense of rhythm from Gladys and his blond good looks from Vernon. He learned to play the guitar that his parents had given him for his tenth birthday and sing songs like 'Old Shep'.

'I remember Elvis crossing the levee carrying his lunch in an old molasses bucket,' said Janelle McComb. 'He was going to the Lyric Theater, where Mr John Glower had a talent show every Saturday morning. Anybody could go and do their act: play the comb, sing, dance or whatever. That particular Saturday, Mr Johnny looked at Elvis and said, "Elvis, what are you going to sing?" And Elvis said, "I'm going to play 'There's a Hole in the Bucket'." And Mr Johnny said, "Do you know it?" And Elvis said, ' "Sure I do – and there really is a hole in my bucket." He was around 10 at the time.'

The Presley's first home, which Vernon had built with his own sweat on a $180 loan, had been repossessed while he was in prison, and the family now lived near the black Shakerag district of Tupelo. It was here that Elvis first heard the blues. Steaming up from the bayous, distilled in the cotton fields and scented with a whiff of honeysuckle, the bitter-sweet sounds flowed out of the ghetto in the sweltering hush of evening.

Black blues, white country and multi-racial gospel were the sounds of Elvis's childhood and he drew upon them all in his music. He loved the country numbers he heard on WELO, the local radio station, which featured the brother of one of his classmates, an itinerant singer called Mississippi Slim. Elvis followed his hero around Tupelo like any other kid and picked up some new chords. On Sundays, he joined Vernon and Gladys singing hymns at the First Assembly of God church on Adams Street.

'Since I was 2 years old, all I knew was gospel music. That was music to me,' Elvis recalled. 'We borrowed the style of our psalm singing from the early Negroes. We used to go to these religious singings all the time. The preachers cut up all over the place, jumping on the piano, moving every which way. The audience liked them, and I guess I learned from them.'

At the age of 3, Elvis had climbed on to his first stage, the choir platform of the church, where he clapped his hands in time to the music.

'He was too young to know the words, but he could keep the tune,' said Gladys.

Elvis was a true believer from childhood, says Janelle McComb, who now keeps his memory alive at his birthplace on Elvis Presley Drive. 'He placed his talent in the hands of God, God touched it and that talent became so magnified that the entire world knew him by his first name,' she said.

According to Vernon Presley, he had passed out at the moment of Elvis's conception, and he told of how a mystical blue light had appeared in the sky above his home on the night of the birth. The infant had seemed to be bathed in light as he struggled for life in the makeshift crib. 'Could it have been for me?' Elvis was to ask. He came to believe that it was, uttering the mystifying words at his last concert: 'I was – and I am.'

Elvis not only became a great singer, a great entertainer and a great personality but also great icon, virtually a religion in his own right, he was, said his musical mentor Sam Phillips, an avatar, or messenger from God signalling the Second Coming. 'We've lost the most popular man who ever walked on this planet since Christ was here himself,' Carl Perkins said in homage.

Janelle McComb observed: 'The Elvis I knew was as gentle as the wind that blows across your cheeks, as compassionate as a benevolent priest, but he could be tempered with steel if somebody stepped on his blue suede shoes. Underneath it all he had a heart that conquered the entire world.

'Everybody asks, "Why do you think the legend still lives?"'

And the answer is that, when Elvis Presley walked on that stage, that little clerk in the audience instantly became the office manager. He gave hope and inspiration to all of those who dream the impossible dream.

'I never knew the superstar in the rhinestone cape. I knew the young boy from Tupelo in the denim jeans who looked at his daddy and said, "Some day I'm going to buy you and Mama the biggest house you can buy."'

When the Presleys did eventually leave Tupelo, it was very much a matter of necessity. Like his father-in-law Bob Smith, Vernon had become involved in the moonshine racket, although his role was that of delivery man for another bootlegger. He was caught by the sheriff, put in the cells and told he could either get out of town or face the consequences. Vernon didn't need any further prompting. After one stretch in prison, the last thing he wanted was any more trouble with the law. Hastily, he gathered up his terrified wife and shy 13-year-old son and headed across the Tallahatchie River on US Highway 78 bound for Memphis, 104 miles to the north.

'We were broke, man, broke, and we left Tupelo overnight,' said Elvis later to explain how he became a Memphian. 'Dad packed all our belongings in boxes and put them on the top and in the trunk of a 1939 Plymouth. We just headed to Memphis. Things had to be better.'

Leaving the hill country behind, Highway 78 cut through the Holly Springs national forest, where great growths of kudzu vine snaked up the trees, the road emerging into green pasture as it neared the Mississippi in Shelby County, Tennessee.

In the autumn of 1948 when the Presleys arrived, the 'Bluff City' was a tough metropolis of 300,000 people. The family encountered more hard times, but at least they were travelling in the right direction. In the Old South, there was hunger, hardship and wounded pride. In the North, there was money, glamour and the promise of a new beginning. Memphis was halfway between the two.

The Presleys lived in a variety of homes, the most wretched of which was a one-room, rat-infested slum at 572 Poplar Avenue, and the most famous a red brick, two-bedroom, ground-floor apartment at 185 Winchester Avenue on a Federal housing project called Lauderdale Courts. Elvis attended the L. C. Humes High School on Manassas Street in North Memphis, Gladys escorting him the few blocks there every day until he was 15. A head-down swagger disguised the fact that he was self-conscious about an outbreak of adolescent pimples, and his face and back were to be badly marked by acne scars. Gladys told him to hold his head up. 'You might come from poor country people,' she told him, 'but you're as good as anybody.'

Bullied for being a mother's boy, Elvis affected the appearance of a screen hoodlum by adopting a Tony Curtis hairstyle and wearing flashy punk clothes. This enraged his crewcut classmates. According to Elvis, they would chase him down the street, shouting: 'Hot dang, let's get him – he's a squirrel, he's a squirrel, get him, he just come down outta the trees!' But he could play the guitar, he could sing and he could dream. 'In those days, he was lost in dreams,' said his friend Marty Lacker.

After three-and-a-half years, the family had to move once more because the combined earnings of Gladys, who worked as a nurse's aide at the nearby St Joseph Hospital, and Vernon, who packed tins of paint into boxes at the United Paint Company, exceeded the maximum $3000 a year allowed to those living on the housing project.

They were evicted in early 1953, the year Eisenhower was sworn into the White House and Marilyn Monroe was elected America's favourite pin-up. The middle-class certainties of the Ike era, which included the flourishing new suburbs of Memphis, did not extend to the Presleys. Gladys could only rave about the first pink Cadillac she had ever seen while walking home from the hospital. 'I'll buy you one of those one day,' her son promised, and he meant it.

The Presleys' next abode was a dilapidated, two-room apartment at 398 Cypress Street in the centre of town. But before Elvis graduated from Humes High later that year, they had found a slightly nicer, though still down-at-heel, place at 462 Alabama Avenue, just across the street from Lauderdale Courts.

'When I met Elvis, he was living on Alabama Avenue in a rough apartment-type house,' the Memphis-born singer/guitarist Johnny Burnette told me in 1962, two years before his death. 'You looked in the front door and saw straight out through the back. I must have seen it a million times, but he wouldn't ever let me go inside. No, sir, me and

Elvis were pretty good friends, but he never let me go inside that house – only look.

'He used to wear the wildest clothes. He always seemed to be wearing those purple pants with black stripes down the side, white buck shoes and a white sports jacket. He'd always have his shirt collar turned up and wear his hair real long.

'There was never anything false about him. He didn't talk much, but he knew what he was capable of doing. Wherever he went, he'd have his guitar slung across his back – never did he bother with a case like the rest of us boys. He used to go down to the fire station and sing to the boys there – they were the only ones round Memphis who seemed to have a lot of listening time.

'Every now and then he'd go into one of the cafes or bars and slouch across a chair. He never sat up straight, he'd just sort of lie there with that mean look on his face. Then some folk would say, "Let's hear you sing, boy," and old El would stroll up to the most convenient spot, looking at the ground all the time. Then all of a sudden he'd slide that guitar round to his front and he'd near raise the roof with that real rockin' sound of his.'

Some of the dives Elvis frequented were on Beale Street, which had smartened itself up since its notorious heyday. Encouraged by bribes, Boss Crump had turned a blind eye to its iniquities for thirty years until he shut it down overnight in 1940 as a wartime measure.

After the war, Memphis became a recording centre for musicians heading for Chicago or Nashville, and Beale Street was back in business as the natural habitat of all species of the blues. By this time, Elvis was sure that music was the key to his salvation.

He had always had part-time jobs to bring in extra money, including employment as an usher at Loew's State Theater, but there was rarely ever enough. After graduating, he drove a truck for Crown Electric for $35 a week, but his prospects were no better than those of any other young man with sideburns, an engaging smile and a headful of dreams. There had to be another way.

'When I was 18, I saw my dad sitting on the edge of the bed with his head in his hands,' Elvis recalled. 'Things were going so bad he couldn't see his way out. I prayed for a miracle and my prayer was answered.'

Even at 18 as Elvis flashed his new pink and black threads from Lansky Brothers, he was really going for it on Beale. Once he got behind a guitar, sex was his talisman and he wore it like a mantle in the dives where he played with the bluesmen. 'Sex is part of nature,' Marilyn Monroe had sighed. 'I go along with nature.' Elvis seemed to concur. He might have been unsure of his natural, God-given talent, but he knew where to go to express it, and, like Marilyn, he was a fast learner.

The sexual vibes came through when Elvis sang. He experimented with his range from deep primitive to high-pitched falsetto, scaling octaves like an opera singer. The physical exertion of moving while he played and sang produced the breathy quality that would make him famous.

The Mississippi Delta, so the locals say, begins in the baroque lobby of the Peabody Hotel on Union Avenue. A dozen blocks away at No. 706, Sam Phillips opened the Memphis Recording Service in January 1950 in time to greet the new decade. Half of the population of Memphis was black, and three of his early recording artists were B. B. King, Howlin' Wolf and Little Junior Parker.

Sun Records, Sam's own label, was only two years old when he recorded Elvis for the first time in July 1954 with two country musicians, Scotty Moore on guitar and Bill Black on bass. They cut four songs, but it was 'That's All Right (Mama)', the Arthur 'Big Boy' Crudup number enhanced by a haunting slapback echo, that launched Elvis on his singing career. Crudup was black, and Elvis, for one, had no illusions about the origins of his music. 'The coloured folk been singin' and playin' just the way I'm doin' now, man, for more years than I know,' he said in 1957. 'Nobody paid it no mind till I goosed it up.'

When Elvis laid down the up-tempo ballad 'Blue Moon of Kentucky' as the flip side of 'That's All Right', Sam Phillips let him know that he had finally discovered his unique talent. 'Fine, *fine*, man, hell, that's different!' enthused the studio boss. 'That's a pop song now, little guy. That's good.' They were the sweetest words Elvis had ever heard.

The money started coming in. His first royalty cheque from Sam Phillips amounted to $200, and he spent it on a dress and some shoes for Gladys. Her feet were too swollen from years of neglect to wear the fashionable footwear, so she kept them in a plastic bag under her bed.

Elvis was determined to give his parents everything money could buy: a new four-room rented home, made of brick, on Lamar Avenue, a better car and more food than they could eat. Old-time religion and the new-fangled music, which DJ Alan Freed had renamed 'rock 'n' roll', brought earthly rewards that the Presleys had previously only studied in catalogues or shop windows. Material things that could take away the misery assumed a religious significance in Elvis's mind.

In mid-1955, he moved the family to a three-storey house at 1414 Getwell Street with a lawn in the front and back. Luxuries that were to follow, such as air-conditioning and a swimming pool, were gifts from God and they were within reach. Keep praying and He might give your mother a pink Cad.

When Elvis started to find work out of town as a singer, Gladys fretted so much that he might come to harm driving down the dark country roads that she turned to alcohol to calm her fears. Vernon took her to bars, where she drank beer and tried to socialize, but the fear always came back in the morning. It remained until Elvis walked safely in the front door.

'She wasn't used to the music or entertainment business and she was worried about her boy,' said Todd Morgan, the resident Elvisologist at Graceland. 'It was bewildering, traumatic and overwhelming for her. I'm sure that this was happening so fast it was frightening.'

Gladys put on a great deal of weight and deep, dark circles formed around her panda-like eyes. Her doctor prescribed diet pills and sleeping medication.

'Gladys had a tremendous influence in turning Elvis into a very polite and courteous southern gentleman, but she was very concerned that something might happen to him,' said the Memphis disc jockey George Klein, who had met Elvis in high school. 'She said to me, "George, Elvis has this habit of sleepwalking. If it happens, you just talk to him softly. You say, 'Come back to bed, Elvis, everything is going to be OK.' And if he talks in his sleep, you answer him and carry on a conversation with him." It happened a couple of times when we were on the road in the early Fifties. I did exactly as she had said, and it worked. He went back to bed.

'The other thing Gladys said was, "When you get in the hotel, Elvis has this tendency to leave his money in his pockets, maybe two or three hundred dollars. When you send his clothes down to the cleaners, be sure you go through his pockets and get the money out." I thought that was kinda cute.'

Everything changed for Elvis when he met the flamboyant Colonel Tom Parker, a virtual Barnum & Bailey rolled into one. In a flash of inspiration, the Colonel decided that he had been born for the sole purpose of running Elvis's career. To be on the safe side, he took chance out of the equation. From the beginning, the Colonel marketed his eager young charge in the manner of a carnival attraction.

'You stay talented and sexy and I'll make us both rich as rajahs,' he promised. He seemed to see Elvis as an exponent of writhing male burlesque set to strangled guitars and thumping bass, more a curiosity than a musician. But what his methods might have lacked in finesse, they made up for in results.

'I met Elvis backstage and became his manager in the fall of 1955,' said the Colonel, whose previous musical experience had been with the country singers Eddy Arnold and Hank Snow. 'In those days, he was on the *Louisiana Hayride*. He was being booked into small towns where he went in and got $200 a time, and that went on for a while until I got him on to television and it all blew up nationwide.'

Actually, the Colonel's first master stroke had been to buy out Elvis's Sun contract and sell the recording rights to RCA Victor for $25,000 and the music publishing rights to Hill & Range for $15,000. With a $5000 royalty settlement from Sam Phillips in his back pocket, Elvis got to work with producer Steve Sholes at the RCA studio in Nashville, a converted church, where he warmed up by singing hymns. Then he went out and spent the money on a pink Cadillac for his mother, even though she couldn't drive.

Two days after his twenty-first birthday, he recorded 'Heartbreak Hotel' with Scotty and Bill plus Chet Atkins on rhythm guitar, D. J. Fontana on drums and Floyd Cramer on piano. Sholes laid on so much echo that the song sounded as though it had been recorded in a catacomb.

Elvis made his first television appearance on *Stage Show,* the TV showcase of the ailing jazz brothers Tommy and Jimmy Dorsey, on 28 January 1956. His first number was a medley of 'Shake, Rattle and Roll' and 'Flip, Flop and Fly'. He gave the two Big Joe Turner million-sellers such a wallop that it seemed as if the truck driver from Crown Electric had been plugged into the main circuit. For sheer audacity, that first performance was not so much a debut for Elvis as an initiation of the incredulous TV millions into what was to come. His face was podgy, his brownish-blond hair was dishevelled and his teeth, later capped, were in need of attention, but the screaming had started the moment he began to shake his left leg. Elvis was invited back five more times, although it wasn't until the third show that he let rip with 'Heartbreak Hotel'.

The reaction was phenomenal. 'Heartbreak Hotel' became his first No. 1 hit and went on to become the biggest-selling single of the year. Other TV moguls could no longer ignore the pulling power of 'Elvis the Pelvis', a title that Elvis hated from the moment he heard it. In March, he left New York and drove to Los Angeles to play the Coliseum and then went down to San Diego in early April to appear on the *Milton Berle Show*, which was being transmitted from the aircraft carrier *Hancock*. He also played two concerts at the San Diego Arena, where 'the effect on bobby soxers was like that of Frank Sinatra's old black magic days,' according to the *Memphis Press-Scimitar*. 'The arena manager had to call out police and a platoon of Shore Patrol to handle the mob which pursued Elvis to a barricaded dressing room.'

In the audience on one of those two nights was a young girl destined to become the sex symbol of another decade: Raquel Welch. She has never forgotten the impact that seeing Elvis perform 'Heartbreak Hotel' made on her.

'The first time I saw Elvis was at a show he gave in San Diego when I was only about 14 and still a virgin,' she told me. 'The only thing I knew about sex was girl talk, but when I saw this raw sensual package called Elvis up there on stage, I felt something stir within me, and I said, "My God, this is it! This must be what sex is all about." He was *that* exciting.'

On his second outing for Berle, Elvis gave a performance of 'Hound Dog' that caused a national scandal. Shoulders hunched in a drape jacket, he seemed to pivot on tiptoe and hang there, gyrating, as though suspended at the end of invisible wires. It was his sexiness on this show that damned him to everlasting fame.

For his next TV appearance, Steve Allen tried to calm things down by dressing Elvis in white tie and tails and getting him to sing 'Hound Dog' to a woeful basset called Sherlock. Elvis hated the gimmick, later calling it 'the most ridiculous performance of my entire career', but even standing still, he pushed the show's ratings past those of Allen's arch rival, Ed Sullivan. The latter had stated publicly that he would never book Elvis on the grounds that his act was obscene. Ratings, however, spoke louder than morality, and Sullivan signed him for three shows.

The only setback that Elvis suffered in his first year of living famously was an ill-advised booking that the Colonel had made for him to play the New Frontier Hotel in Las Vegas. 'He was the opening act for a Mickey Mouse band called Freddie Martin in the Venus Room,' Liberace's manager Seymour Heller told me. 'He was bombing because the older customers didn't know him and the kids couldn't get in because they were under 21. Lee [Liberace] had heard him on the radio a lot and he said to me, "This kid Elvis Presley is great. I'd like to meet him." We went over to the Frontier that afternoon and I introduced them. An agency photographer was called in to snap some pictures, and Lee said to Elvis, "Let's swap jackets, you play piano and I'll play guitar." That picture went around the world three times. Lee was gentle, generous and good-hearted, but he was also clever. He never let anyone go without an autograph unless he was running for a plane.' However, Liberace's generosity failed to rescue Elvis in Las Vegas. He was dropped down the billing and the Colonel finally tore up the contract so that Elvis could leave the desert and head for greener pastures. Seymour Heller recalls: 'I met Elvis many times after that and he'd always say, "Nice to see you, Mr Heller." I'd tell him to call me Seymour, and he'd say, "Sure thing, Mr Heller, OK, Mr Heller." He was polite, sometimes over-polite, but he was one of the nicest gentlemen I ever met.'

Elvis dyed his hair black, and *Variety* gave him the title 'King of Rock 'n' Roll', to which he replied: 'There is only one King and that is Jesus.' Even in second place, Elvis had no complaints about his sudden popularity. Hal Wallis, the film producer of *Casablanca* fame, had signed him to a seven-year deal with Paramount Pictures, saying that, in his screen test, Elvis had reminded him of a young Errol Flynn. However, the year's hectic schedule of recording, touring and making his first film, *Love Me Tender,* with Debra Paget and Richard Egan, had made Elvis ill. He had been taking Benzedrine to keep him going, and sleep became more of a problem than sleepwalking. 'I'm six feet tall and weigh 195 pounds – I've gained about twenty pounds in the last year,' he said at the time. 'I can't understand that because my appetite isn't as good as it used to be. I can't seem to relax ever and I have a terrible time falling to sleep.

At the most, I usually get two or three hours of broken sleep.' Sleeping pills were prescribed to knock him out. The Marilyn Monroe/Judy Garland syndrome had begun.

When John Lennon was just climbing out of short pants, Elvis knew that the miracle he had prayed for was coming true. He said: 'My daddy and I were laughing about it the other day. He looked at me and said, "What happened, El? The last thing I can remember is I was working in a can factory and you were driving a truck." It just caught us up.'

Elvis had recorded 'Hound Dog', his first Jerry Leiber and Mike Stoller rocker, during a session at the RCA studio at 155 East 24th Street in New York City. He put down thirty takes and was pleading to do it one more time when the engineers turned out the lights and went home. Steve Sholes was satisfied that he had a massive hit in the can, but Elvis the perfectionist still wanted to make it better.

'My first meeting with Elvis was in summer 1956 when he came to the office of Hill & Range in New York with Colonel Parker,' said Freddie Bienstock, the manager of Elvis's music publishing company. 'It was at the time he was recording "Hound Dog" and doing the *Steve Allen Show*. He was staying at the Warwick Hotel and I chauffeured him around Manhattan. I also remember walking with him down the street and he had a kind of white sports coat and there were lipstick marks on it from girls who had obviously tried to kiss him.

'I got to know him better when I went down to Memphis just before Christmas when he was planning his second picture, *Loving You*. He picked me up from the airport with some of his gang and brought me to the house in Audubon Drive.'

Elvis had paid $40,000 for the new green ranch-style house with a tiled grey roof and black shutters at 1034 Audubon Drive. There were two Cadillacs (one pink) in the carport. This was the Presleys' first Christmas in a home they could truly call their own, and they were in a mood to celebrate. Elvis and Gladys had bought the biggest tree they could fit into the living room.

'The first thing I remember is that Elvis asked me to sit down in a particular chair,' said Freddie Bienstock. 'Unbeknownst to me, he pulled a switch and the chair started to vibrate wildly. The sensation was such that I was scared, but he said, "It's very relaxing, Freddie, I'm very proud of this chair. I want you to enjoy it."

'That night Hal Kanter, who was directing *Loving You* for Paramount, came to the house for dinner,' Freddie related. 'Elvis had a maid at the time called Petunia who was very nervous about cooking for a Hollywood director. The food was southern deep fried, but there was nothing to drink on the table, not even water. Kanter asked Elvis politely if he could have some water. Elvis was embarrassed and screamed, "Petunia! Water!" The maid was so nervous she brought in a pitcher of water with ice but no glasses.

'So Kanter kept looking at this and didn't know what he should do. When Elvis realized what the problem was, he screamed, "Petunia, you forgot the glasses!" Kanter said, "It's all right – a straw will do."'

Elvis was due to appear on the *Louisiana Hayride* at Shreveport. Hal Kanter was anxious to accompany him on the trip, to get to know him better and to observe him in action on stage.

'Elvis wanted me to come along, too,' said Freddie. 'He said to me, "Listen, Freddie, you've got to come because I'm not getting on with this Kanter too well. You heard the remark about the f***ing straw. This guy is supposed to be my director, but he turns out to be a comedian!"'

Kanter was a southern boy himself, from Savannah, Georgia. Elvis fascinated him so much that he included many of the details of the singer's rise to fame in the screenplay of *Loving You*, in which Elvis played a rising rock star called Deke Rivers. Shrewdly, Kanter described Elvis as 'the young man with the ancient eyes and the child's mouth', an apt early description of the Elvis enigma.

Lizabeth Scott, who co-starred with Elvis in *Loving You*, was also mesmerized by his blue eyes. After describing him as 'the most remarkable young man I had ever, ever encountered', she said: 'He was very young and very adolescent, but he had the most mature eyes. I shall never forget his eyes, so beautiful, so exquisite. And he was so talented. I had great fun making that film.

'Elvis had an entourage of young men around him and he was untouchable. He was one of the most polite young men I have ever met in my life. "Ma'am" this and "Ma'am" that, "Yes, sir", "No, sir" and whatnot. For what he was doing, he was absolutely excellent. He came in prepared, he had a photographic memory, he was on time, he was a gentleman to the very core of him. He was a simple man, a simple little boy. But I feel that he could have been so much more than he was because he had the potential.'

His much hyped first film, *Love Me Tender* ('Mr Rock 'n' Roll in the story he was born to play'), had its world premiere at the Paramount Theater on Broadway on 16 November 1956. It shared the box-office honours for the year with *Giant*, the dynastic Texan epic starring James Dean, Elizabeth Taylor and Rock Hudson. The critics panned Elvis as an actor, but he was as big as those three Hollywood stars put together.

George Klein, the Memphis DJ, was witness to the impact that Elvis and the Colonel made on the movie capital. As he was planning a career in television himself, George was fascinated to watch the Colonel in action, but he was also baffled.

'Why do you need the William Morris Agency when you're his manager – and why give them another 10 per cent?' he asked the Colonel one night.

'George, I know everything about recording contracts and personal appearances, but I know nothing about movie contracts,' the Colonel answered. 'The sharpest guys in the world are in Hollywood and they will eat you up and spit you out. They know how to manipulate things. Abe Lastfogel is president of the William Morris Agency and he handles the biggest stars in the industry. If Mr Lastfogel and I both walk into a producer's office, there is no way in the world they are going to cheat us.

Mr Lastfogel knows how to handle the movie people and I know how to handle Elvis.'

'It ended up with Elvis getting a $1 million advance and 50 per cent of the picture,' says Klein. 'You know, Elvis was making more money at that time than Brando and Taylor.'

Elvis had declared at the outset: 'New York and Hollywood aren't going to change me none.' But in the same way that 'Heartbreak Hotel' had altered John Lennon and Raquel Welch, there was a fair chance that Elvis just might change Hollywood. On Merseyside, John slicked back his hair and practised his guitar on the front porch. In his head, he was composing the first stanza of 'The Ballad of John and Elvis'. It was destined to run and run.

CHAPTER THREE

Hollywood Hound Dog

BY HALLOWEEN 1957, Elvis had achieved the impossible and he knew it. The shimmering iridescence that was the King of Rock 'n' Roll glowed in every corner of the globe. Even in silhouette, his image was unmissable. At 22, he was already the star of two successful movies, *Love Me Tender* and *Loving You*, while *Jailhouse Rock* had just been given its world premiere in Memphis.

That night, Paul McCartney and John Lennon made music together for the first time. John had met Paul at the Woolton village fête on 6 July. 'There's a photo of me with a checked shirt on, holding a little acoustic guitar and I am singing "Be-Bop-a-Lula",' John recalled. 'The day I met Paul I was singing that song for the first time on stage.' The cocky leader of a high school skiffle band called the Quarry Men, John had consumed several pints of the local beer and was quite tipsy. 'He kept putting his arm around my shoulders,' said Paul. 'His breath smelled, but I showed him a few chords he didn't know. I left feeling I'd created an impression.' He was right. John had been greatly impressed by Paul's white sports coat, black drainpipe trousers and Tony Curtis haircut. 'He looked like Elvis,' said John. 'I dug him.'

He invited Paul to join the Quarry Men for a performance at the New Clubmoor Hall in Liverpool. Anxious to show what he could do, Paul played lead guitar, but it was to be for the first and last time. As he didn't know how to restring a guitar for a left-handed player, he played the instrument backwards, making a hash of his solo on 'Guitar Boogie'.

'The Quarry Men started at the time of the skiffle boom, and the first big influence on the group was Lonnie Donegan,' said Bill Harry, the founder of *Mersey Beat,* a newspaper that avidly charted the Beatles' rise. 'But John had got into Elvis at Quarry Bank High School and he began singing Elvis Presley numbers in the act.'

The group, minus Paul, had already made its debut at the Cavern, where they were upbraided for doing 'Hound Dog' and 'Blue Suede Shoes'. 'You weren't allowed to play rock 'n' roll – it was jazz or skiffle,' said Bill Harry. 'When John sang an Elvis number, the manager sent him a note saying, "No bloody rock!" But John was really into the Elvis thing and he wouldn't give it up. He loved Elvis.'

Although the Beatles later appeared to come from nowhere, they did, in fact, serve a very tough apprenticeship. They played gigs wherever they could find them, including the Jacaranda, a humble coffee bar that charged fourpence for buttered toast and another penny for jam. They played from the back of a flatbed truck on one occasion, fought with their rivals and often dodged hostile fans. Their experiences in the North of England were not unlike Elvis's own baptism of fire in the Deep South, where he hadn't been too proud to play from the back of a flatbed truck either.

For Elvis, fame had provoked notoriety and jealousy even in his home town. When he returned to Memphis to see Gladys and Vernon after finishing *Loving You,* he was confronted with danger the moment he stepped out into the real world.

'Elvis and I were dragging Main Street, just cruising around looking for some girls our own age to come to a party at Audubon Drive,' recalls George Klein. 'We found some who recognized him, so Elvis pulled up. I went to tell the girls we were having a party and to follow us. I got back to Elvis and there were ten Marines surrounding him. Without realizing it, we had pulled up right in front of a recreation hall for the military. They'd seen Elvis in the car and had come out. They were angry about something and I said to this great big Marine, "What's going on?" Lil ole me, five feet eight inches tall. "Presley has been going out with my wife," he said, "and I'm gonna beat him up."

'I said, "Man, you must be crazy – Elvis just got back in town from making a movie two days ago." They said, "Is that right? Oh, man, we're going to find out what a movie star is made of!" They had us backed up against the car like a scene from a gangster movie. Elvis reached in his coat and took out this gun and put it right up between the guy's eyes and said, "Now what did you say there?" The guy put his hands up and all the uniforms started backing away, and Elvis said, "Now back up and get out of the way."

'And they started saying, "Mr Presley, don't shoot! Don't shoot! We were just kidding around. Don't shoot!" We eased into the car, Elvis keeping the gun on the Marines, and we drove off. I said, "God, Elvis, where did you get that gun?" He laughed and said: "It's not real – it's a Hollywood prop gun." He had brought it home as a souvenir. It only shot blanks, but it got us away from there.'

The incident shows that Elvis had become a target for anyone with a grudge, and before long he was toting real guns for his own protection. Red West, an old school friend who had once saved him from a beating because of his long hair, became his bodyguard.

The chance for Elvis to sing live again came a few weeks later when the Colonel organized a concert tour starting in Chicago and working its way through St Louis, Philadelphia and Buffalo to Toronto, Montreal and Ottawa. Squeezed in between the end of filming *Loving You* in March and the start of *Jailhouse Rock* in May, the tour proved so successful that Elvis was back on the road in late August, covering the Pacific North-west centres of Spokane, Tacoma, Seattle and Portland. In Vancouver, he flapped his wings so freely that he was accused of inciting a full-scale rock 'n' roll riot among the fans. Elvis revelled in it.

But there was serious trouble waiting in Los Angeles, where Elvis ached to give the best show of his life at the Pan-Pacific Auditorium in the heart of Hollywood. More by accident than design, the first performance ended in a bizarre climax, which even Elvis found hard to explain after the damage had been done.

Bathed in white light and clad in a tuxedo woven of golden thread, its lapels and cuffs sparkling with rhinestones ($10,000 from Nudie's of Hollywood), Elvis was at the height of his powers. Even before he opened that first night, 28 October, with 'Heartbreak Hotel', a mounting crescendo of ear-splitting squeals told him he had died and gone to teenage heaven. The vast majority of the audience were impressionable girls of junior high school age: white, affluent and sexually alive. Some were as old as 15, others as young as 10.

Decked out from top to toe in Elvis fashions and waving his publicity picture over their heads like sails in a high wind, they let him know that they were here for some action. He was only too happy to oblige. This was the Teddy Bear Army, its battle colours of Hound Dog Orange, Heartbreak Pink, Love Ya Fuchsia and Cruel Red shining brightly on moist young lips. His own likeness smiled boldly back at him from a multitude of scarves, dresses, dungarees, blouses, sneakers and charm bracelets. He knew he was among the faithful.

Instantly, he was Presley the Performer, a master illusionist who created magical shapes with his flowing torso and liquid limbs. These combined with nerve-tingling sound bites from those curling, bee-stung lips to summon up the libido even in those too young to know they had one. The black pompadour slicked back into the classic ducktail, the kiss curl hanging over the high, noble forehead and the long sideburns now stamped him as arrogant, delinquent and dangerous. Cosmetic artistry had firmed up the classical features and eliminated even the merest hint of any blemish. Some said that he had had a nose job and that skin had been grafted from his backside to cover up the acne scars. Even if such darkly handsome good looks, surrounding a pair of improbable pale blue eyes, owed not a little to trickery, the girls saw only what they wanted: the epitome of white male sexuality.

As he cast his spell, the dynamic that came into play made anything, anything at all, seem possible for a few fleeting moments: the most improbable sexual fantasy might just become reality for the truly devout believer. And these were truly devout believers.

As the vision Elvis created became momentarily real, yet more squeals, tearful cries and ecstatic screams ripped the night air, only to rise even higher the instant the pivotal, pump-action pelvis stopped moving. Once the radioactive particles ceased to vibrate, the illusion faded and the sudden withdrawal was unendurable. All too aware of what he had done, Elvis looked curiously contrite. Standing motionless beneath the spotlights, he was human again and noticeably vulnerable. But still they begged for more and, once again, he obliged.

Maurice Kinn reported that night in the *New Musical Express*:

> Throughout the fifty minutes of Presley's shattering antics, the entire auditorium was a seething, contorting mass of wriggling humanity, reacting with shrill screams and convulsive jerks to every breath of the Presley voice, every twitch of the Presley hips. This was not just audience reaction, but sheer mass hypnotism. Fans fainted in dozens, falling like ninepins in the aisles and across the rows of seats.
>
> He deliberately sets out with an almost sadistic intent to arouse the fans to fever pitch. They say that Elvis is the only singer who wears out his trousers from the inside – and now I know just what they mean.

In a final burst of high spirits, Elvis concluded the show by rolling over and over on the stage with his arms and legs wrapped around a stuffed version of Nipper, the dog normally seen cocking an attentive ear to a wind-up phonograph on the RCA Victor logo. Elvis had ended each performance on the tour by serenading the mascot with a fast and furious rendition of 'Hound Dog'. In Los Angeles, when he suddenly seized Nipper in this undignified and unscripted embrace, the foreplay had been so great that some outraged members of the press thought he was simulating sex with it. Exciting young girls to orgasm was bad enough, but having sexual intercourse with a dog was going too far. The final taboo had been broken.

The LA deputy police chief ordered the Vice Squad to instruct Elvis to eliminate any 'sexy overtones' from his next performance. To underscore the caution, the Colonel was also warned that obscenity charges would be brought against his star if the Nipper act were repeated at the second concert.

Three 16mm movie cameras were hastily despatched to the Pan-Pacific Auditorium to shoot Elvis from different angles. In the event of a further infringement, the film would be produced in court as evidence.

Bunkered down in the Presidential Suite of the Beverly Wilshire Hotel, Elvis stuck to his usual rejoinder: 'They all think I'm a sex maniac, but I come from a respectable family and I wouldn't do anything to embarrass them. I just act natural.' He rang his mother to reassure her that everything was all right. Gladys worried just the same.

So it was that Dixie's prodigal son came before the West Coast philistines on the most critical night of his life. The powerful overhead lights had already dimmed when an armed escort directed two ticket holders, Ricky (later Rick) Nelson and his girlfriend Marianne Gaba, to their front-row seats. For a few moments, the excited hubbub subsided into a hush. Everyone waited tensely for the King to make his most eagerly awaited appearance.

Slipping unseen into their seats alongside Ricky and Marianne were some of the biggest box-office names on the Hollywood scene: Russ Tamblyn, Carol Channing, Sammy Davis Jr, Nick Adams, Tony Franciosa, Rita Moreno, Vince Edwards and Tommy Sands. Elvis was the hottest ticket in Tinseltown. Edgy officers of the LAPD had insisted that they arrive after lights out to prevent an outbreak of hysteria even before the spotlight picked out Elvis's gold-laméd figure on the blue velour-draped stage.

'I remember we all had to come in late because the crowd was so excited,' recalls Marianne, then a beauty queen of 17. 'It was dark inside and we had police to get us in so everyone would stay quiet.'

No Presley concert had ever been staged in front of such a dedicated turnout of his peers or in such a high-voltage atmosphere of official disdain. He came on with the eyes and ears of the world upon him, with the Vice Squad waiting in the wings and the *créme de la créme* of Hollywood's young talent watching in rapt anticipation from their ringside seats. It was a big moment. Elvis stood briefly speechless as he caught sight of the famous faces. Some he knew well, like Nick Adams and Sammy Davis, but he had never met Ricky Nelson or the entrancing girl seated beside him. Ricky shifted uncomfortably when he realized Elvis was looking at them.

Addressing the crowd, Elvis said: 'I'm sorry this came up, but we're not gonna let it stop us from putting on the best show we can for you people. If they think it's obscene, that's their problem, not mine.'

Before going into his act, he winked at one of the spy cameras, inscribed a halo around his head with a circular motion of his hand and said: 'I'm gonna be an angel tonight.' Pandemonium.

Whatever the city fathers might have thought, the roar of endorsement from the crowd showed that, in their eyes at least, Elvis could do no wrong. After the show, a spokesman for the Vice Squad said that, as Elvis had 'reduced the orbit of his gyrations and gone through no bumps and grinds', he would not be charged with any offence.

'Elvis recognized Ricky in the audience and we were invited to a big party he was holding at the Beverly Wilshire,' Marianne told me years later, reliving that night.

Even by the epic standards of Los Angeles, the Wilshire was special. Host to European royalty and Hollywood celebrities, it had never seen anything quite like Elvis Presley. By the time he moved in, the brown

Tuscan stone facade had already survived at least one major earthquake. However, the new rock-age hysteria that followed Elvis wherever he went sent tremors of a very different kind coursing through the tree-lined streets of Beverly Hills. As Ricky and Marianne were swept past the massed ranks of police and security guards, it seemed that the fever of the concert had invaded the hotel. They moved past the arches containing chic Parisian boutiques into the lobby, where they gazed at Corinthian columns that stretched up to glass mosaic skylights. Marianne was dazzled.

'The whole of the Memphis Mafia were there and a lot of the celebrities I had seen at the concert,' she recounted. 'I was only 171/2 at that time and very star-struck. As soon as we walked into his suite, Elvis spotted Ricky and came dashing over. He shook my hand politely and then grabbed Ricky in a bear hug and lifted him up.

'Ricky had just had a hit record of his own and become a huge idol, but he was completely in awe of Elvis. We both were.'

To Elvis, however, Ricky was an important figure not because of his budding rock career, but because he starred with his parents in the *Ozzie and Harriet Show,* one of his favourite TV series. Far from taking offence that Ricky had mimicked him in a recent episode, he was flattered that the Nelsons should regard him as important enough to include in their show. He kept pumping Ricky with questions about his family that Ricky had difficulty in answering. He was so nervous and excited that his throat had seized up and he could barely speak.

'As we left the party, I said to Ricky, "I'm never going to wash my hand again," and Ricky said, "Nor me" and laughed,' said Marianne.

Elvis had started filming his fourth movie, *King Creole,* when news of the summons he had been dreading finally arrived at the Wilshire.

'Elvis was sitting down with all of his cronies at this big dining-room table in his suite,' said Freddie Bienstock. 'Colonel Parker came in with the unhappy news that Elvis had been drafted and he had to go in the Army. One of the boys jumped up. "What the hell is going to happen to us?" he said to the Colonel. "I gave Elvis the best years of my life." At that point, Elvis got very sore indeed. It was the only time I ever saw him really angry.'

Elvis returned to Graceland for Christmas and his call-up papers were delivered by hand on 20 December 1957. Uncle Sam had claimed his most famous recruit. Paramount managed to secure a sixty-day deferment to enable him to complete the movie.

'They were grabbing him off the set to get him in the Army,' said Carolyn Jones, who co-starred with Elvis. 'I had one of my bouts of flu on that picture. We went down to New Orleans and I caught a bug. When we came back to Paramount to finish the indoor scenes, I had a high fever and they were saying, "We don't care if you're dying, he's going into the Army." So I was doing love scenes with him, with a temperature of 104, saying into his ear, "Oh God, I hope you've had a shot of penicillin. You're never going to make it." And he was very nice and kind.'

Two things happened to Elvis while he was in the Army that were to shape the rest of his life: Gladys died soon after he went in, and he met Priscilla just before he came out. Gladys had taken to drinking vodka during Elvis's long absences in Hollywood, often accentuating the effect with amphetamine-based diet pills. The single trip she made to California with Vernon, driving both ways because she was terrified of flying, only added to her anxiety. She had cirrhosis of the liver, developed hepatitis and died of a heart attack on 14 August 1958, while Elvis was completing his basic training at Fort Hood in Texas. He was still in bits when, as a private first class, he arrived at Bremerhaven with the 32nd Battalion of the US Third Armored Division in the *General Randall* on 1 October.

At first, the Germans were sceptical about the arrival of the dangerous American they called 'Lardhead' or 'the Yowling Boy' on their soil, but he gradually won them over with his natural southern charm. 'Would you like to meet Brigitte Bardot?' a reporter asked him at his first press conference. 'Yes, I would,' Elvis grinned. 'But she's engaged,' the reporter shot back. Elvis saw the trap and explained: 'I meant I wanted to meet her as a performer.' According to the German press, he came across as 'likable', 'modest' and 'a well-mannered, intelligent young man'.

German teenagers besieged the base at Friedberg, and whenever his Spearhead platoon went on manoeuvres, Elvis had to slip out quietly to prevent fans blocking the road. 'The only way to avoid people is to post him out in some field under a tree at two o'clock in the morning,' said his sergeant. Elvis took Dexies to keep him awake on these lonely dawn patrols.

The last thing he was looking for was trouble. Grieving for his mother, he moved Vernon, grandmother Minnie Mae Presley, Red West and a couple of the Guys to a rented house at Goethestrasse 14 in Bad Nauheim to see him through his tour of duty. His respect for his father and grandmother and his devotion to the memory of his mother endeared him to many older Germans. He also befriended two GIs: little Charlie Hodge from Decatur, Alabama, and tough Joe Esposito from Chicago.

Elvis astounded the Germans by doing his share of dirty jobs, standing in line on pay-day to pick up his $135-a-month wages, showing respect for rank with eager 'Yes, sirs' by the dozen, while still managing to be popular with the other men. Off-duty, he zipped around in *Der Elviswagen,* a white BMW sports car, but instead of antagonizing the local constabulary, he drove so carefully that they asked him to lend his name to a road safety campaign. He was even spotted queuing up to donate blood to the German Red Cross.

However, Elvis came close to over-stepping the boundaries of acceptable behaviour when he dated Vera Tschechowa, a respected teenage actress. He spent one four-day leave with her at her home in Munich and attracted a *Blitzkrieg* of abuse from her fans. Once again, he was 'a cheap, uncouth, American gangster'. But Vera defended him loyally 'Elvis is very much misunderstood,' she said, posing on his arm. 'He is a sensitive, honest and good-hearted friend.'

However, Elvis took the hint and looked around for an American girl to share his spare time. Two months before he was due to leave for the States, a friend called Currie Grant brought to Elvis's home Priscilla Ann Beaulieu, the 14-year-old step-daughter of a newly arrived Air Force officer. It was a blind date that was to have momentous consequences. For his part, Elvis was much taken with this dark-haired young girl who seemed so at ease with him and his family. One of the first questions he asked her that first night was: 'Who are the kids listening to in the States?'

'Why, everyone is listening to you,' the ninth-grade student replied truthfully.

'What about Ricky Nelson?' Elvis wanted to know.

RCA had released several pre-recorded songs to keep the Elvis name alive during his Army service, but he was desperate to make up for lost time and the careers of Ricky Nelson and the new generation of rock singers were an important factor in planning his re-entry. Although Elvis thought that Priscilla was 'the most beautiful girl I have ever seen', he knew that she was too young for a serious relationship. Besides, he was about to return to making movies in Hollywood. Secretly, he wondered whether Ricky was still going steady with the gorgeous girl he had brought with him to the Wilshire. One thing that had not escaped his attention during his exile was the flowering of Marianne Gaba. Her looks had by now excited the attention of Hugh Hefner and his fellow connoisseurs at *Playboy*. The magazine had an eager following among US troops in Germany and Elvis read it like any other homesick GI.

'I was a Playmate centrefold in 1959 and I was chosen as Playmate of the Decade,' Marianne told me at her Beverly Hills home. 'But it was actually very, very mild – just a little tushy showing. It would be nothing now, but it was a big deal in those days before the sexual revolution. I went steady with Ricky for three years until 1960, and then Elvis came out of the Army and we made *GI Blues*.'

Elvis returned in March 1960 to find that the United States had changed as much as he had. The decade began with Fidel Castro's revolution in Cuba and it would end with Jimi Hendrix's finale at Woodstock. Elvis wasted no time.

During a 24-hour recording session in Nashville, he recorded the No. 1 hit 'Are You Lonesome Tonight?' (a suggestion of the Colonel's) and 'It's Now or Never', an adaptation of the Neapolitan love song 'O Sole Mio'. Then he flew to Miami to appear on Frank Sinatra's *Welcome Home Party for Elvis* in a six-minute guest appearance for which the Colonel demanded, and got, a record fee of $125,000. 'Elvis, I tell you something, it's great,' smarmed Frank, who had insisted that Elvis wear a look-a-like tuxedo on the show. 'I'm glad to see the Army hasn't changed you.' Sinatra had once called Elvis's music 'a rancid-smelling aphrodisiac', but that no longer applied. Elvis even sang one of Frank's old songs, 'Witchcraft', while Sinatra warbled along with 'Love Me Tender'. Elvis smiled like good guys should and laughed all the way back to Hollywood.

The plot for *GI Blues* involved Elvis playing Tulsa MacLean, an American soldier stationed in Frankfurt, who tries to win a bet with his buddies that he can bed a long-legged cabaret singer called Lili. The fact that Juliet Prowse, who played Lili, was engaged to Sinatra didn't prevent Elvis from commenting: 'She has a body that would make a bishop stamp his foot through a stained glass window.' When Elvis tried his luck with Juliet, he was quietly but firmly told that Frank wouldn't like it. He backed off and switched his attentions to Marianne Gaba.

'I had the part of a German waitress in a frilly outfit,' she said. 'I had about twenty lines, most of which were cut. One evening, somebody came up to me and said, "Elvis would like to go out with you." So I said, "Oh, of course," and they said, "Can he have your number?" and I gave it to him.'

Marianne had just become engaged to Michael Starkman, a young stockbroker who worked for Prudential Securities. She told him: 'If Elvis asks me out, you will have to understand: I love you and we are going to get married, but back in high school I remember watching him on TV and I have to go out with him.'

'Well, you have to do what you have to do, right?' stammered Mike, swallowing his fear. This was the stuff of which bad Hollywood movies and tabloid headlines were made: ELVIS PRESLEY STOLE MY GIRL.

'We'd only been engaged for a week and I was very jealous and upset,' recalls Mike, now senior vice president at Prudential. 'I threatened to call off the engagement, but Marianne said to me, "If I don't go, I'll resent it for ever." So she went.'

'Elvis did call and they sent over a gold, bullet-proof limousine to my little apartment right at the back of Saks, three blocks from the Beverly Wilshire,' said Marianne. 'My roommate gasped, "Oh, my God, look at that big gold thing – it's as long as the block!" The windows were dark so I didn't know if Elvis was in there or not, but it turned out that he wasn't. When I asked where we were going, the driver said, "To the Beverly Wilshire." I thought, "Oh aye, aye, he thinks I'm going to jump into bed with him."

'There were so many screaming people outside the Wilshire that I had to go in through the back entrance. Elvis had two floors, the 8th and the 9th, and there were people everywhere, maybe twenty men and a few girls running around. Then something happened which told me what type of person Elvis really was.

'They were all ordering food from room service because it was too big a hassle to go out. Everybody was ordering *escargots* and Chateaubriand, all these fancy, expensive things, and they asked Elvis what he wanted, and he said, "Peanut butter, jelly and mashed banana on white bread." And I thought to myself, "Oh my God, he is just a homespun, sweet young man." He didn't need all this stuff; he wasn't trying to impress anybody. After a while, he told everybody to leave, and there I was in the room with Elvis alone.

'He brought out his guitar and he started playing and my heart was pounding. He was wearing a pretty shiny silk shirt and I was in skin-tight toreador pants. We sat and we necked for a long time. Oh, gosh, yes, he was adorable and a fabulous kisser. It was before birth-control pills and I was certainly afraid that, if I went to bed with someone, I would end up embarrassing my mom and dad who were working back home in Chicago to support me to be out here. But he never even suggested it.'

Mike spent the most nerve-wracking evening of his life with his brother, the artist Shel Starkman. 'I was with Mike and it was serious stuff,' said Shel. 'This was an historical moment. His fiancée was out with Elvis Presley, the sexiest guy in the world. Mike was devastated. He was almost in tears.'

Unaware of this drama, Elvis carried on as though everything was under control. Around midnight, he was ready for some action.

'He had another car come and we were driven to Cyrano's near the Playboy Club on Sunset,' said Marianne. 'I remember driving in the limousine and there were girls looking at him and it was so funny to watch the reaction when he pulled the tinted windows down. People would just look at him and go absolutely crazy. They'd start screaming and try to follow. It was like he was toying with them. He would laugh and roll the window up, then he'd want the same reaction and he'd roll it down again. He'd wait two seconds until someone drove up, see him and go absolutely crazy.

'They must have called Cyrano's to tell them that he was coming because, although everything was taken, they had put a table for us right next to the stage. I can't even remember who was playing. We left before the show finished and he dropped me off at my home.

'Michael rang as soon as I got back in, about 2.00 am, and my roommate said he had been calling every hour on the hour. He made me promise that, if Elvis asked me out again, I wouldn't go. So I told Elvis that I had a boyfriend and couldn't date him again.

'About two months later, we were staying at the Desert Inn in Las Vegas, about to get married at the Little Church of the West. Michael ran into Colonel Parker and told him that we were getting married. The

Colonel must have told Elvis because a big hound dog, bigger than life-size, turned up in our room. A note around its neck read: "To Marianne, with love from Elvis and The Colonel."

'I kept this huge thing in my bedroom for the first year of my marriage and then my husband said, "Either that goes or I do." So it went.'

Hal Wallis and the studio were delighted with the success of *GI Blues* because it extended the base of Elvis's appeal. 'I think possibly some of his fans might have outgrown him, but there were others to take their place,' he said. But like many early Elvis purists, John Lennon was dismayed: he hadn't outgrown Elvis, Elvis had betrayed him. 'He was disappointed in the way Elvis had changed,' said Bill Harry. 'John said he was saddened that Elvis had turned into just a middle-of-the-road singer.'

In truth, the change had gone much deeper than Elvis's singing style. When he first returned to Memphis, he was asked: 'Do you have any advice for boys of your age who are going to put in a certain amount of duty in the services?' Elvis replied wisely: 'Well, the only thing I can say is to play it straight and do your best because you can't fight 'em. They never lost yet.' He strongly advised against 'trying to be an individual or trying to be different'.

King Creole had marked the last rendition of the rock-age rebel, and *GI Blues* confirmed in John's eyes that Elvis's capitulation to the military amounted to total surrender. It was the equivalent of watching your greatest ally go over to the other side. But, by now, John had plans for his own career, big plans that would take him on a ten-year roller-coaster ride to the top and down again. 'I came out of the sticks to take over the world,' he boasted.

When Elvis flew across the Pacific to make *Blue Hawaii* in 1961, he was delighted to find himself once again in the company of his old friend Patti Page.

'In Hawaii, we would sit around at the Coconut Palm Hotel after dinner,' Patti remembers. 'Elvis would bring out the guitar and we would all sing any song that he or I remembered from childhood, as well as gospel songs and hymns.

'Elvis always seemed happiest when he was performing because he liked the acclaim, and I was happy for him, but I always noticed the sadness. I couldn't define it when he was young and we never had a deep conversation about it, but he would just say casually, "My Mama liked that song" or "My Mama loved that dish of food." I liked him very much from the start and I've always thought he had a talent that was never really brought out as far as it could have been.'

CHAPTER FOUR

The Last Pre-Beatle Christmas

JUST EIGHT years after 'That's All Right (Mama)' had teased and tantalized a new generation of white youth, fame had made Elvis a virtual recluse in his down-home mansion. Surrounded by an imitation southern countryside that was quickly yielding to fast-food fortresses, Elvis souvenir shacks and advancing columns of one-armed gasoline pumps, he rarely dared to venture out alone.

But a few days before Christmas in 1962, he did just that. Elvis turned the black Cadillac off Highway 51 and was instantly admitted through the 'Music Gates' at No. 3764. Sitting beside him was Priscilla Beaulieu, tired but elated after her flight from Germany. She took in a nativity scene that had been set up on the lawn for the Christmas festivities, and then, enthralled, she entered the big house called Graceland for the first time.

Of all man's temples dedicated to the love of a woman, none surpasses the Taj Mahal, but Elvis had done his best for Gladys with Graceland. In August 1957, he had paid $100,000 for the colonial-style mansion set among towering oaks in fourteen acres of rolling countryside at Whitehaven on the outskirts of Memphis. Just one mile north of the Mississippi border, it was about as close as you could get to Tupelo and still call yourself a Memphian.

Built in 1939 by Dr Thomas Moore and his wife Ruth, Graceland was named after a favourite aunt of theirs, Grace Toof. What the house lacked in historical significance, it made up for with presence, once Elvis had finished with it. The limestone facade and the four Corinthian columns of the massive portico were illuminated with pale blue spotlights, which gave Graceland an aura of gentrified grandeur, even if Gladys had kept chickens in the backyard.

Priscilla, just 17 years old, loved the look of the house and she was excited at the prospect of spending her first Christmas with Elvis. To help her sleep that first night, he gave her two large red 500-milligram Placidyl tablets. She woke up two days later. Now the King himself was fast asleep, the famous face in repose.

At 27, Elvis was at his most handsome. The dyed black hair, cut shorter for his movie roles, was slightly ruffled, but the classical features remained unmarked. The sideburns were neatly trimmed, the spit curl somehow less pretentious. Even the sneer had temporarily departed from the celebrated lower lip. Elvis slept, seemingly at peace.

He lay in a pair of midnight blue pyjamas on a double king-size bed, the black silk sheets crumpled. The decor of his bedroom was Rockin' Fifties, the furniture black and white. Heavy blue drapes shut out the pale wintry light, but the black velvet ceiling sparkled with a constellation of tiny spotlights. At the foot of the bed, several TV sets were permanently turned on. The pictures danced and changed silently, the sound turned down. On the bedside table was a photograph of Gladys in a silver frame, and another of Jesus.

Outside, two stone lions guarded the portico of the mansion. Fairy lights twinkled in strands wound down the length of the white columns. The curved driveway swept through bare trees and the rolling lawn down to a group of fans clustered outside the Music Gates.

To the faithful millions that last Pre-Beatle Christmas, Elvis Presley was still the undisputed King of Rock 'n' Roll, and the fans accorded him the worship due to such drugstore majesty. No other rock star, white or black, had ever come close. The singer who rated second to him in record sales was the country singer/guitarist Johnny Cash and they weren't even competing in the same race. It seemed Elvis just couldn't lose.

At the start of December, the catchy Otis Blackwell/Winfield Scott offering 'Return to Sender' was riding high in the US charts, and Elvis had had three other *Billboard* successes during 1962: 'Can't Help Falling in Love', 'Good Luck Charm' and 'She's Not You'. RCA had abandoned the echo chamber and the rocking guitar in favour of a more mellow, romantic lyricism with only occasional flashes of the old boogified blues. The new style suited Elvis and, more important to the money men, it appealed to a wider audience. The Hillbilly Cat of Western Bop had transformed himself into a sophisticated balladeer who was fully aware of his vocal and erotic powers.

The movies released that year – *Follow That Dream, Kid Galahad* and *Girls! Girls! Girls!* – all followed the tried and tested exploitation formula that had already seen millions queuing at the box office. The studio system worked for Elvis whatever medium he was using, whether it was at RAC Victor, United Artists or Paramount.

In Hollywood terms, Elvis was bigger than Valentino had ever been, and if his acting skills failed to compare with those of his heroes Tony Curtis, James Dean and Marlon Brando, no Elvis movie ever made a loss at the box office. 'A Presley picture is the only sure thing in show business,' growled Hal Wallis. The money kept rolling in.

On Christmas Eve, snow fell at Graceland and Elvis's happiness seemed complete. He gave Priscilla a poodle puppy, which she named Honey. She gave Elvis a musical cigarette case that played 'Love Me Tender'. They ran outside to play in the snow like a couple of kids. Nothing was going to spoil their dream.

In London, early in 1962, a young record store executive called Brian Epstein was having no success whatever in attracting interest in an unknown group he had just signed under their latest stage name, the Beatles. The bosses of the big West End record companies scoffed when he told them in all seriousness: 'My boys are going to be bigger than Elvis.'

It sounded ridiculous. Even the top flight of British stars – Cliff Richard, Billy Fury and Frankie Vaughan among them – had failed to make more than a tiny impression on the US market. No one, least of all a British challenge, had ever got near Elvis.

The sages of Denmark Street, Britain's Tin Pan Alley, listened to a demo tape that the baby-faced manager had brought with him and politely showed him the door. But Brian Epstein had listened when John Lennon told him: 'Elvis is finished, but he doesn't know it yet.' He was convinced that he and John had spotted a gap in the market and that the Beatles were the group to fill it. Brian had kept trying. Finally in May he secured a recording contract with the EMI organization for the Beatles to record on its unglamorous Parlophone label.

No one except Brian and the Beatles, certainly not the King himself, his young sweetheart nor the fans shivering at the Music Gates, knew that Elvis Presley's reign was about to end in the most unlikely manner. The Mississippi was about to run into the Mersey.

Like the young pretenders to the King's throne, Epstein came from Liverpool, the great transatlantic port on the east side of the Mersey estuary. Historically, it had one vital connection with Memphis: Liverpool was linked to the Old South by iron chains. In the 18th and 19th centuries, fast-moving clippers had brought raw cotton from the southern states to the Lancashire mills, and then carried woven goods to Africa, where they picked up cargoes of slaves for the American plantations. The misery of human bondage was given voice in the blues. In the second half of the 20th century, Liverpool gave birth to its own bluesy sound: the Mersey beat, which created the Beatles and Beatlemania.

Bill Harry, founder of *Mersey Beat* newspaper, remembers: 'John Lennon and Stuart Sutcliffe were my closest friends at Liverpool College of Art. John used to dress like a Teddy boy and had a wild reputation.

But he was a wonderful line drawer, who could give an amazing feeling of a fat bird or a shaggy dog with just a few lines. Stuart was a fantastic artist.

'The three of us used to go to the local college pub, *Ye Cracke*, and talk about the American cultural domination of Britain in films and music. We had hardly any money at all, just our student grants of £24 a year, and all we could afford were halves of bitter. We made a vow to make Liverpool famous: John with his music, Stuart with his painting and me with my writing.

'Next door to the art college was the Liverpool Institute, which Paul McCartney and George Harrison attended. They used to rehearse in the art college with the Quarry Men.'

At John's insistence, Stuart had joined the band as bass guitarist, even though he was a second-rate musician. Paul and George objected strenuously, but being mere grammar-schoolboys, they had to give in to their persuasive leader. Stuart wore dark glasses and played with his back to the audience to hide his lack of expertise.

'In 1958, they weren't regarded as one of the top Liverpool groups,' said Bill Harry. 'We were booking them for art college dances, although they didn't have a proper sound system. Stuart and I were on the Students' Union committee, and we voted for union funds to be used to buy them PA equipment. They didn't even have mike stands, so John's girlfriend Cynthia and the other girls used to sit opposite them on chairs holding brooms with the mikes attached to the handles. John used to make Cynthia dress up like Brigitte Bardot. He had a life-size poster of Bardot pasted to the ceiling of his bedroom.

'Pete Best, whose mother ran the Casbah Club where the Quarry Men sometimes played, joined as drummer in August 1960, shortly before the group made its first trip to Hamburg.

'The Beatles were very much a last choice for Germany because Allan Williams, the owner of the Jacaranda who recruited the acts, didn't think all that much of them. He had asked Gerry and the Pacemakers, but they wouldn't do it, and he asked Rory Storm and the Hurricanes, but they were booked into Butlin's. So in desperation he took the Beatles. They played in Hamburg for four-and-a-half-months and came back tremendous.

'When they appeared in December 1960 at Litherland Town Hall, the posters announced "THE BEATLES DIRECT FROM HAMBURG". All the local girls thought they were a German group, and said to them, "For Germans, you don't 'arf speak English with a Liverpool accent.' "

In Hamburg, Stuart Sutcliffe had fallen deeply in love with Astrid Kirchherr, a blonde with the film star looks of a Mae Britt, who was a regular at their first venue, the Indra Club. Their romance signalled the end of Stuart's friendship with John, who was consumed with jealousy that anyone should come between him and his best friend. When the group returned to the club for a second engagement, John made his dislike plain whenever Astrid turned up, taunting her with oblique references to Hitler and the Third Reich.

'The group was George on lead guitar, Stuart on bass, John and Paul on rhythm guitars and Pete Best on drums,' said Bill Harry. 'Paul didn't like this. Originally, he wanted to be on lead guitar, but he knew he couldn't match George. So the only other thing was bass guitar.

'The Beatles were on stage with Tony Sheridan at the Top Ten Club one night when Paul and Stuart had a big fight after Paul made some comment about Astrid. Paul was surprised at how tenacious Stuart was, although he was only slight. They whacked hell out of each other and the audience loved it. They thought it was part of the act. After that, Stuart got out of the group.'

He tossed away his guitar, picked up his paints and joined his sweetheart in the attic flat she occupied above her parents' house. John forgave him and wrote moving letters telling him how bad things were at home in Liverpool. 'I've only got one ciggy to last until Thursday,' he wrote in one letter. Plagued by headaches ever since he had been attacked and kicked in the head during a fracas outside a pub in Bootle,

Stuart collapsed with a fatal brain haemorrhage at Astrid's home just as his art career was taking off again.

Bill Harry asked John to pen a few lines about the group, and in the rustic style he sometimes liked to mimic, he told of the 'Dubious Origins of the Beatles': 'Why Beatles? It came in a vision – a man appeared on a flaming pie and said unto them, "From this day on you are Beatles with an A." Thank you, Mister Man, they said, thanking him.' In fact, it had been Stu, a devotee of Buddy Holly and the Crickets, who had suggested that the group should change its name to the insect-like Beetles. John agreed, but substituted the famous 'a' for the second 'e'.

Bill Harry took some copies of the first issue of *Mersey Beat* around to the Whitechapel branch of NEMS (North End Music Stores) and politely asked to see the manager. 'Brian Epstein came down and said he'd take a dozen copies,' said Harry. 'He phoned me that afternoon and said he'd sold out and ordered another twelve dozen. The Beatles were all over the cover. Epstein kept inviting me back to his office for sherry to find out more about what was happening. I asked him to write the record review column for me. He started writing about classical music and jazz, and I told him it had to be about rock 'n' roll, so he started doing Elvis Presley and Billy Fury.'

When he became famous, Brian liked to claim that he had gone in search of the Beatles after a young fan, Raymond Jones, had requested a copy of 'My Bonny' at his family's record store in Liverpool's city centre on a Saturday late in October 1961. Jones gave the singer's name as Tony Sheridan and his backing group as the Beat Boys. Brian said he discovered that the track had been recorded in Hamburg, but that the Beat Boys were, like Sheridan, from Liverpool. Playing as the Beatles, the backing group were currently appearing at the Cavern, a jazz club in the cellar of a converted warehouse only a few minutes from his store.

Brian dropped into the club on 9 November 1961 with his personal assistant at NEMS, Alistair Taylor, and was astonished by what he saw. 'They smoked as they played, and they ate and talked and pretended to hit each other,' he remembered. 'They turned their backs on the audience and shouted at them and laughed at private jokes.' Afterwards, he met John, Paul, George and Pete Best, and listened to their copy of 'My Bonny'.

'I don't know why I asked them to come round and see me, although I'd loved their act,' Brian recalled. 'They had some indefinable charm.'

Alistair Taylor remembers that day in November very clearly indeed. 'That was the day I turned down two-and-a-half per cent of the Beatles,' he said. 'Brian and I went on to lunch at Peacock's and he asked me what I thought. I said it was going to take money and I couldn't put any up. Being Brian, he said, "I'm not asking you to. If you come with me and we sign them up, I'll give you two-and-a-half per cent of the Beatles' earnings." And I said no, I just wanted a better salary. It was the most monumental gaffe of all time.'

'I had no idea of being a manager,' said Brian. 'But it somehow happened in conversation and we felt we ought to have a contract. None of us had ever seen such a thing so I got one drawn up. It was iniquitous and enslaving in my view, although many stars work under such terms, I know now. So we tore it up and drafted our own. I still haven't signed it.' He never did.

Bill Harry, a reliable witness to the rise of the Beatles, is definite about their first encounter with Epstein: 'Nobody has ever heard of Raymond Jones, and even after all the publicity, he never showed up. I arranged for Brian to go down to the Cavern to see the Beatles. I phoned up and said that Brian Epstein from NEMS would like to come down, and he was so nervous that I told them to make sure there was no hassle about letting him in. When he got there, they announced from the stage that Brian Epstein from NEMS was in the audience.

'The Beatles laughed because they knew him. They were in his shop all the time going through his records. Brian was there while queues of kids were coming in to buy *Mersey Beat*, which had the Beatles all over it.

He also sold tickets for rock concerts and there were posters advertising the Beatles at the Tower Ballroom. After all that, how could he possibly make out that he never knew them? But people keep going along with the false story.'

Brian's first action as manager was to tackle the group's unruly appearance and Hell's Angel image.

'The Beatles were very much John Lennon's group – it was his band – and they were a rough-and-ready, hard-swearing lot in black leather doing tough R&B music,' said Bill Harry. 'Brian wanted that to change and smooth them out to make them more acceptable. So he sent them all these neat little typed-out memos saying, "Do not smoke on stage, do not swear on stage, do not talk to the fans." John didn't like all this because he thought he was being channelled into a false image, but Paul loved it. Paul was doing numbers like 'Till There Was You' from *Music Man* and 'A Taste of Honey' and all these sweet numbers, whereas John was into rock.

'Brian got his tailor to run up mohair suits for them. What he was effectively doing was changing it from John's group into Paul's group. When he eventually realized that he was becoming estranged from John, he took him on holiday to Spain and explained why the group needed to change. And he was right. In their old rough way, they were more exciting and better as a group, but Brian made them acceptable.'

However, the rough edges were still showing when I first met the Beatles – completely by accident and just before the explosion that would rock the music world to its very foundations.

CHAPTER FIVE

Rockin' With Little Richard

THE STAR Club was a dive in the St Pauli district of Hamburg, which is Liverpool with a red light over the door. On a rainy November night in 1962, hookers, drug dealers and groups of seamen ebbed and flowed through the puddles of the Grosse Freiheit, a cobbled thoroughfare running off the Reeperbahn. I found the Star Club at No. 39.

Three long-haired youths, in jeans and black leather, and their girlfriends, similarly attired, pushed past me into the entrance. Inside, a frantic piano was playing. Black, heavily ringed fingers stabbed at the keyboard with lightning speed. The pianist played a heavy rolling bass and fast triplets on the treble. Richard Penniman, a.k.a. Little Richard, sounded as though he had never been away from the rock scene despite a period as a gospel-singing preacher.

Wild-haired, wide-eyed and resplendent in purple drape jacket, purple trousers and white kid shoes, he was standing at the piano on stage in front of a backdrop of the Manhattan skyline. Smoke and hard looks came from the floor. It was a tough audience. As I entered, he was singing 'Good Golly, Miss Molly'.

I paused, taking in the crowded, smoke-filled room. I was 21 years old and I'd just lost my job on the *New Musical Express*. The consolation prize was ten days in Hamburg with Little Richard.

The youths sat down at a table, a fat German waiter slopping steins of beer in front of them. There was a low murmur from the other tables. A glass broke somewhere behind me.

Barely two years after Sergeant (First Class) Elvis Presley had kissed Priscilla goodbye and flown out of Frankfurt with his unit to resume civilian life in the United States, I was about to meet his successors as the giants of rock 'n' roll – in Germany of all places, where Elvis had been converted into a clean-cut American hero, and in a nightclub similar to the one in *GI Blues,* his comeback movie that showed how much he had changed. Strange things happen in the music world, but few could be stranger than this.

As I drew level with the leather-clad youths, one of them rose and shouted: '*Beatles! Beatles!*

Little Richard played harder and sang louder to drown out the interruption. He caught sight of me as I passed the stage on my way to the dressing room, and flashed that big porcelain smile of his in welcome. But in the dressing room, he was petulant.

'Hello, child,' he said, posing sulkily in the doorway. 'You missed my show.'

'Hi, Richard,' I said, not taking much notice of his mood. I had seen his show several times in England. I had also accompanied him on the train to Hamburg because he was frightened of flying.

'What's this beetle thing?' I asked to change the subject.

The eyes rolled and he sat down in front of the globes surrounding a stage mirror.

'Lawdy! Those cats!' he sighed, repairing his make-up with a stick of mascara. 'That mother John is the devil's own child. I tell you, Chris, he's a *mean* dude.'

At this point, the door burst open and four guys about my own age scrambled into the room and headed straight for the buffet supper set up on a table. They were scruffily dressed in jeans, T-shirts and leather bomber jackets, their hair long and unkempt. They were, it immediately became apparent, ravenously hungry.

'Watch him, wack, he's a religious maniac,' the one called John said between mouthfuls.

Little Richard placed a jewelled hand on my shoulder.

'Pay no attention to the hired help,' he said. 'They only come by for the free food.'

'Shaddup, grandfather!' said John.

I slipped away from Richard's grasp and approached the group.

'I'm Chris Hutchins . . .'

'. . . from the *NME*,' volunteered the one called Paul, stuffing a piece of chicken into his mouth. 'Fab. I've read your stories.'

'You ought to be writing about us,' said the one called Ringo, also eating with gusto.

'Sure, if you'll let me into the secret.'

'We're the Beatles,' said Paul.

'From Liverpool, y'know, Merseyside,' obliged Ringo.

The fourth, the one called George, kept eating. He was extremely thin.

'You spell that B-E-A-T-L-E-S,' said John, interrupting an assault on the now-legless chicken.

'Who's influenced your music most?'

'Little Richard,' said Ringo.

'Chuck Berry,' said George.

'Elvis,' said Paul.

'Yeah, before Elvis, there was nothing,' replied John, aiming the shot at Little Richard.

'Excuse me!' the rocker interjected, thumbing the lapels of his purple jacket like a big shot.

'*Ah* am the King of Rock 'n' Roll. *Ah* was singin' rock before anybody even knew what rock was. Sure, Elvis was one of the builders, but *Ah* was the architect.'

'Sure thing, grandfather,' said John.

Since we had met in London a few weeks earlier, Little Richard and I had talked about Elvis at length. He was kinder than most black singers, who claimed Elvis had simply stolen their music.

'Any records out yet?' I asked John to steer the conversation in a different direction.

'Sure, "Love Me Do" made it to No. 1 in the *Mersey Beat* Top Twenty – you should know that,' he replied in the superior Northern tones I came to recognize well. Those involved in the London music scene had never heard of the Beatles, but I let that pass. 'We're signed to Mr Brian Epstein of NEMS. He's got big plans for us,' said John. 'So are you going to put us in the *NME?*'

'Actually, I just got fired from the *NME* for talking to Don Arden [a music impresario] about launching a rival newspaper. He arranged for me to make this trip and I'll be doing a piece on Little Richard for *Disc*. But I'm free to write about anyone I like and I will write something about you.'

'I'm doing *you* a favour,' John said in that irritating tone of voice. 'One day you'll have to queue up with the rest to interview us. We're going to be big. In fact, Brian says we're going to be bigger than Elvis.'

I'd never heard of Brian Epstein either, but when I saw the Beatles perform later that night, I realized that John hadn't been kidding. Fuelled by amphetamines and strong beer, the Beatles' rock style set the place alight. They had a vitality that was new, fresh and young. The 'leather boys' danced on the tables with their girlfriends to a rousing rendition of 'Blue Suede Shoes'.

Little Richard and the Beatles were, in fact, old chums. I discovered that he had met them when they had shared the billing with him and Gene Vincent at the opening of the Star Club back in April. They had also been booked as main supporting act on one of his shows I'd missed in England, appearing on the same bill at the Tower Ballroom, New Brighton, on 12 October at a concert organized by Brian Epstein.

After the show, John had asked Little Richard for his autograph and address in the US. Little Richard had written across a programme featuring his photograph: 'To John, May God bless you always, Little Richard. 1710 Virginia Road, Los Angeles, California.' So the exchanges

I'd witnessed between John and Little Richard had been just friendly banter.

'They've got plenty of energy,' I said to Richard as we watched.

'Man, they're fabulous. If I hadn't seen 'em, I'd never have dreamed they were white. They have a real authentic black sound.'

'Do you think they've got a chance?'

'It's always been individual performers so far: Elvis, Jerry Lee, Chuck Berry, Gene Vincent, yours truly. But if any *band* can make it, this is it.'

'John Lennon seems a big-headed sod.'

'Believe me,' said the true King of Rock 'n' Roll, 'there's somethin' troublin' that cat deep down in his soul.'

There was something troubling Little Richard as well, though not in his soul. He had, it emerged, become wildly attracted to Ringo Starr. A few nights later, he invited Ringo and me to join him and his keyboard player Billy Preston for a late supper in his room at the Atlantic Hotel. It was late, after 3.00 am, and 'supper' was a plate of sandwiches rushed up by the night porter. Neither the hour nor the shortage of food mattered to Ringo or me. We had taken our quota of purple hearts, which would keep us awake as well as suppress our appetites.

It soon became obvious that the rock star had an ulterior motive in inviting us to his bedroom. He made it clear that he wanted to have sex with Ringo, and suggested that I should do the same in the next room with Billy Preston.

Ringo and I regarded this suggestion with some alarm. Aided by the pills, we started talking our heads off, mainly about girls. I rattled on about my girlfriend Jan, and Ringo told the story of one of his most disastrous dates.

'I turned up in me best gear – a real Ted suit complete with crepe sole shoes,' he gabbled as Little Richard listened impatiently. 'Thought I was going to knock her dead with that lot! Anyway, we went to the cinema on the bus, walked into the foyer and I bought the tickets. She started heading towards the best seats – upstairs. But I took her arm and led her down to the stalls where the only two seats left were right in the front row. It was as much as I could afford, you see. We sat there for three hours with our necks aching agonies. Funny, I never saw her again!'

Richard nodded understandingly.

'Women are trouble,' he sighed. He picked up a copy of the Bible and read out quotations that, he said, proved that the good Lord would not pass judgment on Ringo if he consented to what he had in mind. I had an answer to that.

'You also told me in London that the Bible said you'd be struck down dead if you ever played rock 'n' roll again,' I reminded him. 'Yet you've been playing nothing else since this tour began and you're still alive.'

Little Richard was still trying to figure out a suitable reply when Ringo and I made our excuses and escaped into the dawn. But Richard did not hold a grudge. One night I heard him remark to the club owner, big, blond Manfred Weisledder: 'The Beatles are so good. Watch them, man, they could be the biggest thing in the world.' When Manfred complained about the higher fee that the Beatles demanded for their fifth, and final, appearance in Hamburg, Brian Epstein told him something he had been saying all year: 'These boys will soon be bigger than Elvis.' By then, Manfred was beginning to believe him. He paid up.

At this point, however, the Beatles were struggling to make ends meet. Each week, John sent all his modest wages to Cynthia in Liverpool. The couple had married quietly in August and she was pregnant with Julian. It was a well-kept secret – even Ringo didn't know – but John confided in me, making me swear not to tell anyone.

'How do you manage to send *all* your money home?' I asked him.

'Easy,' he replied. 'Between sessions with the band, I go down to some of the strip joints and play guitar for the girls. That earns me my grub money.'

John's love for Cynthia failed to curb his lust towards Bettina, a buxom German barmaid in whose company he always behaved like an overgrown schoolboy.

'Bettina keeps me in drink and pills, and Cyn keeps me in love,' he told me. 'Bettina calls out for her favourite numbers when we're on stage. You can always pick out her voice.'

John loved the bustle – and the hustle – of the Reeperbahn. He enjoyed talking to the hookers who operated near the group's one-room flat. He found the prostitutes among the most honest people he'd ever encountered. 'They've got nothing to hide,' he told me. Honesty was very important to him, but it was a personal honesty rather than anything to do with the law.

I grew closer to John than to the other Beatles once I came to appreciate his wicked sense of humour. When we found we were on the same wavelength, he accepted me as a day-to-day ally in the battle of life. He didn't exactly go looking for fights, but he seemed to attract trouble whenever he drank.

He was deeply observant, though, even when he said nothing. This detachment meant he could ignore whatever he considered trivial or boring, but it enabled him to engage his intellect the moment something caught his eye. Many of the things he jotted down on scraps of paper ended up in his songs.

When he did speak, he had a savage way of pointing out the obvious. But there were some things he couldn't bear to talk about, which made him seem secretive. They were, I learned, just too private, too painful.

'Even at college, John was very closed about his mother,' Bill Harry told me. 'He never mentioned her. In fact, he never mentioned much about his family at all. Everything was secret, even his marriage to Cynthia. I had known Cynthia since she was 13, but he kept that from everybody. When the Beatles were doing gigs in Liverpool, Cynthia was hidden away to stop the fans from knowing he had a girlfriend, let alone a wife. A rough seaport like Liverpool was very much a male chauvinist place. The guys were tough and the girlfriends had to do what they said. It was very macho.

'When I said to John in the Cracke one night that I'd heard he wrote poetry, he denied it because poetry isn't the macho thing. Eventually, I coaxed him into showing me a poem he had on him in his pocket. It was a rustic poem, very English, and I loved it. He wasn't copying the American type of stuff, the San Francisco Beat poets who were popular at the time.'

The Beatles' equivalent of the Memphis Mafia was Neil Aspinall, a slight, fair-haired trainee accountant who had joined them as road manager shortly before I met them. 'John's mother, Julia, was killed in a road accident when he was 17, but even before she died he was brought up by his Aunt Mimi in a semi-detached house in Menlove Avenue, Woolton,' he told me at the time. 'I suppose we look upon John as the most affluent Beatle because Mimi owned her own house, although they certainly weren't rich. The other three Beatles were all brought up in council houses.

'George's parents still live in theirs in Speke, near Liverpool Airport. His father was a bus driver. George's mother is named Louise, the same as his married sister who lives in America.

'Ringo's parents are also still in their council house in the Dingle district. His stepfather Harry works as a decorator. Ringo's mother Elsie (he calls them by their first names) once told me that Ringo had offered to buy them a new house, but they live among their lifelong friends and they would never be happy if they moved. A pink telephone is one of the small luxuries Ringo has had installed in their house – though they still haven't got a bathroom.

'Paul also comes from the Woolton district. His mother died when he was in his early teens and his father – we call him Mr Mac – brought up Paul and his brother Mike. Their mother was the district nurse.'

For as long as he could remember, the only thing that had mattered to Paul was music. 'I never cared about a career and a future and all that stuff, but I had a bit of a conscience towards me dad,' he told me. 'One day he told me to go out and get a job, so I went down to the Labour Exchange in me donkey jacket and jeans. The fellow sent me to an electrical firm called Massey & Coggins. I told the boss I wanted a job. I wasn't particular, I said. I'd sweep the yard if he wanted. But he asked me where I'd been educated, and when I said Liverpool Institute, he started making big plans.

'They gave me this job of winding coils for about £7 a week – big money then. At work they called me Mantovani because of the long hair. Anyway, I was hopeless. Everybody else used to wind fourteen coils a day while I'd get through one and a half – and mine were the ones that never worked. After a bit I started getting lunchtime dates playing at the Cavern. I had to whip out of work over the back wall at lunchtime and go in the next day and say I'd been ill. One day I just didn't go in and that was that.'

Wherever he went, Paul, the strolling minstrel, composed songs in his head.

'I used to walk home if I didn't have enough for the fare, but I never minded that,' he said. 'I wrote lots of songs on those walks home: "World Without Love" and "Love of the Loved" included, though John helped me polish them up. I used to go to his house and I remember those walks home very well. I had to cross this horrible, pitch-black golf course. I'd always be singing, but if ever I came across somebody in the dark, I'd shut up and try to pretend it hadn't been me. Met a copper like that once. I had a guitar round my neck and was quite cheerfully playing and singing at the top of my voice. Thought he was going to arrest me! But he walked up and asked if I'd give him guitar lessons.'

Ringo had the toughest childhood, spending more than three years in hospital at different times suffering from peritonitis and pleurisy. The

Dingle was in the centre of Liverpool not far from the docks and Ringo was constantly troubled by bullies.

'There was a pub at each end of our street, Admiral Grove, and because I was working, the local Teds used to say, "Lend us a shilling," ' he told me some time later. 'It was their entrance fee to either pub – the price of the first drink. At first I gave them the money, but I was only earning two pounds five shillings a week out of which Elsie gave me fifteen bob pocket money. So I got fed up with the scroungers and started refusing. They would wait for me to come home from work and chase me from the top of the street to my home. One night I didn't make it. Need I say more?

'Ever since I was 12, I've drummed around on anything handy. I used to play on tin cans – even played that way at a party once. There was a music shop I used to pass on the way to school, which had a tom-tom in the window. It cost six pounds. I used to look at it every morning, but we could never afford it. But one Christmas Elsie and Harry bought me a full drum set. It cost ten pounds and I knew they couldn't spare the money.

'Around the end of 1957, my best friend Roy Trafford and I started going to the Cavern Club. I used to admire the groups who played there and wished I could join one. Then I formed a group with the fellow who lived next door, Eddie Clayton, and his brother-in-law. We used to play in a cellar at lunchtime and all our pals would come to listen. I didn't take the full kit – just a snare drum, a cymbal and a pair of sticks in a shopping bag with me sandwiches each morning.

'Then I joined the Cadillacs in November of 1958. The leader had a car and used to pick me up, so for the first time I was able to take out the full kit. I still dressed like a Ted and I was going to dances and always getting into fights. So when I got a chance to join Rory Storm's group, I jumped at it. After all, I was fed up with getting beaten up and it was a better way of meeting girls.

'Early in 1960 Rory got this offer for the group to play at Butlin's camps, but it meant giving up our jobs. I went home and asked me mother and father what they thought. They said "No," and for a fortnight I just thought about it. Then I went and told the boss at the factory where I'd been working that I was leaving to play fulltime in a group. He said, "You'll be back here in three months asking for your job back." There's not much chance of me going back for me job at the moment.

'Then we took the group to Germany to play at the Kaiserkeller in Hamburg. The boss of the club also owned the Indra and the Beatles were playing there. Then the Indra was closed, and the Beatles came to alternate with our group at the Kaiserkeller.

'In between sessions we used to stand at the back and request numbers from the other groups. I always remember John used to ask for me to sing "Alley Oop" every night. John and I got to know each other really well. We used to have breakfast together when the club closed in the morning. When our group came back to England, the Beatles went to play at the Top Ten Club. We met up again when they came back to Liverpool to play at the Cavern.

'Then one day their drummer Pete Best went sick. A car came for me and the driver asked if I would play drums for the Beatles at a lunchtime session at the Cavern. What a laugh it turned out to be. Our group did the same numbers but we did them differently, and I didn't fit in very well as a Beatle on that first session.

'After that, I occasionally filled in for Pete Best. Then Rory Storm's group got a booking at Butlin's at Skegness for a short season. By this time I had replaced me 1950 Standard Vanguard with a Ford Zodiac and was able to drive home every Saturday. The Beatles were playing at a place called the Hot Spot, and one Saturday morning Elsie said that George Harrison had called and would I go down to see them at the Hot Spot? It was my night off and I couldn't think of a better way to spend it.

During a break, John, Paul and George invited me to join them at the Blue Angel later on. Pete Best wasn't coming, they said.

'At the Blue Angel I was introduced to Brian Epstein. We shook hands and he seemed a bit surprised at my appearance: I had a beard and a grey streak in my hair then. I thought no more about the meeting until the following Tuesday when, early in the afternoon, I received a message asking me to phone Mr Epstein at midnight. I did and he said, "Would you like to join the Beatles?" I said I would, and he asked me if I could make it the next day as Pete Best had left, so I said no, but I would join them on the following Saturday afternoon.

'I turned up that afternoon in black corduroy jacket and trousers and a black polo-neck sweater. John said I looked like Billy the Kid.

'My first date as a Beatle proper was at Port Sunlight. Half of the hall was in my favour and the other half called out, "Pete Best for ever, Ringo never!" One fellow kept shouting it and George yelled back at him, "Shut up!" Later on the fellow butted him for it.

'About a month later, we went to London for our first recording session at EMI. I was very nervous and the others kept saying, "Don't crack up now, Ringo." The recording manager George Martin laughed at John playing the mouth organ on "Love Me Do". Soon after the session there were two big hits "Hey Baby" and "I Remember You", both strongly featuring mouth organ. I think, since then, George has realized that we know what we are doing.

'The next time we went to the studio, I was horrified to see a set of drums that weren't mine and a man who definitely wasn't me getting ready for the Beatles' session. George said we were going to do "Love Me Do" again and I played tambourine. Fortunately he decided afterwards to issue the first version as a single, although the one on which I don't play drums is on our first LP.'

I found it harder to get close to George Harrison. As the youngest Beatle, he tended to back off rather than try to compete for the limelight with the extrovert John and Paul. But he was a great guitar player and his urchin-like good looks made him extremely appealing to fans. George was the original Little Boy Lost.

'George was regarded as the kid and kept very much in the background,' said Bill Harry. 'They kept him down most of the Beatles' career, which he always resented. He was upset by the way they treated him. The only original Beatles number they recorded in Germany was "Cry for a Shadow", which had originally been called "Beatle Bop". It was done by George and John, but mainly George, and it was an instrumental skit on the Shadows. So the first original Beatles number was one written by George.

'When they started happening, I used to see George in the clubs at night. I told him, "Listen, everything is Lennon and McCartney. Why don't you start writing – after all, you were the original Beatle songwriter?" He said, "Nobody would be interested."

'But I kept at him until finally I saw him at the ABC Blackpool and he said, "I want to thank you. You made me a lot of money. I was going out to a club one night in Liverpool and I thought, "Oh God, I'm going to see Bill Harry again and he's going to hustle me and bother me about writing a song, so I sat down and started a song called 'Don't Bother Me'. It's on our new album *[With the Beatles]* and I've already made £7000 out of it.'"

It wasn't until 1969 that a Harrison composition, 'Something', gave him his first hit single. No less an authority than Frank Sinatra described it as 'the greatest love song of the past fifty years'.

By then, Hamburg was just a memory, but it had served its purpose well. 'I knew we were going to make it to the top,' John told me later. 'We learned a lot in Hamburg playing twelve hours a day. It was hard work, but it made us tough and we knew we'd earned our chance. No one gave us anything for nothing. We worked for it all.'

CHAPTER SIX

The Epstein Revolution

AFTER THE Star Club, I was astonished at how fast the Beatles 'happened'. Only John, drawing on his own script, seemed able to anticipate the moves.

'Love Me Do' had been recorded on 4 September 1962 in EMI's No. 2 studio on Abbey Road in London's St John's Wood. The backing was taped fifteen times before record producer George Martin was satisfied. As the clock struck midnight, he finished putting down the vocals.

Martin was an imposing figure, well over six feet tall, who dressed in executive business suits and combed his short-back-and-sides hair in the manner of a matinee idol of the period. He had been wrestling with a problem ever since he had signed the group: he wanted to make one of the Beatles a star, but he could not make up his mind which one.

John, the obvious leader, was five foot ten inches tall with brown hair and brown eyes, and he appealed to the rebel in us all. Paul, as tall as John with hazel eyes and black hair, was more cuddly. George, although as tall as the others, and with dark brown eyes and brown hair, seemed positively to demand mothering. But when George told him at their first meeting, 'I don't like your tie,' the producer realized that he could be as abrasive as John. Ringo, at five foot eight inches, with blue eyes and dark brown hair, was the unknown quantity.

'This was the age of the solo star — Cliff Richard, Billy Fury and so on,' said George Martin. 'Even after we'd signed the Beatles, I spent hours going through each one trying to work out which one would be the star. And then it came to me: why not treat them equally?'

When 'Love Me Do' was released on Parlophone in October 1962, people far from Merseyside began to take notice, but not much. The song reached No. 17, then stalled and dropped. However, their second single, 'Please Please Me', another Beatle original that John had insisted they record, hit No. 1 in the British charts on 16 February 1963, and they were on their way. At first, it was the unique sound of vibrant guitars and pleasing harmonies that caught the ear. But once they started to appear before a wider public, the Beatle look delighted the eye in a way that no other group, before or since, has ever managed to do.

No one has ever bettered the description that a Liverpool housewife gave journalist Maureen Cleave, an early Beatle *aficionado:* 'Their physical appearance inspires frenzy,' said the woman. 'They look beat-up and depraved in the nicest possible way.'

The Epstein Revolution was taking place and I was in the middle of it. Brian doubled the size of the Mersey Mafia, bringing in as Neil Aspinall's deputy a genial giant in horn-rims called Malcolm Evans. Elvis had Joe, Sonny, Red, Marty, Charlie *et al.,* and the Beatles had 'Nell' and Mal.

The Beatles were easy to spot in the midst of a crowd. Their mop-topped haircuts – 'pudding basins with a fringe', which the innovative Astrid had pioneered on Stuart Sutcliffe in Hamburg – had become an immediate trademark, and they were pursued through the streets of London by hordes of marauding girls determined to capture a piece of them as a souvenir. Their dress was also distinctive. I went with the 'Fab Four' to Dougie Millings' tailoring shop in Old Compton Street, Soho, to be fitted for new suits. Dougie stood beside John, a piece of chalk in his hand, to mark out the material. John ran his fingers around his exposed neckline.

'Hey, where's the bleeding' collar?' asked John.

'They put it on later,' I said, laughing at his apparent ignorance of bespoke tailoring. 'This is just a fitting.'

Astrid had produced the no-collar look in Hamburg, once again for Stuart, and Brian Epstein had been intrigued by her trend-setting ideas. A stylist himself, he now looked at Lennon approvingly.

'No, I think it looks rather better without one,' he said. 'Make them up like this, Dougie.'

The new-look Beatles were soon dashing down Carnaby Street in smart, lapel-less, grey suits. This was the age of the escapist fad, and the Beatles joined the Mini motor car, the miniskirt and Ian Fleming's 007 hero James Bond as the symbols of a new Britain.

Brian had already stopped the group from smoking, eating and swearing during their act to make them more acceptable to the very particular tastes of BBC television producers. Soon, the same elitists would be begging for a chance to book the Beatles.

If Elvis even noticed the emergence of the Beatles, he gave no sign, although he was concerned about his own music. The man who knew the problem as well as he did was Freddie Bienstock, who could justifiably claim that 'for the first twelve years Elvis hardly ever looked at a song unless I had seen it first.'

'Elvis was always a worrier even though one could not always detect it,' he said. 'But he was also extremely street-wise – not really educated but brilliant in his own way. He was perceptive. He really knew what motivated people and the way it worked as far as songs were concerned.

'It got to be a real pain in the ass when he was doing three or four pictures a year. All the music had to be commissioned. The producers would send me twelve scripts, and I would have to find the scenes where the song might fit. Elvis hated to break out into a song if it didn't fit into the action somehow.

'I would get four or five of our songwriters to write a song for that particular spot and end up with maybe three or five versions for each spot. Elvis would select the ones that he wanted to do, but it was really mass production. Not much attention was being paid to the songs themselves, particularly as each producer wanted a title song from the film. With titles like *Kissin' Cousins* and *Wild in the Country*, it was difficult to come up with a hit. The quality undoubtedly suffered.'

The Beatles, on the other hand, had the creative genius of George Martin, now the honorary 'Fifth Beatle', to turn the song-writing talent of Lennon and McCartney into one brilliant single after another. 'From Me to You', 'She Loves You (Yeah, Yeah, Yeah!)' and 'I Want to Hold Your Hand' followed in rapid succession. In the cut-throat world of the charts, it was no contest. The Beatles just couldn't lose – but some people are never satisfied. I would one day listen to Paul playing 'Yesterday' on a piano to Dick James, the group's musical publisher. 'Very nice, Paul,' responded Dick, 'but haven't you got something with "Yeah, yeah, yeah!" in it?'

At heart, I was still an Elvis fan, and my biggest ambition was to get him to Britain. So I rang the Colonel's office at Paramount and somehow managed to get through to the man himself.

'Is your call paid?' asked the Colonel, the first words of a conversation that has, so far, lasted thirty years.

'Yessir, it's paid at this end.'

The Colonel's attitude was puzzling. He was running a multi-million-dollar Elvis industry yet he was worried about the price of a single transatlantic phone call. I asked him if Elvis were planning to visit his fans in Britain and, if so, suggested the Colonel might consider the Beatles as a supporting act.

'Beatles? Never heard of 'em,' he said dismissively. 'Sounds like something out of a flea circus.'

As for a British tour, it was a distinct possibility once Elvis had completed his obligations in Hollywood. Maybe some time in the next six or seven years, maybe sooner.

It was hard to imagine two more diverse personalities than Colonel Thomas Andrew Parker and Brian Samuel Epstein: one a very brash American, hiding many secrets, including the facts of his birth; the other very British, hiding the secret of his homosexuality. They did, however, have two things in common: both could be remarkably mischievous, and both were equally hell-bent on achieving the success of the superstars they managed.

Brian's first-floor office at No. 13 Monmouth Street near Cambridge Circus, headquarters of the Official Beatles Fan Club, was humble and poky. Still only in his 20s with brown, wavy hair, he would greet me with his engaging smile. He was so much one of the original 'suits' that I suspected he had been born in one. He was exceptionally neat in dress and fastidious in manner, a boyish whine competing with his public school accent. He would be seated behind his desk, sipping water from a glass and taking purple-heart amphetamines. Uppers were as common as aspirin in the pop world.

Brian came from Knotty Ash, one of the more select suburbs of Liverpool, where his mother Queenie and father Harry still lived in style. Despite this enviable background nothing had ever been easy for Brian. He told me he had been so shy and sensitive as a boy that he had been expelled from Liverpool College at the age of 10 for being below standard. He eventually attended seven schools before leaving altogether at the age of 16, the despair of his Jewish parents.

Business, however, was his forte; as he put it, he had the 'knack of knowing what people want'. He liked to divide the world into winners and losers. 'You and I', he declared over lunch in an expensive West End restaurant, 'are winners. We're prepared to sacrifice everything to get what we want. The Beatles are going to be very big because they've got nothing to lose.'

Brian's biggest problem was coming to terms with his homosexuality, which the Beatles knew about but chose to ignore. When, on a trip to Liverpool, Brian and I called at his parents' house, he asked me to wait outside in the car. 'I don't want them to jump to the wrong conclusion,' he said, apologizing profusely. But I was grateful to Brian, whom I regarded as a friend. Our association had given me the inside track on the biggest rock story ever likely to break in Britain.

However, a wild new group had started to build up a following down among the suburban lanes of Surrey. The Rolling Stones created chaos whenever they appeared at their version of the Cavern: the Crawdaddy Club in the *outre* Station Hotel in Richmond. The Beatles, looking like gunfighters in long leather overcoats, went to see them on 14 April 1963. 'The beat the Stones laid down was so solid it shook off the walls and seemed to move inside your head,' George recalls. 'It was a great sound.' After the gig, the two groups adjourned to the Stones' flat in Edith Grove, Chelsea, to talk about their respective careers. John came away angry, resentful and jealous. 'They've stolen our image,' he stormed. 'They're like we used to be before Brian ponced us up. I'm in the wrong band.'

I saw a lot of John and he talked quite freely to me, knowing that the *NME* – to which I had recently returned, at twice my previous salary – was then only interested in positive stories. 'BEATLE JOHN WANTS TO JOIN THE STONES' was just one of the stories I never wrote.

'John went bananas about all the publicity the Stones were getting for being rough,' said Bill Harry. 'He knew the Stones were middle-class boys from the Home Counties, not leather-jacketed Teds at all. While the Beatles had been swearing and whoring in Hamburg, they had been attending trendy schools. John hated it. He really hated it.'

The Beatles were mobbed after a concert at the Royal Albert Hall and had to dash for the safety of their getaway car, an Austin Princess. Countless hands beat a frantic tattoo on the roof. The Beatles were shaken by the enormity of the reaction. They had started calling on me at my flat in Chelsea at all hours, famous but mystified – except for John, who expected fame as his due.

That particular night, John, George and Ringo turned up with a young actress friend, Jane Asher. The old Regency furniture in the cramped living room was hastily pushed aside to make space for the unexpected guests, and they squatted on the dark green pile carpet. As the only woman, Jane was in the centre.

She was pale-faced and suitably thin for the period that spawned Twiggy. But her crowning glory was the mane of ginger hair that cascaded down below her shoulders. When she spoke, her voice reflected her Wimpole Street background, singling her out as upper middle class, yet her kindly smile made the rest of us feel comfortable.

Jane later became Paul's fiancée, but their engagement ended after she caught him in bed with another girl. Tonight, however, she would leave holding hands with George.

'I nearly had me bleeding' head ripped off,' complained Ringo, sampling his drink. 'If this goes on, someone's goin' to get seriously hurt.'

'Yeah, or seriously rich,' said John, never missing a chance.

I raised my glass of Mateus rose, then the sophisticated drink for young Chelsea trendies. None of us knew anything about vintages or high living, but we were willing to learn. We wanted it all.

'To the Beatles.'

John narrowed his eyes and spoke in that superior Scouse drawl. 'Yeah, the group the fans love so much they want to tear us to pieces.'

Jane laughed. 'Oh, John, you're such a cynic. Admit it . . . you adore the attention.'

He tasted his drink and licked his lips. 'Sure I'm a cynic. What we play is only rock 'n' roll under a new name. Rock music is war – hostility and conquest. We sing about love, but we mean sex – and the fans know it.'

'The fans think you're decent, clean-living chaps,' I said.

'It's just an image,' said John, 'and it's the wrong one. Look at the Rolling Stones. Rough as guts. We did that first and now they've pinched it.'

'You can't blame them for that,' Ringo cut in reasonably.

'The fans have to dream that one day they might marry a Beatle,' said Jane.

'Yeah, but only those who haven't reached the age of puberty,' said John. 'I give some girl an autograph and she wants my tie or some of my hair. Then she wants to have sex. Then she tells me she's only 15. Jailbait. Is there any more booze?'

I poured the last of the wine from the flask-shaped bottle into John's glass. 'That's the last of it. I wasn't expecting company.'

John narrowed his eyes, a sure sign of displeasure.

'OK, there's no booze. Let's talk about sex. Jane, how do girls play with themselves?'

Miss Asher was shocked but cool enough not to let it show for more than a moment: 'I'm not going to talk about that,' she replied.

John started to turn nasty. This was the dark side of his character, which his friends grew to fear. At times like this, no one was spared.

'You're the only girl here and I want to know,' he insisted. 'How do you jerk off?'

'There's only one jerk here,' I ventured.

This hit the target. John could dish it out but he didn't like taking it.

'*Oh fab!* No booze, no birds, insults from the host . . . what kind of a rave is this?'

A silence fell on the room. All eyes fastened on Jane. She was quietly weeping.

'Bleedin' marvellous,' said John, rising. 'I'm going in search of some crumpet. Call me a taxi.'

Jane recovered her composure with the help of gentleman George.

'You know, John, you can be very cruel sometimes,' she said.

John turned at the front door, before leaving to find his own taxi.

'It's just the beast in me,' he said, pinching a line from Elvis in *Jailhouse Rock*.

This was John, yearning to be a rock rebel like the Elvis of old and having to shake hands with city councillors instead.

The following month the Beatles went on a tour of England with Gerry and the Pacemakers and Roy Orbison. The likable Texan, having followed Elvis on the Sam Phillips' Sun label, had become a star in his own right. Dressed all in black leather, his hair dyed black, his eyes hidden behind dark shades, he told John: 'You would be tremendous in America.'

'Don't be daft,' replied John. 'They wouldn't understand a dicky bird we say.'

Just as he had been turned down by British record labels, Brian encountered the same resistance in America.

'When the Beatles had their first big hit with "Please Please Me", the deal was that Capitol, which EMI owned in the US, had to be offered first option,' said Bill Harry. 'They turned it down, so it was released by another label but without success. Capitol just weren't interested.'

Not without some difficulty, Mr Sidney Bernstein, formerly of the Bronx, plotted the Beatles' rise to prominence on his side of the Atlantic. One of his problems in advancing their cause was that he had never actually heard them sing, let alone seen them perform. But he was instrumental in getting the Beatles into New York and into the American market – at great cost to Elvis and every other US star.

'I had been reading about them in English newspapers and I guess nobody else in the music business was reading English newspapers,' Sid remembers. 'I got Brian Epstein's number in Liverpool and in February '63 called him.'

According to Sid, the conversation went like this: 'Mr Epstein, my name is Sid Bernstein. I am a promoter here in New York and I would like to present your group in America. I have been reading about them for four months, never hearing a song. There are no records being played here and nobody in America seems to care about British music, but I would like to play the Beatles.'

'Why would you want to do that?' asked Brian. 'I know there's no airplay – in fact, nothing is happening for us in America at all.'

'They will be heard,' Sid assured him. 'How much do you want?'

'You know, the other night we got the equivalent of $2000 for one show and we have all the work we can handle.'

'Mr Epstein, I would like to offer you $6500 for two shows in one day. That's $3250 per show.'

'Wait until I tell the boys in Isow's!' Brian said, referring to Jack Isow's' restaurant where all the big shots of the music industry hung out. 'Where would you play them?'

'At Carnegie Hall.'

'My boys at Carnegie Hall?'

'Yes.'

'As fate would have it, I've just seen an MGM movie called *Carnegie Hall*, which featured all the great classical musicians and opera singers who have performed there. My boys playing there? Wait till I tell them at Isow's! When do you propose to play them?'

'How about three months from now?'

'No, that's too soon. But I'll agree to this time next year, provided we've had a hit in the American charts by the year's end.'

'All right, February twelfth next year: it's a Wednesday, Lincoln's birthday.'

By the autumn of 1963, a headline writer at the *Daily Mirror* had coined the term 'Beatlemania', and the fever had spread like an epidemic. Sid's rash deal, which he admits he'd ad libbed as he went along, plucking both the fee and the venue out of the air, was looking good.

For the first time in the history of pop music, not only had Liverpool taken over from London, but Britain was poised to seize the international market from the United States. However, Capitol was still reluctant to accept the Beatles. After turning down 'From Me to You', another British chart-topper, Alan Livingston, the Capitol president, sent a memo to London saying, 'We don't think the Beatles will do anything in this market.' Epstein flew to New York in November 1963 to try and stir up some action.

'We'd watched the American charts with envy but they seemed unobtainable,' Brian said. 'Frank Ifield was very successful in Britain, but he had only had limited success in America – like every other British artist since the war. There is an American *sound* on disc, and in November 1963 I felt a certain American feeling. This feeling, I was certain, existed in "I Want to Hold Your Hand". I knew that if the Beatles were to mean anything in the US, then "I Want to Hold Your Hand" was the record to do it.'

John and Paul composed the song at Jane Asher's house and the Beatles had recorded it on 17 October 1963.

'By accident, all these lucky things happened one after the other,' said Bill Harry. 'It was the most incredible amount of luck that had ever been known in the history of pop. It just so happened that Ed Sullivan was in London when the Beatles arrived back from their tour of Sweden.'

When he reached New York, Sullivan told Sid Bernstein about the scenes he had witnessed.

'Ed said that, when he and his wife Sylvia were changing plans at Heathrow in October '63, he had seen the signs: "THE BEATLES", "LONG LIVE THE BEATLES", "THE BEATLES FOR EVER",' said Sid. 'He asked an airport attendant if that were an animal act because he was into animal acts, you know, but the airport attendant laughed and told him that this was England's most popular singing group.

'Ed said he had never seen a display like that: three or four hundred kids at the airport. He called to find out who represented them and found out that a New York promoter by the name of Bernstein had booked them for the following year at Carnegie Hall.

'Right away, he called me up and asked me what I thought of them, and I said they were a phenomenon. I still hadn't heard them, but to me they were a phenomenon because of the progress they had made.'

Sullivan invited Brian Epstein to visit him at his suite in the Delmonico Hotel. 'Ed bought them to appear on his television show on Sunday, 9 February – three days before Carnegie Hall – and another appearance a week later,' said Sid. 'This ensured my bet, because anybody who played *Sullivan* two weeks in a row became a star.'

Epstein's lucky roll kept going without any pushing on his part.

'The next thing that happened was that an American disc jockey got an advance copy of "I Want to Hold Your Hand" – his girlfriend was a BOAC hostess and she brought it to him from London,' said Bill Harry. 'He began to play it and he got all these phone calls, so he kept on playing it. Capitol had finally agreed to release the record in January 1964, but they brought it forward to December and put $40,000 into promoting it. It was amazing how all these strands came together, just incredible luck.'

Roy Orbison's prediction came true when 'I Want to Hold Your Hand' hit No. 1 in the *Cash Box* chart in the New Year. The Beatles, who were at the George V in Paris when the news arrived, celebrated with a party, during which Brian Epstein stuck a chamber pot on his head. They sent me a postcard dated 27 January, which I have kept, showing the George V flying a drawn-in flag marked with a huge letter 'B' for Beatles. John had scribbled on the back: 'Having fun. We've ordered *NME* (just to read "Alley Cat", of course). See you soon. Ta-ta. John, Paul, Ringo & George.' 'Alley Cat' was a column of pop gossip, required reading for pop stars and their managers.

One of the sanest contemporary explanations of the impact the Beatles were making came from Archie Bleyer, head of Cadence Records, who had piloted the Everly Brothers to stardom:

The reason the Beatles are so successful is that they have produced a new, original sound. The important word is 'primitive', meaning belonging to the beginning, or original, not derived from something else. You might say the Beatles sound is a progression of rhythm & blues and skiffle, but it is neither in the true sense. It is original.

When Brian Epstein read this opinion in the copy of the *NME* that the Beatles had ordered in Paris, he took in every word. The Epstein Revolution was about to go global.

CHAPTER SEVEN

First Blood to the Beatles

THE BEATLES went to America for the first time in February 1964 and I went with them. They called me Chrisp Hutchy or, sometimes, Chrispy Hutch. It really didn't matter; we were friends. In New York, we were at the Plaza.

From a window on the 12th floor of the vertical French chateau, John gazed across Central Park and saw the Dakota building for the first time. The forbidding Gothic mansion block excited nothing more than mild curiosity in him. This was his first visit to New York, not an augury of his own death.

Looking down, he took in the chaotic scenes in the street below. He forced the window open for a better view and a sound like cannonfire exploded in his ears.

On Fifth Avenue, thousands of girls were being crushed against the police barricades that had been set up almost a block away from the hotel. The girls sang, 'We love you, Beatles, oh yes we do' between orchestrated bursts of screaming. A siren wailed above the confusion. Paul joined John at the open window.

'I guess the same thing happens every time Elvis hits town,' said Paul, genuinely overawed by the reception.

'Elvis?' John said dismissively. He closed the window to muffle the sound.

'Oh, aye, Elvis Pretzel.'

John made a rude face in the direction of the hysterical fans. 'Elvis has never even played New York. We're bigger than Elvis.'

I overheard this exchange as I talked to George and Ringo. 'So you'd meet Elvis if I could fix it?' I asked them.

Ringo nodded his head eagerly to signify that he at least was willing.

John, as ever the Beatle who bit, said: 'He can visit us any time he wants . . . like his fans are doing.'

He was a capricious character. Sometimes I felt close to him; at other times, the gap between us was as wide as the Mersey. However, there was no doubting that John, Paul, George and Ringo had taken Manhattan, the Bronx and Statten Island, too.

'They put a smile on America's face,' said Bill Harry. 'America was still in mourning for John F. Kennedy and people were in a state of deep depression. Suddenly, the Beatles were there with funny haircuts and funny accents. This was the extra thing that made them a hit.'

That night, the group performed on the *Ed Sullivan Show,* the programme that was famous for having made Elvis famous from the waist up. In the dressing room at the CBS studios, four radios blared Beatle songs and Beatle chat from four different stations. 'It's like Liddypool on Saturday night,' joked Ringo.

Paul shouted, 'It's from Elvis!' as he opened one of the hundreds of good luck cables to arrive before the show.

'Elvis who?' quipped John Lennon, still playing hard to get.

'Shirrup!' yelled Paul, reading the message:

CONGRATULATIONS ON YOUR APPEARANCE ON THE ED SULLIVAN SHOW AND YOUR VISIT TO AMERICA STOP WE HOPE YOUR ENGAGEMENT WILL BE SUCCESSFUL AND YOUR VISIT PLEASANT STOP SINCERELY ELVIS AND THE COLONEL

Only minutes before they were due to appear, John realized he had no cufflinks. He asked if he could borrow mine and I handed them over.

The cufflinks were two theatrical masks: one a happy face, the other sad – just like John himself. He put them on hastily and dashed down three flights of stairs to the stage, arriving with only seconds to spare.

Sullivan, no slouch at exploiting a good thing even at the expense of his own prejudices, opened his show with the Beatles doing three numbers: 'All My Loving', 'Till There Was You' and 'She Loves You'. They returned in the second half with 'I Saw Her Standing There' and 'I Want to Hold Your Hand'. An estimated 73 million people tuned in to watch, compared with the 54 million who had seen Elvis's first performance on the show in 1956. Across America on Beatle night, teenage crime dropped to almost zero.

Realizing that the Colonel and I were playing the same game, even if our motives were different, I phoned his number at Paramount the following morning.

'How much did Mr Epstein get?' he wanted to know. 'What was the fee?'

'$10,000, I understand.'

There was a derisory snort down the line from Tinseltown.

'I knew that,' said the Colonel. 'I was just checking. He should have let me negotiate for him. I got $50,000 for Elvis and that was back in '56.'

I tried to sound impressed, hoping that would give me some leverage in the favour I was angling for.

'Colonel, I'm sure you've thought of it already, but what about fixing a meeting between Elvis and the Beatles?'

He considered the angle for a few moments.

'You know these guys pretty well, huh?'

'If you watched the TV closely – John was wearing my cufflinks.'

'A meeting, huh? It did cross my mind. Sure, why not? *They* can visit *us* any time they like.'

'They sort of thought Elvis might visit them.'

The Colonel became business-like and quite gruff.

'Let me tell you somethin', son. Elvis is an international entertainer and a Hollywood movie star. Two weeks ago I told him I hoped American teenagers would be as good to the Beatles as they have been to us. El said he felt the same way. He's on holiday in Las Vegas at the moment, but I'll discuss the matter with him.'

The Beatles had awoken to a New York covered in snow, but nothing short of a blizzard would have driven away the fans camped outside. Reviews of the *Ed Sullivan Show* had also been decidedly frosty. Asked at a press conference how he felt about scathing comments in the *New York Times* that morning, John declared, to the delight of the TV and radio interviewers: 'It's all lies.'

Told by another reporter that long-haired mammoths in the Natural History Museum resembled the Beatles, John borrowed a line from George: 'I don't like your tie.'

The group performed their first live US concert at the Coliseum in Washington, D.C. I watched from the back with Brian Epstein. Nearby, a cop stuck a bullet in each ear to shut out the shattering sound. Jelly beans, much harder than the jelly babies fans threw in Britain, rained down on the stage. 'Throw peppermint creams,' Paul suggested. 'They're softer when they hit.'

After the concert, the Beatles were guests of honour at a masked ball held by the ambassador, Sir David Ormsby-Gore, later Lord Harlech, at the British Embassy. What should have been a triumphant night for Britain turned into an embarrassing farce for all concerned. One woman took a pair of nail scissors out of her handbag and blithely snipped off a lock of Ringo's hair as though she were taking a cutting from a house plant. Ringo cringed, but kept the peace. 'Did you see that woman cut off a piece of my hair?' he asked incredulously. 'I'm ruddy mad. This lot are terrifying – much worse than the kids.'

When a pink-faced young Britisher shoved an autograph book in front of John's face, he refused to sign his name. The assault on Ringo had raised his working-class hackles.

'You will sign this and like it,' the obstreperous one persisted.

'Oh really?' said John. He walked out of the reception and went back to the hotel in a rage.

The following day, the Beatles caught a train back to New York for their two concerts at Carnegie Hall on Lincoln's birthday, making Sid Bernstein the happiest man in America. 'The box office sold all 6000 tickets for the two shows in twenty minutes,' he said. 'We could have sold 200,000 tickets.'

John finally unwound when we took a pleasure cruise on the yacht *Southern Trail* off Miami, courtesy of a friendly millionaire.

'Foony 'ow these people have swimming pools when the sea is just at the bottom of their gardens,' said Ringo as we skirted white-walled mansions lining the waterside.

'Well, this isn't Merseyside – they wear mink bikinis here,' said John.

As the yacht passed a small beach, someone recognized the Mopheads, as the Beatles had become known in America, and dozens of hands waved in greeting. Paul gave his familiar wink and thumbs-up sign.

Over on the West Coast, Elvis wasn't allowing himself to be completely upstaged. He posed obligingly on his yacht *Potomac* for a picture that would appear in a double-page feature on the Beatles. 'I wish they were here in person,' he said disingenuously, adding: 'They aren't competition, they're an asset to the music industry – keeping it fresh and alive.' The King confined his true thoughts to his buddies in the Memphis Mafia.

The Beatles were in Miami to broadcast the second of their three *Ed Sullivan* shows, from the Deauville Hotel. They became excited when they were told that Elvis was sailing his yacht to Florida and intended calling on them. But although they kept their hopes up until the last minute, Elvis did not appear. They had been the victims of a hoax. Elvis's yacht stayed in the coastal waters off California. He had never had the slightest intention of going anywhere near Miami Beach or the Beatles.

Hearing of their disappointment, the Colonel phoned Brian at his hotel the morning after the *Ed Sullivan* show and, once again, offered his congratulations.

As an introduction to the American market, the short tour had proved a runaway success. They deserved every cheer they got when we flew back into Heathrow. It had become apparent even to their worst enemies that the Beatles were no seven-day wonder.

In April, they made a TV special for Rediffusion called *Around the Beatles*, which included a sketch from *A Midsummer's Night Dream* as well as a selection of their hits. John appeared as Thisbe, Paul as Pyramus, George as Moonshine and Ringo as the Lion, each Beatle reluctantly dressed in Shakespearean costume.

P. J. Proby, the Texas-born singer who was making a solo career after doing demo tapes for Elvis, appeared on the special as one of the supporting acts. He told me: 'I was suspicious of those guys at first apart from Ringo, who was friendly from the start. The others didn't seem to want to know me. Then somebody told them I did good impersonations and they started to talk to me. "Do your one of me," said Paul. "Do Rosie and the Originals," said John. But I do Elvis best of all and everybody loved that.'

The Beatles made a highly successful movie with Dick Lester, *A Hard Day's Night*, about twenty-four hectic hours in the life of the group. John wanted to call it *Authenticity*, Roy Orbison suggested, during a visit to the set with me, that it should be named *Ben Hair* and promoted as a biblical epic. Finally it was Ringo who came up with *A Hard Day's Night*, a phrase he had contributed to John's first book, *In His Own Write*. But it was the literary drummer who cracked first under the strain of the group's many, many hard day's nights.

'Ringo has never been particularly strong, so I suppose I keep an eye on him the most,' Neil Aspinall told me at the time. 'He collapsed during a picture session just a couple of days before the Beatles were due to leave for a tour of Scandinavia, the Far East and Australia in June. I was with them when it happened and got quite a fright when I saw Ringo sink to his knees.

'I immediately took him to a doctor, who said that Ringo would have to go to hospital. I phoned Brian and told him that, despite the tour, there was no alternative: Ringo *had* to go to hospital. He did, and Jimmy Nicol stood in for him.

Ringo, who had his tonsils removed at University College Hospital, London, rejoined the group in Melbourne. The Beatles never played without him again.

Soon after they arrived back, the group were in Liverpool for the northern premiere of *A Hard Day's Night*. Still exhausted after the long flight, they found the route from the airport to the Town Hall packed with well-wishers. At a civic reception, one dignitary grabbed John's arm just as he picked up a sandwich.

'Careful, that's my bad arm,' said the Beatle, sounding a note of warning. But the interloper was oblivious to John's mood. He thrust an autograph book and pen under his nose.

'Sign this,' said the notable.

This was practically a re-run of the incident in Washington, only, this time, John was on his home patch and had no intention of running away. For a moment, I watched him hesitate. Then he took the book and pen with one hand and thrust the sandwich into the man's mouth, saying: 'Hold this.'

After signing his name, he handed the book and pen back to the owner and crossed the room to join the other Beatles, leaving the not-so-dignified dignitary with the sandwich clenched between his teeth.

Parlophone continued to release first-class records such as 'Can't Buy Me Love', one of the songs from *A Hard Day's Night*. The only recording Elvis put down while the Beatles were back in England for those six months was the soundtrack of *Girl Happy,* which included such forgettable numbers as 'Fort Lauderdale Chamber of Commerce' and

'Do the Clam'. Elvis had become a Hollywood recluse, afraid or unwilling to face up to the challenge of the Awesome Foursome.

'He found all sorts of excuses not to go into the studio and record unless he absolutely had to,' said Freddie Bienstock. 'He would say he had broken his ankle and I should feel the broken bone, or that it was too hot and he could not go on. That was his way of showing he was unhappy.'

The Beatles continued to eat up the public acclaim, but with their impudent humour firmly intact. I scribbled down the Beatle-isms whenever I heard them.

Someone asked Ringo how he liked girls to dress.

'In dresses,' he replied.

A girl asked George: 'What do you think of topless swimsuits?'

'Fine,' he said. 'I've been wearing them for years.'

No similar one-liners were coming out of Memphis or Hollywood. To ease the frustration of his self-imposed exile, Elvis was closely inspecting swimsuits himself, and one in particular. It adorned the voluptuous figure of Ann-Margret, his Swedish-born leading lady in *Viva Las Vegas*. In one scene, Elvis, dressed in a suit and holding a guitar, found himself standing on a diving board with Ann-Margret playing the role of a swimming instructor. 'Now you push him into the pool,' ordered the director. And she did. Before long, Elvis and Ann-Margret were pushing each other into bed.

I rang the Colonel to check out the truth of the rumours that had drifted out from the closed film set.

'Listen, our boy had one hobby last year, he has the same hobby this year and it'll be the same next year: pretty girls,' said the Colonel. 'I've met Ann-Margret and she's real pretty, but there'll be others to follow.'

It didn't suit the Colonel's purpose to mention that Elvis had a live-in girlfriend back at Graceland. Elvis the stud was good box office, but there were limits. Priscilla found out about the affair anyway, and Elvis withdrew even more, abandoning the stage to the Beatles, the Rolling Stones and the other supergroups of the Sixties.

Roustabout, Elvis's next film, found him working with an unknown extra in whose life he had played an unsuspecting role. Once again, Raquel Welch found herself studying the Presley form.

'When I got to Hollywood, my first-ever job in the movies was as an extra in *Roustabout*,' she told me. 'I was just a girl in a blue blouse behind a booth – you see me in one shot, that's all. When Elvis came on the set, I was really disappointed: his hair was dyed so black he looked like Wayne Newton, he was covered in make-up and I remember he had these polyester pants on with permanent creases stitched in. It was definitely not the raw sex machine I had seen on stage in San Diego.

'Anyway, on the third day one of his boys came over to me and said, "Elvis is having a party tonight up at the mansion. Would you like to come?" I thought, "Oh, no, there's going to be him and his boys and a bunch of girls and they're going to be working out between them who has who, I can do without that," so I didn't go.'

To the casual observer, Elvis couldn't appear to have cared less. Looking plump and uninterested, he carried on a mindless existence in the company of the Memphis Mafia. A 'big night out' might be watching a movie at the Memphian Theatre.

However, P. J. Proby saw the truth with his own eyes. 'Last time I was at his home, Elvis just sat there glaring,' he said at the time. 'He's got a jukebox full of Beatles records and he plays them all the time.'

None of this made things easy for the Colonel, but he was cunning. Working on the principle that, if you can't beat 'em, join 'em, he made an overture of peace. From his office at Paramount, he sent a telegram welcoming the Beatles to California during their second US visit, a full-blooded tour of North America beginning in August 1964.

TO BRIAN EPSTEIN AND THE BEATLES STOP IF THERE
IS ANYTHING I CAN BE OF SERVICE WITH AS A

FRIEND DO NOT HESITATE TO CALL ON ME STOP
GIVE MY BEST TO CHRIS HUTCHINS AND IF YOU
HAVE TIME GIVE ME A CALL WHEN YOU COME TO
TOWN STOP ELVIS AND THE COLONEL

This Western Union cable was later sold at auction at Sotheby's and now has a place of honour on a wall in the Hard Rock Cafe in London's Piccadilly. The message seemed to confirm a report that had already reached the Beatles: Elvis had bought several tickets for their concert at the Hollywood Bowl. Alas, this turned out to be yet another hoax.

At the time of their performance, Elvis was driving from Los Angeles to Memphis in his customized Greyhound bus, with Scatter, his pet chimpanzee, and the Guys. Once again, he had no intention of turning up to support his deadly rivals.

CHAPTER EIGHT

The Lennon Lemon Acid

THE NOTEBOOK, a Walker's Tablet Refill No. 4, is scuffed at the edges, the blue-lined pages yellowed by age. But it contains my notes about the Beatles tour of the US in August and September 1964. These jottings formed the basis of a newspaper series I wrote called *Living with the Beatles*. They begin:

> On the thirteen-hour flight to San Francisco, we whooped it up with champagne and caviar. Flight began hilariously with boys sending up hostess attempting to demonstrate safety apparatus. Later we relaxed with lemonade and Scotches – Coke is out now – John, George and I sitting on back of a double seat. John talked at length about the inferiority complex which prevents him dining out. 'I'm terrified to even lift a phone and book a table,' he told me . . .

There was a great deal more to come. We arrived in San Francisco safely and checked into our rooms on the 15th floor of the Hilton. Here, John confided more about the fears that even the money and fame that went with being a Beatle had failed to erase from his life. He said he had a premonition that he would die in tragic circumstances. He was, he admitted over more Scotch, 'paranoid about somebody trying to bump me off'.

I knew he was serious, having seen him soaked in sweat *before* a concert, terrified at facing 'the mob' as he called the crowd. When we scanned the tour itinerary together, he stopped at one name and said: 'Dallas – that's where Lee Harvey Oswald shot Kennedy. That reminds me, I've got something to show you.'

He produced a piece of typewritten paper and read from it: '"Kennedy was assassinated on a Friday – so was Lincoln. They were both shot from behind, in the head, on a Friday and in the presence of their wives. Lincoln was elected in 1860, Kennedy in 1960, both of their successors were named Johnson and were southern democrats. Lincoln's killer shot him in a theatre and ran to a warehouse. Oswald shot Kennedy from a warehouse and ran to a theatre."'

John folded the paper and handed it to me. 'It's uncanny,' he said. 'These psychopaths must follow some sort of pattern. I wonder if Kennedy ever thought it would happen to him?'

Although risks were cut down to a minimum, it was still highly dangerous being a Beatle in America in 1964. To say that everybody was nervous was putting things mildly. The Beatles asked Brian to ensure that the limousines sent to meet them at San Francisco airport were closed cars instead of the open models originally planned. George jokingly added: 'And we'd like bulletproof vests.'

Security was tight, but despite heavy police guards on the hotel and on the floor occupied by the Beatles, the fans slipped through. Two passed my room at four o'clock one morning, crying and moaning, 'Ringo, where are you?'

George explained: 'Previously pop stars have been put on a pedestal – unreachable. But our image is a different one. We were the ones you can come and shake by the hand and say, "You're doing a great job, wacker." We liked it that way, but now it's just impossible.'

The tour, which would cover twenty-four cities in the US and Canada, opened at the Cow Palace, San Francisco. To avoid fans, the group were collected by a limousine that drove up an interior road that winds up inside the hotel. With sirens wailing and police motorcyclists on either side, we sped the wrong way down the busy main road to the stadium, where 17,000 Beatle People were waiting.

After meeting Shirley Temple and Joan Baez backstage, the Beatles performed ten numbers in a hail of jelly beans. Then they dashed backstage and a decoy police car sped off. But the ruse failed. When the Beatles did leave in a closed limousine, so many fans jumped on to the roof that it was in danger of collapsing. Police officers pulled the Beatles to safety and put them in the back of an ambulance, which had been taking to hospital several drunken sailors who had been hurt in a brawl.

Finally, we got to the airport and flew to Las Vegas, arriving at 2.00 am to find the night life still in full swing. Once incident here proved that John's fear of people could make him react in a callous way. I was enjoying a drink with the group at the Sands Hotel when a bespectacled teenage girl, not the usual Beatle groupie, burst in unannounced. We were trying to work out how she had managed to slip past the security guards when she explained in a loud, friendly voice: '*Hi, guys!* I'm Donald O'Connor's daughter.'

John did not hesitate. Eyes narrowing, he looked up and said: 'Oh, I'm sorry, luv, I really am.'

Puzzled, Donald O'Connor's daughter said: 'Whadda ya mean, you're sorry?'

'Just heard it on the radio,' replied John, straight-faced. 'Your dad's dead.'

Donald O'Connor's daughter reeled beneath this dose of what we called the 'Lennon lemon acid'. She broke down in hysterics and had to be sedated. The last I saw of her, she was being driven away in an ambulance.

John could be cruel sometimes, but I now knew that his sharp cutting edge was a protection against his own insecurity. He was, in a distressing way, his own worst enemy. This came out when, much later that night and showing no signs of remorse, he talked about the incident.

'Soft cow,' said John. 'Why the hell did she think we'd care about who her father was? It's always, "I'm the mayor's wife" or "My brother knows the President." Well, *I'm* a Beatle but I don't go round announcing it.'

As one of the four most famous human beings on Earth, John, of course, had no need to state the obvious to anyone he met. However, his inability to grasp the difference between himself and a nervous, excited fan showed that the strain of living up to his fame was beginning to tell. John Lennon never liked living up to anything.

'John never gets openly angry, but when someone annoys him – and fools always do – he can tear them to shreds with his sarcasm,' Neil Aspinall told me. 'It's impossible to fight a verbal battle with John and win. I've seen many famous and important people learn that lesson the hard way.'

John was also scornful of the way people imitated Beatle fashions. He could not conceal his contempt when a TV news bulletin reported that showbiz stars including Steve McQueen were flocking to a Hollywood barber who specialized in Beatle haircuts. 'How soft can you get?' he snorted.

He was equally disdainful when it was reported that those without sufficient hair of their own – among them, the world's richest man at that time, J. Paul Getty – were wearing Beatle wigs. 'The only rich guy I'm interested in is Howard Hughes,' John said. 'I bet he doesn't wear a Beatle wig.'

John was, indeed, vastly intrigued by Hughes, who was living at the Desert Inn just a block away from the Sands. Hughes had arrived in Las Vegas one midnight the previous year, travelling incognito in the back of an ambulance. Guarded by his Mormon entourage, he had entered the hotel through the back door and occupied all the high-roller suites on the ninth floor. There he had stayed, seeing no one. Not even the armed Mormons stationed at the entrances to his suite had set eyes on him.

Hughes' reclusive lifestyle so fascinated John that he took a big risk with his own safety. While thousands of fans were camped outside the Sands hoping to catch a glimpse of the Fab Four, it was John's only wish to see Hughes' hiding place. When he put his request to the security guards, they told him it was impossible and refused to take responsibility for any Beatle venturing beyond his own heavily guarded suite. But John was so determined to visit the Desert Inn that he recruited the help of Irving Kandell, the concert programme concessionaire who was a staunch Beatle fan.

Kandell borrowed a hotel doorman's uniform and a catering van, and together we smuggled John down the back stairs, through the kitchens and into the forbidden world beyond. No one recognized the Beatle, disguised in doorman's coat with his hair tucked up beneath a braided cap, as we drove the one block to the Desert Inn in the early hours of the morning.

There were just the three of us standing by the dusty roadside. Lights blazed from every part of the Desert Inn except for the heavily curtained ninth floor.

'That's it?' asked John, awe-struck. He was stoned.

'Yeah, that's it,' murmured Irving Kandell. 'That's where Howard Hughes lives.'

John stood there silently gazing up, lost in the experience. Someone famous was asleep behind those drapes and no one could reach him. He was untouchable.

For days afterwards, he talked about Hughes, quizzing anyone who might know about him. If there was one person John wanted to meet in the whole of America it wasn't Elvis Presley but Howard Hughes.

'That would suit me,' he said. 'In one place for ever, instead of all this travelling. Total privacy, nobody to bother you, scream at you, poke your hair or ask what your favourite colour is. (Black.) I just want to meet him and tell him I understand.'

Despite his desire for seclusion, John still entertained numerous young women in his bedroom, sometimes two or three at a time. He liked to watch the sexual antics of others and he liked being watched himself. It was in Vegas that he had a very narrow escape when he relaxed his rule about 'jailbait' and allowed a pretty 14-year-old girl to join in. When the girl failed to return home late that night, her anxious father contacted a friend who had been with her earlier in the evening. Told that his daughter was with John Lennon at the Sands, the man dashed around to the hotel and started to raise hell. Mal Evans spirited the girl out of John's bedroom and she slipped quietly home. Unaware of this, the father threatened to ask one of the police officers on guard to find his daughter. It took all of Brian's gentle persuasion and a fistful of dollars to placate the angry parent. Had he complained to the police, John would have faced a charge of statutory rape and might have spent the foreseeable future in a Nevada penitentiary.

Not long afterwards, he had good reason to fear for his life – and in Dallas, as he had predicted. When the Beatles' chartered prop-jet landed, it was directed to a parking position some distance from the terminal after ground controllers warned the pilot that the police could not control the 20,000 waiting fans.

No sooner had the pilot cut the engines and the aircraft had come to a halt than the crowd broke through the barriers and surged all over the plane. Like an excited swarm, they climbed on to the wings and peered in through the cabin windows.

I was sitting beside John when the captain explained over the intercom that he was powerless to move the plane. Just starting up the engines would mean slicing dozens of Beatle admirers to pieces.

'If someone doesn't do something soon, we'll all be dead,' John told me seriously. 'It only needs one lighted cigarette to get near the fuel tanks and we'll be singing "She Loves You" in heaven.

Eventually, a laundry truck was manoeuvred beneath the plane, the Beatles were dropped through the luggage bay into it and they were driven to safety. I didn't know it then, but the Colonel had tipped off Brian about that little trick. It worked a treat.

CHAPTER NINE

Jayne Mansfield Can't Help It

WHEN WE reached LA, I met the Colonel face to face for the first time. He sent a car to pick me up early one morning to take me to the Westwood apartment where he had been laid up with a bad back for two months.

In his lavishly furnished first-floor suite at the Beverly Comstock, I found him taking business calls from a hospital bed. As I arrived, he was just agreeing a deal for the sale of half-a-million framed colour portraits of Elvis. The photographs of the Colonel himself didn't do him justice. Pale blue eyes and plump nose sat in a moon-shaped face like ornaments on a pudding, and his ample chins told a story. Yet even semi-crippled, he exuded the ferocity of a rogue elephant. (He later informed me that the elephant was his favourite circus animal.) When he finished making money over the phone, he welcomed me cordially, and I asked him for news of Elvis.

'He's long wanted to meet the Beatles, but he arranged ages ago to spend this break between filming in Memphis,' said the Colonel, ever the diplomat.

Although he had not been out of the apartment for eight weeks, the Colonel insisted on getting up and taking me down to his offices at Paramount. Before we left, I phoned Brian Epstein, who invited us to lunch at the Beverly Hills Hotel.

At Paramount, an illuminated sign above a doorway advertised Elvis's latest picture. The walls of the outer office and the corridors that connected it to the outside world were decorated with Elvis likenesses: billboards for Presley films, advertising material for Presley records, posters for Presley lipstick, handbags and pyjamas. The centrepiece was a cardboard replica of the cellblock in *Jailhouse Rock*.

The walls of his own office were covered with pictures of the Colonel with famous politicians and celebrities: the Colonel with President Lyndon B. Johnson, the Colonel and Elvis with the Speaker of the House, the Colonel with Frank Sinatra. He pointed his cane at the rear wall behind his cluttered desk. 'This here is my dead wall. When anybody dies, I move their picture over here. All these people are deceased.'

Later, we drove to the Beverly Hills Hotel, where Brian was staying. There were screams of 'Elvis' and 'Beatles' as the two most famous rock managers in the world shook hands warmly in the foyer. Over lunch, the thing that seemed to concern Brian most was the tight security necessary to protect the Beatles. The Colonel wasn't impressed.

'You don't have to protect the Beatles the way we protected Elvis because, with them, there is no jealousy,' he snorted. 'You don't have to fear the boyfriends because your artists are characters loved in a different way. The boyfriends would throw things at Elvis on stage. We never had to send in the police to get them – the girls always got them first. Your problem is to protect the small fans from getting hurt in the crush. We never had them so little.'

'Will Elvis ever tour again?' asked Brian.

'Put it this way – I'd like him to tour again some day because I'm a showman, but at the moment we can earn more money and entertain more fans by making films. One day you will discover the same situation with the Beatles . . .

'Elvis has required every moment of my time, and I think he would have suffered had I signed anyone else, but I admire you, Brian, for doing it your way with other performers as well. Obviously you have a different organization, but remember, too, that when Presley soared to fame I was 44. When the Beatles happened, you were 28. That helps.'

When the Colonel recalled how he had launched Elvis in the early days by doing rough jobs like selling tickets at dance halls, Brian retorted: 'So did I in little Lancashire towns. I took around my own posters and sold tickets when they were earning less than £20 a show.'

Whatever the rivalry between their superstars, I noted that the two managers displayed a fair degree of one-upmanship themselves.

The following afternoon, which was hot and humid, I took the Colonel to meet the Beatles. We drove to their rented mansion in Saint Pierre Road, Bel Air, in a station wagon loaded with presents. 'I put on a tie specially for these guys,' said the Colonel.

The Beatles had just finished lunch when we arrived. Still in trunks after a morning swim, John regarded the Colonel with barely disguised curiosity. I prayed that he wouldn't sabotage the deal I was carefully piecing together.

The Colonel made himself at home at the dining-room table where the remains of lunch were waiting to be cleared away. He told the Beatles: 'Elvis phoned me this morning to say he was sorry he wasn't here to greet you, but he'd welcome you at Graceland if you'd like to stop over in Memphis.'

(In fact, Elvis was telling his bodyguards: 'I don't want to meet them sonsovbitches.' He was becoming quite aggressive about it.)

Ever hopeful, the Beatles discussed the idea, but Brian shook his head with the sort of reluctance he would adopt to turn down £50,000 deals. 'I don't think our schedule will permit,' he said solemnly. The Colonel shrugged. Secretly, I believe he was relieved. He knew Elvis's state of mind and he wasn't physically well enough himself to deal with his recalcitrant client.

From a huge box, the Colonel handed out his presents like a midsummer Santa Claus. For each of the Beatles, there was a table lamp in the shape of covered wagons and a valuable leather gun-belt. Brian got a gold one and the Colonel gave me a silver one spangled with rhinestones. Ringo dashed into the kitchen and borrowed a cowboy hat from the chef. The Beatles already had imitation six-shooters and a gunfight started around the dining room.

'Bang, bang!' said Paul, aiming his gun at the Colonel. 'You're dead!'

John found a more symbolic target. He pointed his gun at his own head and shouted: 'Bang!'

'I wish we had real guns,' said George.

John caught the implication and frowned.

'Have fun,' said the Colonel, taking his leave.

That evening, Paul, George and Ringo went across to Burt Lancaster's neighbouring mansion to watch Peter Sellers' latest movie, *A Shot in the Dark*. Once the film had ended, they ventured down to the Whiskey-a-Go-Go on Sunset. John had stayed at Beatleville, the name we gave any temporary residence, to receive Bobby Darin and Sandra Dee. After they had departed, John and I were watching TV in the living room when Jayne Mansfield and a male companion appeared unannounced in the open doorway. We were both in a mad, mischievous mood.

'Only two Beatles left around here?' she asked, disappointed.

'Why it's *the* Jayne Mansfield,' said John, greeting the blonde star of *The Girl Can't Help It* as though he was really impressed. 'And Mickey Hargitay,' he said to the complete stranger with her. 'Good to see you.'

'Oh, silly,' giggled Jayne, loving it. 'Mickey's my ex. This is another friend.'

'I'm John,' said the lone Beatle. 'This is Chris. The others have gone to the Whiskey-a-Go-Go.'

'Well, let's go and join them,' she giggled again, breathing in deeply.

'No, thanks, I'm staying in,' said John. 'Would you like a drink?'

'I'll have a cocktail,' said Jayne, fluttering her eyelashes.

'I'll get it,' I volunteered. I'd never poured a cocktail in my life, but I went into the kitchen and started to examine the bottles. John followed me.

'What do you put in a cocktail?' I asked.

'A drop of that, that, that and that,' he replied, pointing to every liquor bottle on the shelf. 'And then you pee in it.'

I poured gin, vodka, red wine and several liqueurs into a large glass, added ice and handed it to John, who added some liquid Lennon. Jayne pronounced the drink a real humdinger and got even more excited when John told her it was a Beatle Special. Playfully, she tugged John's Beatle cut and asked: 'Is this real?'

John hated to be touched. Dropping his eyes, he returned the compliment.

'Are those real?' he asked.

Jayne took a deep breath and replied: 'There's one way to find out.'

Her companion interrupted by flourishing a pack of tarot cards. In return for the hospitality, he said, he would read the cards for John.

'He's going to tell you your destiny . . . and mine,' breathed Jayne, her massive bosom heaving in John's direction.

No one knew at this stage that Elvis had been one of Jayne's conquests. She had bedded him after the Colonel had deliberately demanded an astronomical fee for him to appear in *The Girl Can't Help It*. The Colonel didn't want Elvis to share the billing with Little Richard, Eddie Cochran, Fats Domino and a host of other rock stars. After their one-night stand, Jayne asked Elvis if he would reconsider. 'Ask the Colonel,' Elvis yawned. The Colonel refused to budge, but Elvis gave Jayne a pink motorbike as a consolation prize.

John tolerated the tarot reader while he went through a glib recital of the group's much chronicled success. Then he drew a card that made him stop. He dropped the cards with an expression of mock horror and exclaimed: 'My God, this is terrible. I see an awful ending to all this.'

At this point, John lost his temper. He was wildly superstitious and his anger covered up his fear about what fate might have in store.

'*Out!*' he ordered America's most famous living sex symbol, taking her and her companion by the arms and propelling them through the doorway. His sudden hostility stunned them so much that they went with barely a murmur. Incensed, John suggested we join the other Beatles at the Whiskey-a-Go-Go for some real cocktails.

'What a phoney that guy was,' he said, relaxing in the cab. 'He told me things everyone knows, then tried to scare me witless.'

It wasn't easy to get into the club. Thousands of fans were being manhandled by the police outside, but John was easily recognizable and we were shoved through the door. Inside, another thousand patrons plus a score of photographers were jostling to join George and Ringo. Paul had found better things to do and had gone off on his own. No sooner were we seated than a familiar voice was heard above the clamour.

'Hi, you guys – fancy seeing you here!'

Jayne Mansfield swanned into view with a photographer in tow and squeezed her breasts into the middle of our group. John studiously ignored her, but the cameraman snapped a picture of three of the Beatles apparently out nightclubbing with Jayne Mansfield. To show his disgust, George flung the remains of his Scotch and Coke at the photographer. An ice cube hit one of the spectators, the actress Mamie van Doren, in the face. As Gentleman George tried to apologize, John whispered to Jayne what had really been in the Beatle Special. Before she could hit him, we made an undignified exit.

The ironic thing was that the 'phoney' tarot card reader had got it absolutely right. Both John and Jayne died violent deaths, the actress being decapitated in a car crash in New Orleans only two years later. The next time John and I discussed predestination, he remembered that day and worried even more about his future. By this time, he was heavily into numerology under the tutelage of Yoko Ono, and he was obsessed by the number nine, the date of his birth.

'Jayne was born on 19 April and she died on 29 June,' he said. 'April is the fourth month and June is the sixth. Add them together and you get ten. I was born on 9 October, the ninth day of the tenth month. She died two months after her birthday, which means I'm going to die on a day with a nine in it, in December.'

A much more welcome guest than Jayne Mansfield or any of the other Beatle-eaters was Bob Dylan, who visited them at the Delmonico Hotel when we reached New York.

After midnight one night, I returned there with Neil Aspinall and Mai Evans. We had been to see *Spartacus* at a cinema on Times Square. Neil quietly opened the door of the Beatles' suite and we entered the outer room. Through the half-opened door of the living room, a curious ritual came into view. Mal nudged me and said: 'Christ, look at that!'

Six chairs were lined up in a row. The Beatles occupied the centre four, Bob Dylan sat at one end and Brian Epstein at the other. As we watched, Dylan elbowed the Beatle next to him and the gesture was passed along the line to Epstein, who promptly fell off his chair. All six broke into helpless laughter. Brian climbed back on to his chair and the procedure began all over again. Brian fell to the floor once more and everyone burst out laughing.

'If I'm not mistaken, the boys have discovered pot,' I whispered as we crept quietly away.

The Beatles had tried hashish before, but this was their first experiment with potent grass. I raised the subject with Brian the following day while we were having coffee in his suite. He didn't look at all well.

'What was that scene about last night?'

'Were you there? I can't remember.'

He popped two amphetamines, washed them down with a glass of water and shivered.

'All I can say about the drug culture is: plenty of drugs but not much culture.'

I finished my coffee and left. I didn't see Brian again for several days and all my enquiries as to his whereabouts were met with mystifying shrugs. Something was clearly wrong. It was John who told me what had happened.

'Brian went out the other night and picked up a sailor. The guy roughed him up and stole his watch, bracelet, pen . . . all solid gold from Asprey's. He's flown back to London to get replacements.'

'What? For the whole lot?'

'Yeah. He thinks people will notice they're missing and jump to conclusions.'

The image-conscious Brian was normally very cautious about his homosexual entanglements. But once he had downed a few drinks and taken some drugs, he would seek out rough trade in the low dives on 42nd Street. The confident young impresario, immaculate in Saville Row's finest, would become a silly, giggly drunk.

His technique was to make a pass at another man, not necessarily a homosexual, and risk everything on the outcome. The distinct possibility of being hit added to the thrill. Drugs, both uppers and downers, had started to erode his sanity. Like Elvis, he would throw tantrums, then reward the victim of a black mood with extravagant presents.

There is no doubt that part of Brian's problem was his unrequited love for John Lennon. He was obsessed by John's sardonic wit and artistic genius as well as being attracted by his good looks. In many ways, John was the man Brian most wanted to be: he saw John as wildly outspoken, incredibly brave and extremely talented.

Unfortunately for Brian, John was a dedicated womanizer, a veritable conquistador of the opposite sex. The sexual traffic flowing in and out of his hotel bedroom far exceeded that of any of the other Beatles, and his lovers were always female. Since many of the groupies were under-age girls like the one in Las Vegas, John had developed a liking for the professionals. I could relate many instances of this, but one particular night in Paris will make the point.

We were at the George V when John suddenly felt a desire for some exotic female company. An aide was despatched into the Champs-

Elysees to bring back some street-walkers, but it was 4.00 am and the streets were deserted. When he returned to the suite to report failure, he found John surrounded by eight glamorous women. The Beatle had made other arrangements with the help of an obliging night porter.

'Take your pick,' he said to the three men who had stayed behind after a business meeting with Brian. 'This one's on John.'

As each man chose one or more of *les belles de nuit*, John, dressed in a white bathrobe and looking like Caesar in his Beatle cut, stood at the door handing out 100-franc notes to each girl to pay for the services she was about to render.

John, of course, knew of Brian's lust for him and exploited it to get his own way. They had shared a Spanish holiday in the summer of 1963. Brian personally told me that, in Barcelona, he had not got further with John than a single kiss, so he had switched his attentions to a more amenable Spanish bullfighter. John's version was slightly different. He omitted any mention of kissing.

'A lot of rumours floated around about that holiday,' he told me. 'But I just went to sort Brian out. We sat in cafes and talked and talked and talked, mostly about people we'd been in love with. I convinced him that, while I didn't condemn his way of life, I was into women as far as sex was concerned.

'I really didn't want to hurt him by saying something stupid like "I can't stand queers." I could understand what was in his head. By the end of the holiday, he understood me better and the subject will probably never come up again.'

Brian believed that John had never got over the death of Stu Sutcliffe or his mother. 'Much of John's anger towards the world is grief over Stu and Julia,' he said. 'He thinks about death a lot.'

My biggest coup of this tour was to arrange a telephone conversation between Paul and Elvis. After they left Los Angeles, the Colonel frequently phoned the Beatles to keep in touch with their progress. When he was unable to get through to the hotel in Atlantic

City, he sent a cable asking me to call him urgently. I contacted him and he gave me Elvis's secret number at Graceland. According to my battered notebook, this was '901 EX(PRESS) 7-4427'. 'You can contact the artist through Marty Lacker,' said the Colonel, wary of eavesdroppers. 'He is waiting for a call from you fellows, so don't let him down.'

'How do you do?' enquired Paul when we got through to Elvis. 'I want to tell you we all think it's a drag that we weren't able to get together with you, but it's just one of those things. We would still like to meet you if it can all be arranged.'

Elvis told Paul that he was disappointed, too. 'I've taken a great big interest in your career and wanted very much to have a long chat with you guys,' he said. 'I've bought an electric bass guitar and I'm learning to play it. The darn thing's given me callouses all over my hand.'

'Well, keep practising,' said Paul. 'You'll get used to it. When are you coming to England, then?'

'Soon, I hope. I'm definitely coming.'

'Great! You can count on us having front row seats for your first show.'

'When are you going to invade the Hollywood studios?' Elvis wanted to know, giving voice to one of his greatest fears.

'Oh, you mean make a film?' answered Paul. 'I don't think we will, really. We like it in Britain and there's no need for us to film in Hollywood, although I appreciate it's the natural thing for an American star to do.'

'Well, I guess you've got a manager to take care of that kind of thing anyway.'

'Too true. I've got no brain for business. I couldn't look after a couple of dollars.'

'Talking of dollars in a pretty modest sort of way, I've bought every single one of your records and we play them all the time up here at the house. I like the cover of your new album [the unsmiling Beatle faces depicted in half light on *With the Beatles*]. It's kinda weird and I like weird things. Your faces on that cover remind me of the faces in that movie, *Children of the Damned*.'

This was more like it, a genuine double-edged compliment.

'Talking of films,' said Paul, 'That manager of yours is a laugh. He told us he had an offer from a producer to make a film with both you and us in it. The producer said he was offering a million dollars for Elvis and a million dollars for the Beatles. But Colonel Parker said, "I told him that he had forgotten there were four Beatles and they'd want two million dollars." We thought that dead funny.'

'Yeah, that sounds like the Colonel all right,' chuckled Elvis.

At this point, Paul covered the mouthpiece with his hand and said to John: 'Have a word with him, man.'

'No, thanks,' John answered. 'Can't think of anything to say.'

Paul signed off diplomatically and hung up his extension. I took over the conversation. When I asked Elvis about his Beatle collection, he replied: 'I guess I've got every record they ever made here. I'm looking at a copy of *A Hard Day's Night* right now and I've also hired a copy of the film which we're going to show up here at the house tonight.'

He added: 'That's how I spend most of my evenings, watching pictures privately. Coming down to Memphis and just kicking around this house is the only way I get to rest. We have a lot of fun out here. We have some wild parties. It's a pity y'all couldn't have made it over.'

I repeated the offer to John, who wasn't impressed by the thought of visiting Graceland. 'If he ever comes to England, he can visit *my* country estate,' he said. 'But I bet he won't set foot in England until we're history.'

CHAPTER TEN

Love Me Do, Alma Cogan

JOHN HAD paid £19,000 for his own retreat – a mock Tudor mansion called Kenwood – just before we had gone on tour. Tucked away in vast grounds at St George's Hill in the stockbroker belt of Weybridge, Surrey, it was infinitely more graceful than Graceland and more deserted than the Desert Inn.

In December 1964, the would-be recluse invited me down for a visit. John greeted me wearing a green corduroy suit over a bright red sweater and black suede boots. 'How about the suit then?' he asked. 'I've got a flat cap to match.' We climbed a narrow flight of stairs to the top floor and entered a small, comfortable room, modestly furnished.

While the main part of the house was being converted and decorated to the Lennon taste, John, Cynthia and Julian were confined to this small flat, which would eventually accommodate their chauffeur and his wife. As Cynthia made tea, I got the impression that this was a warm, cosy home far removed from the world of show business. This wasn't John Lennon the scathing cynic as he often appeared, but a contented, homely man secretly embarrassed by the comfort of his surroundings.

'I'll play you the Animals' LP – it's great,' he said, adding thoughtfully: '. . . That's if the record player will work. It gets left on for hours – sometimes all night – and it's a bit burned out.' We listened to the Animals, and John laughed his throaty chuckle as Eric Burdon broke into his version of 'A Hard Day's Night'.

I asked if the house gave him the Howard Hughes-style privacy he wanted.

'Yeah,' he said, 'but we get a few visitors at the weekend, y'know. There's no gate up at the moment. Things will be fine as soon as that little job gets done. George comes around a lot because he only lives ten miles from here. As a matter of fact, I'm expecting him this afternoon with a cat he's giving us. This place is well tucked away, but I've bought a Rolls-Royce so I'll be able to get driven up to town whenever the need arises. And Cyn's got the Mini – she's just passed her driving test.

'Funny, I've never been keen on learning to drive. George, Paul and Ringo have all got high-speed cars now – Paul says he touched 140 miles an hour going up to Liverpool the other day, but I'm just not interested.'

I asked him about a report that he had had enough of globetrotting and would like to settle down in England.

'That's the way I feel at the moment, but I suppose we'll have to go abroad eventually, even if it's only for a holiday. If you could find me somewhere in Britain away from it all, I'd go there. After the Christmas show, we get about a month off, and I suppose Paul and I will have to go somewhere to write the songs for *Help!* But as for settling down, I could never do that. It's nice to get some peace for a week or two, but after that, it would drive me mad. No, we won't be cutting down next year.'

We chatted about the new Beatle record, 'I Feel Fine'. 'I actually wrote it around that riff going on in the background,' said John. 'I tried to get that effect into practically every song on the LP, but the others wouldn't have it. I told them I'd write a song specially for that riff, so they said, "Yes, you go away and do that," knowing that we had almost finished the album. Anyway, going into the studio one morning, I said to Ringo, "I've written this song but it's lousy." But we tried it, complete with the riff, and it sounded like an A side, so we decided to release it just like that.'

We set off on a guided tour of the house. Julian's bedroom was bright red and had its own bathroom. Another bedroom was decorated blue and reserved for any additions to the family, although none was expected imminently. The master bedroom at the front of the house comprised two rooms knocked into one, with sage-green walls and white doors and window frames. Downstairs in one corner was the room that would become John's den.

'This one's being decorated in red to make it look small and cosy,' he said. 'I'll have my books, TV and record player in here – my own private room.'

As I drove back to London, I thought of the man who had been too frightened to pick up a telephone to book a restaurant table and the man who had pointed a gun at his own head. I asked Bill Harry about the Lennon enigma.

'I could never imagine John as Squire Lennon sitting in a nice house admiring the garden,' said Bill. 'From the first time I met him, he was always looking for something. He was a seeker. At art college, John, Stuart and I talked about metaphysical things like the meaning of life, astral travel and mystical dimensions. We talked about how the philosopher's stone wasn't about the transformation of base metal into gold, but rather a code that the alchemists had for the evolution of man.

'John and I got on extremely well because we were rather tougher than other people. John used to humiliate Stuart and put him down because it was in his nature to take advantage and dominate other people if he could. But if you stood up to him, he would back down. He was more intelligent than people gave him credit for. His Aunt Mimi used to phone me and say, "I will always remember you because you were the first one to call John a genius."

'He had this talent as an artist, but he didn't really have proper art tuition. He got expelled from art college because of his wild reputation. So all his lines and illustrations came from within himself. He was self-taught.

'After I published his article "The Dubious Origins of the Beatles", he was so chuffed that he came round to the office with this big bundle of stuff. It was nearly everything he had ever written or drawn: 250 drawings, stories about Small Stan and "The Tale of Hermit Fred", amazing poems. I found them fascinating. He had done all these wicked satires of political figures of the day like Macmillan. I crammed a whole drawer with them and told him I was going to print some in every issue of *Mersey Beat*. I told him I'd run a column called "Beatcomber" because I liked Beachcomber in the *Sunday Express*.

'So I started publishing John's column, and then *Mersey Beat* got so successful, we had to move. We'd started in this tiny attic and now we needed a whole floor of the building. My wife Virginia did the moving while I was out doing an interview. When I opened the drawer to get John's new thing out there was nothing in there. Virginia had thought it was all rubbish and had thrown them in the bin. The dustmen had taken them.

'I knew John was going to go bananas, but I had to tell him, so that night we went down to the Blue Angel and John was there. He cried on Virginia's shoulder.

'John always believed he was frustrated – he had all this creativity within him, but he lacked somebody to recognize it and draw it out of him. He needed to channel his work through a sponsor or a patron. Instead, he found his way into drink and drugs. He liked to think through drink; he believed that being a big drinker would enable him to write better and do things better.

'Then it was on to drugs. The first time he got into drugs was in Liverpool when this poet came back with him to his flat at Gambier Terrace and broke open a Vick's inhaler: he had Benzedrine in there and John chewed the raw Benzedrine.

'When John went over to Hamburg, he got Prellies, which you could buy over the counter at the chemist's, but they made you high. Then he moved on to marijuana and eventually LSD, which helped him to write those songs. But he was still looking for answers when he went to the Maharishi to learn transcendental meditation. He was always trying to find the creative thing. What he really needed was someone to give him a kick up the bum.'

After my first visit to Kenwood, my wife Jan and I were occasionally invited to spend Saturday evenings *chez* Lennon. The first night we arrived, Cyn proudly showed Jan the central kitchen island, which gleamed with new appliances. 'I had to get someone down from London to show me how to work the knobs and switches,' she admitted.

'I'm like you,' John whispered to me. 'I'm used to the stove going up against the wall.'

We sat at the tiled work surface on kitchen stools while Cyn cooked a meal and served it straight on to our plates. None of us had experienced 'kitchen cuisine' like this before, and it was fun. But I could tell that Cyn was as confused about the space-age oddities of her new abode as she was about the direction that her married life was taking. The interior decorators had been called in, and although she and John had been consulted, the house had a strange, glossy magazine feel to it, not at all like John and Cyn.

'The renovation cost twice as much as the bleedin' house,' said John, more in astonishment than anger. 'But I guess it's increased the value of the place.' His financial advisers had suggested that he should invest in property and he had concurred. Cyn, a quiet woman from a modest background, had wanted the house, but she now seemed no more comfortable in it than John.

Around 10.00 pm, we all headed up to London in my Jag to spend a few hours at the Ad Lib, a disco atop the Prince Charles cinema off Leicester Square. This was the hip place for the movers and groovers of what *Time* magazine was to christen 'Swinging London'. John loved being at the Ad Lib because he needed to feel part of something other than the Beatles. He had to be with his own kind – the artists, musicians, beauticians, hairdressers and other young people of the night – not among the aspiring business types of stockbroking Surrey.

We slipped into one of the banquettes and ordered Mateus rosé, still the recommended drink for young trendies, and looked at each other in the glow of the red glass candle holders on each table. John and Cyn were both extremely short-sighted, but refused to wear glasses in public. As they hadn't got around to trying the new contact lenses yet, they had no alternative but to blink myopically at the passing parade. Girls danced in Quant skirts, providing the only floor show. Regular as clockwork, Ringo, the relentless clubman, turned up, and Brian put in an appearance before disappearing on one of his furtive sorties.

However, the showstopper was Alma Cogan, the 'girl with the giggle in her voice'. Even in the semi-darkness, her theatrical make-up glowed brightly. Everybody loved Alma, but John was totally smitten. She was the secret love of his life. He told me that she reminded him in some respects – in temperament if not appearance – of his mother, who had loved being the life and soul of the party. Both had a mischievous sense of humour and both loved singing, dancing and flirting. 'Every time I'm with Alma, it feels right,' said John. 'Julia just couldn't cope with me, but Alma can read me like a book.'

In the Fifties, Alma had risen to be Britain's highest-paid female singer, her strapless ballgowns becoming as famous as the cute songs she sang, such as 'Never Do a Tango with an Eskimo', 'Where Will the Baby's Dimple Be?' and 'He Couldn't Resist Her Pocket Transistor' – the last one made her a household name in Japan.

For John, it had been love at first sight the moment he had met Alma during a party at the Knightsbridge home of Maurice Kinn, then owner of the *NME* and my boss. In the weeks that followed, John and the other Beatles had been regular attenders at Alma's parties at her flat in Stafford Court on Kensington High Street, along with Cary Grant, Noel Coward, Stanley Baker and Lionel Bart. Whenever anyone asked why she had never married, Alma would say, 'Some people go to a psychiatrist, others get married. In any case, I buy my own minks.'

Cyn never wanted to compete for John in such glamorous company. She dressed poorly, being by nature neither ambitious nor free-spending enough to be daring, even though John was by then a millionaire. (I don't believe she thought that the money would last.) This night, as Len Barry's 'One, Two, Three' boomed over the speakers and Alma sparkled for her boyfriend, the Ad Lib's manager Brian Morris, Cyn made suburban remarks and John became annoyed. After the freedom of the bedroom that he had come to take for granted on tour, it was obvious that Cyn was not the one he wanted at his side. There was a frosty silence in the back of the Jag as I drove the Lennons home.

At this stage of his life, John was searching for a woman who could be both lover and mother, a dual role that Cyn could never hope to fulfill. But it was apparent that he was more infatuated with Alma than she was with him, although this never prevented him from trying to win her over. She was accustomed to the attentions of lovesick young men, and John was just one of many who tried to gain her favours.

In retrospect, the similarities between John and Elvis are marked, right down to the search for surrogate mother love, the escapist drug-taking, the spiritual quest and even their problems with food. John had a tendency towards obesity because of his indiscriminate drinking, drugging and eating. When someone referred to him as the 'Fat Beatle', he became obsessed with his weight.

'Every tour we go on, John decides to slim – and, believe me, this involves quite a performance,' Neil Aspinall told me at the time. 'John's natural weight is 159 pounds but he's got a bit of a spare tyre round his middle and he does everything to try to lose it. He sticks to one main meal a day: steak and salad, no vegetables.

'What John can't see is how Paul weighs roughly the same as him and yet looks so slim. It's just that they are built differently, of course. John has two sets of suits – one for when he is his normal weight and the other for when he has slimmed down to a trimmer figure.'

My friendship with the Beatles was getting me acres of space in the *NME,* but I still wanted the big story. More hopeful after hearing the invitation to visit Graceland from the King's own lips, I kept in touch with the Colonel until the Beatles visited the US again in August 1965. This was the year that the Queen awarded them MBEs for services to Britain's export drive. Outraged holders of the award promptly sent their medals back to Buckingham Palace, one pompous Canadian MP saying that he refused to be placed on the same level as 'vulgar nincompoops'. When the Queen asked the Beatles at the investiture: 'How long have you been together?', Ringo replied: 'About forty years, ma'am.' It just seemed like that.

John, the anti-war campaigner, found the idea of medals of any kind repellent. He later claimed that he smoked dope in the Palace loo to express his true feelings and he eventually disowned his honour. 'I thought you were supposed to do something brave in war to get one of these,' he told me. 'Well, there's never been any chance of me doing that. This is just a political gimmick to make Harold Wilson [then Prime Minister] look good.'

More important to John was the fact that President Lyndon B. Johnson had sent 3500 US Marines into Da Nang, the first American fighting troops to be committed to the field in South Vietnam. He hated war in general and Vietnam in particular. When Johnson announced at the end of July that he was sending in another 50,000 troops, John burst out: 'Who does he think he's kidding? That was the idea all along.' John threatened to stage a one-Beatle boycott of the States, but luckily for me, he packed his bags along with the rest of us. We flew to New York on TWA's flight 703.

The date was Friday the 13th, and I kept my fingers crossed.

CHAPTER ELEVEN

Shea: Beatles Roll The Stones

AFTER A freezing winter, the kids of New York City knew what they wanted more than anything else: the Beatles. As he trudged through the sidewalk slush to reach his apartment at 12th Street and 6th, Sid Bernstein resolved to give them just that.

In his mind, he had conceived the greatest rock event since David slew Goliath. Not only would he bring the Beatles to New York again, but he would play them at the city's biggest venue, Shea Stadium. Shea, home of the Mets baseball team, right beside La Guardia airport in Queens, could hold a capacity crowd of 55,600. There was only one minor detail stopping him: he was completely broke.

However, the fact that he owed rent to his landlord and couldn't afford to pay his grocer's bill were mere trifles compared with the magnificence of his scheme. It was Sunday, 10 January 1965, and Sid shook the snow off his boots, picked up the phone and called Brian Epstein.

Brian was delighted to hear from the promoter who had masterminded the Beatles' two concerts at Carnegie Hall, but he was sceptical when Sid mentioned Shea. He became more amenable after Sid offered to recompense him for every unsold seat in the house.

'Brian told me he'd be at the Waldorf in three months' time, and added, "Please don't advertise or publicize the fact that you have got the Beatles until you've given me a $50,000 deposit. Will you do me that favour?" I agreed, but asked him if I could tell my friends. He said, "I can't stop you talking to your friends.'"

Sid was grateful for small mercies. He had a deal even if he couldn't announce it in the press. 'I had just lost an awful lot of money on a road show version of the TV series *Shindig*, which featured Gerry and the Pacemakers, and a number of American rock 'n' roll artists. But the kids in my neighbourhood knew that I'd brought the Beatles to New York in 1964 and they used to talk to me. I lived in Greenwich Village, right outside Washington Square Park, which is a big hangout place for kids. I used to take my only child at that time – Adam, who was one year old – to the park. Kids would ask me, "What's next, Mr Bernstein, who's coming next?" I had something to tell them that Sunday and they went wild: The Beatles at Shea Stadium!

'I decided, after that reaction, to get a post office box six blocks from my home. I took out PO Box 21, told a few more kids, mentioned the price of the tickets, and waited three weeks. I was desperate. If I got fifty letters, I could pay my rent, if it was sixty or seventy I could pay my grocery bill.

'The post office was open until 1.00 pm on Saturday, and walking the six blocks from my house, I arrived at 12.15. When I got there, I found I'd forgotten my post box key. I went up to the enquiry desk and I told the guy I had a box here, but no key. As they were closing soon, could he open it for me? I showed him my driving licence for identification, and he said, "You're Sid Bernstein, Box 21?" I said, "Yes," and he said, "What's your racket, buddy?" I told him, "I'm in the mail order business," and he said, "You must have some hot item." He pulled out three of the biggest duffel bags I'd ever seen. I shot back real fast to get my car and took those three huge sacks to my home.

'On 10 April, I called the Waldorf and got connected to Brian. "Welcome to New York," I said. "If you have time to see me, I've got the deposit for you." We had banked $185,000 and were still counting. In those three weeks, the grapevine had told the world. There were letters from Japan, Italy, Scandinavia, England, South America and most of the fifty States. We had to send back 100,000 letters.'

As summer set in, a Shea ticket was the hottest item on the black market. On 13 August, the Beatles took up residence as the sole occupants of the 33rd floor of the Warwick Hotel on the corner of 54th Street and 6th, not far from PO Box 21. Any thoughts they might have had of setting foot outside were soon abandoned. The New York Police Department had learned from the events of the previous summer that the only way they could protect the Beatles was to imprison them. The night we arrived the group had to cancel plans to go to the Copacobana to see the Supremes.

None of us could quite comprehend what lay in store at Shea. 'I suppose it will be like any other concert, only louder,' said Ringo, pacing around the suite.

John was in a reflective mood.

'I guess this is the turning point,' he said. 'How do you follow Shea?'

He turned up the TV sound to listen to the news. The headlines centred on race riots, which were ripping through the ghettoes of Los Angeles. The Army had been sent in.

'It's incredible – Johnson sends 50,000 troops to Vietnam, but there's a war going on in his own country,' said John. 'I'm glad I just play music.'

Mick Jagger and Keith Richard, who had become good friends with the Beatles, were also in New York, with their manager Andrew Oldham, and they invited me to travel to Shea with them. We went in a yacht called *Princess,* which belonged to the Stones' American lawyer Allen Klein. I talked to the Beatles over the yacht's radio-telephone as they prepared for the biggest event of their lives. Mick chatted to George Harrison about plans for that evening, to take his mind off the concert. Talking through the hotel switchboard, George gave Mick the hush-hush number of a private line to the Beatles' suite. However, he didn't realize that 2000 other vessels in the Hudson River basin had tuned in. Needless to say, that private number was jammed for the rest of their stay in New York.

As we lazed on deck in the sunshine, Mick told me: 'I don't envy the Beatles. Look how much freedom we have and they're locked up in their hotel bedrooms without even being able to take a car ride, let alone do something like this.'

Then he played Bob Dylan's latest single – 'pressed secretly for us eager maniacs' – and danced on deck in the androgynous style that identifies him on stage. At five o'clock in the evening, we sailed under the Queensboro Bridge and headed up the East River towards Flushing Bay.

As the yacht berthed almost in Shea's shadow, we found that a radio station had monitored the phone call with George and had broadcast the Stones' plan to tie up near the stadium. Hundreds of fans locked out of the concert were waiting in ambush. We had to run ashore and jump into a waiting car, which rushed us into the stadium, where we were hit by a wall of sound. Ringo had been right: it *was* louder. To our ears, the roar of the crowd was like a dozen jet fighters taking off simultaneously. And they were only warming up.

'It's frightening,' exclaimed Jagger.

'It's deafening,' yelled Richard.

We dashed in through the artists' entrance and met the Beatles, who were ready to go on stage. They had been flown to Queens in a helicopter and, like bullion, loaded into a Wells Fargo security van for safe delivery.

'It's the famous Stones,' yelled John.

'Who are these people?' demanded an irate cop.

'They're the same as the Beatles,' roared John.

'I don't care who they are,' the cop roared back. 'They can't stand in the aisle. There's a fire regulation.'

'Then put it out,' suggested George.

The cop relented just as the Beatles were due to go on stage. They had to run across the baseball diamond to the rostrum in the centre. We knew beforehand that this had to be the greatest Beatle concert of all time, but nothing could have prepared us for the pandemonium that broke out when the Beatles came into view.

Ed Sullivan, compére for the event, announced: 'Now, ladies and gentlemen, honoured by their country, decorated by their Queen and loved here in America: *Here are the Beatles!*' If the stadium had had a roof, it would have been blown sky-high. Never have I heard such a blast. The screaming, shouting, whistling and stomping swelled into a crescendo that sent me and the Stones reeling backwards in the aisle. The Beatles had literally rolled the Stones.

As Paul kicked off with 'Twist and Shout', the fevered excitement rose even higher and the noise increased in volume with each offering until all I was aware of was a dull, throbbing ache. It reached a peak when John played an organ with his elbow in 'I'm Down'. Many fans broke through the 2000-strong police cordon around the edges of the diamond, only to be brought down in tackles by a second line of defence nearer the stage.

'I've never felt so exhilarated in my life,' said George when the group collapsed back at the Warwick. 'It was unbelievable that so many people wanted to see us.'

'It would have been better still if we could have heard what we were playing,' said John. 'I wasn't sure what key I was in on two numbers.'

No one was really complaining. For a single concert, the Beatles had received $160,000 out of a box-office total of $304,000. After he had paid everyone connected with the show, including $25,000 to Lloyd's of London for insurance, Sid Bernstein's profit was just $6500, his lucky number. He did, however, manage to pay his rent and the grocery bill.

As the tour progressed, I noticed that John was becoming less frightened and more frivolous. Staying stoned most of the time helped him to cope with the danger, such as the incident that happened during our flight to Portland, Oregon, in a four-engined Lockheed Electra. The plane flew through a gorge with towering rocks reaching into the clouds.

'Do you see anywhere we could land?' asked Paul nervously.

A game of blackjack was in progress at the time and I was winning heavily. There was a large pile of dollar bills in front of me as I dealt the cards.

'*Oi, look!* shouted George, pointing disbelievingly out of the window. 'The bleedin' thing's on fire!'

'Stop playing games and play cards,' I said, continuing to deal. George had been nervous of flying ever since a window beside him had burst open while a small plane taking the Beatles from Liverpool to London had been hurtling down the runway. Terrified of being sucked out, George had called for help, and, just in time, an air hostess had stopped the pilot from taking off.

Nor was George kidding this time. The Electra's port engine was indeed spitting flames. Dollar bills and playing cards flew into the air. The seatbelt warning sign flashed on with urgent *pings*. An air hostess checked that the belts were fastened. I looked at George. He was in a state of nervous collapse. He undid his belt, got up and stood by the emergency exit, anxious to be the first out when we landed. 'Now perhaps people will stop joking about how long we're going to last,' he said seriously.

I looked at John to see how he was taking this, and he stared calmly back. Only John, once again revealing his macabre disposition towards death, could see the funny side.

'When this thing gets down,' he shouted to the hostess, 'it's Beatles, women and children first!'

Needless to say, we landed safely. After the group played two concerts at the Portland Coliseum, we took off for Los Angeles at midnight – in a different plane. We landed at LAX in the early hours of Monday, 23 August for a nine-day stay. I knew I wasn't going to get much sleep. Elvis was in town; it had to be now or never.

CHAPTER TWELVE

My Audience with The King

IN LOS ANGELES, I arranged to meet the Colonel outside the Beverly Hillcrest Hotel. I was early and nervously paced up and down, glancing at my watch. The Colonel turned up right on time at 11.30 am. With his assistant Tom Diskin at the wheel of a shooting brake, he swung on to the hotel forecourt.

The Colonel was wearing a beach shirt and slacks that looked as though they had been bought off the peg at a chainstore. He had on a white Panama hat, and was holding a cane topped with an elephant's head. We set off for Paramount.

Leaning forward from the back seat to make myself heard over the traffic noise, I said: 'It's very good of you to see me again.'

The Colonel held his hat on in the wind, streams of smoke trailing from his cigar.

'Let me tell you, son, I never give interviews. Nor does Mr Presley. *Never!* Ain't that right, Mr Diskin?' He glared at Tom Diskin, who nodded his head in agreement. 'It's one of the unwritten rules of Parker Management. Only tell the press what *you* want them to print. Never let *them* ask the questions.' The Colonel paused to exhale more smoke. 'One day I'm gonna write a book. My own story. I'm gonna call it "*How Much Does It Cost if It's Free?*" '

'Everything's got a price, huh?'

'Not necessarily so,' said the Colonel philosophically. 'A couple of city slickers from New York came to see me the other day. Million-dollar merchandising proposal. Lot of money.'

Tom Diskin was already nodding in agreement so I suspected he had heard this story a hundred times.

'At the same time, a friend of mine from the carny days dropped by. He'd fallen on hard times. Wanted to sell me a few hundred balloons. Fifty dollars. I asked Mr Diskin to show these New York guys in, then I said to my old friend, "I'll tell you what – I'll give you twenty-five." I bartered with him for some time before we agreed a price.

'The city slickers are standing there with their mouths open. They can't believe what's happening. I could have given him the fifty he wanted or even five hundred, but I quibbled. Finally, we agreed a price and he left. The New York types couldn't believe it. They were furious. One of them said to me . . .'

The shooting brake turned neatly under the giant Paramount arch. The Colonel acknowledged salutes from the security guards with a wave of his big cigar. He continued his monologue in a Brooklyn accent: '"You kept us waiting twenty minutes to do a million-dollar deal while you bought some balloons for a few bucks?"'

He made smoke to indicate his disdain at this attitude as the shooting brake passed through the studio.

'I told him I didn't like his tone and I'd decided not to do business with them. "That's OK," this guy says. "It's not your name we want on our products. It's Mr Presley's."

'"Fine," I said. "Go find Mr Presley and ask him." Do you take my point?'

'Sure,' I said, fairly confident I'd got the point. 'You're the only one who can make a deal for Elvis.'

The Colonel triumphantly alighted as the shooting brake jerked to a halt outside his suite of offices. 'I knew you'd miss the point. You screwed up there, son. Sure, I do all Mr Presley's contracts. See this here ring?'

He held up a heavily jewelled ring, which carried the initials TCB.

'Mr Presley gave me this ring. See those initials? TCB – "Takin' Care of Business".'

He stood next to me, drilling me with his clear blue eyes.

'But the point of the story, son, is that you can't put a price on a man's pride. Remember that.'

I entered the inner sanctum of the Colonel's little empire for the second time in my life. It was high noon.

'Let's eat,' said the Colonel.

Tom Diskin entered with a large tray of food from the Colonel's private cookhouse. He set it down on a space the Colonel had cleared on his desk with a sweep of his cane. I pulled a chair up to the desk and surveyed the meal. There were pieces of some small fowl surrounded by huge amounts of vegetables.

'What's the best deal you've ever done?' I asked, the hospitality making me reckless.

The Colonel tossed his cane down on the desk, removed his hat and seated himself in a swivel chair.

'Hard to say,' he said, beginning to eat hungrily. His prodigious appetite had become a talking point long before Elvis started to blimp out on food. 'When I discovered our record company was promoting other artists' records on the sleeves of Mr Presley's albums, I billed 'em $100,000 for the advertising space. And they paid up.'

'The word is that Mr Presley pays you 50 per cent of each deal,' I ventured.

The Colonel tried to hide his annoyance behind a show of bravado. '*Wrong!* You screwed up again. I pay *him* 50 per cent.'

He fixed me with a look that could only be described as malevolent.

'How are you enjoying the desert rat?' he enquired politely. I froze in mid-bite on what I had imagined to be a tiny chicken leg. The Colonel roared with laughter, a great belly laugh that filled the windowless room.

'You just qualified as a member of the Snowmen's League,' he said.

'The what?'

'The Snowmen's League. I'm the Potentate. You snow people and then melt away before they can find you. It has a very exclusive membership, including some former Presidents of the United States.'

He gave me a gold medal attached to a piece of checkered ribbon. The words 'COL TOM PARKER SNOW AWARD' were inscribed around the circular rim. I've kept it as a treasured memento.

After lunch, the Colonel, holding a sheaf of papers, led me across the lot. He opened a door and motioned me inside.

'Wait here, son. I'll only be a few minutes.'

After the noon blaze of the California sun, I had to allow my eyes to adjust to the sudden gloom. The soft light provided by a single lamp did little to illuminate the surroundings. I walked slowly into the room and made out an armchair, a coffee table, a settee. A TV set flickered in one corner. I sat down on the settee.

A few moments passed before I realized that I was not alone. My eyes moved across the dark green carpet to a pair of highly polished black cowboy boots studded in silver. Elvis Presley was sitting in the armchair, legs stretched out. So this was it.

Everything had come down to a few square feet in one small room. It was hard to believe that the man quietly sizing me up from his armchair had once been Elvis the Pelvis, the most notorious performer in the history of popular entertainment. This was the same Elvis who had instigated rock 'n' roll riots and inspired a generation of teenage rebellion, the same Elvis who had caused broken love affairs and triggered reckless adventures, the same Elvis who was the maker of young dreams and the breaker of juvenile hearts. Here within easy reach was the world's most outrageous rock-age rebel and jukebox tearjerker turned cult hero and movie matinee idol: just one man, so many myths. When it came to the moment of realization, the indisputable fact that this same Elvis was really only human flesh and blood blew my mind.

'I wasn't expecting . . .' I stuttered. 'The Colonel told me . . .'

Elvis smiled gently. 'Yeah, I know. That old man sure does like to ring the bell. We spoke on the phone. You're the guy who knows the Beatles?'

He rose slowly, a tall figure dressed in a green shirt with puffed sleeves clipped in at the cuff and a pair of tight slacks. He walked to the cocktail cabinet, poured himself a glass of iced water and started drinking. Then he moved closer.

'I didn't realize you were back in Los Angeles,' I said.

'We got through filming in Hawaii sooner than expected, and came straight back to finish the picture in the studio,' he said. 'My girlfriend drove up around the Beatles' place yesterday and said there was a heck of a lot of fans outside. Those guys can't be getting much peace at all. The Colonel tells me you want me to meet 'em. That right?'

With Elvis towering over me, I felt awkward and insecure.

'It would make a great . . . I mean, they respect you. They want to tell you . . . to say thanks.'

He gave a low laugh. It was a great sound.

'What you really mean is that it would make a great story for your newspaper. Reporters are always tryin' to get me to do things. It's phoney as hell. Anyway, go ahead – *shoot!*'

I could feel panic rising in my throat. This was the moment I had been praying for, yet now that it had arrived, I was totally unprepared.

'Look, my mind's gone blank. I have so many questions to ask you and I can't think of a single one.'

Elvis laughed that great laugh again.

'That's OK. I seem to have that effect on people. At least you're honest about it.' He paused and fixed me with his pale blue eyes. 'Well, I gotta question for you.'

He sat down in his chair, facing me across the coffee table.

'This John Lennon. How good is he? What I really mean is: could he have made it on his own?'

'He's a bright guy. Very bright. But the Beatles are a group. None of them could have done what you've done on their own.'

Elvis nodded slowly, taking it in.

'I hear he's a fag. Is that right?'

Now it was my turn to laugh.

'No, that was a misunderstanding,' I informed him. 'He asked a security guard at a hotel to get him some fags. He meant cigarettes. That's what we call them in England. Fags.'

Elvis shook his head.

'English sure is a weird language.'

'If you'd agree to meet them, you'd find they're OK.'

Elvis's next remark gave me an insight into how the manager manipulated his famous client.

'Colonel says they're just after the notoriety. Want to be able to boast that they've knocked me off my perch.'

'No, the meeting was my idea. I've been one of your biggest fans for years. I've known the Beatles since the beginning and they're no big deal to me. They still can't believe what's happening.'

'Yeah, I can identify with that. It happens so quickly it takes your breath away.'

'Will you do it?'

Elvis shrugged. 'Depends. I'll do what the Colonel recommends. He hasn't been wrong so far, though sometimes I wonder. I reckon I could be doing better things, but the Colonel has a policy about remaining loyal to the film companies. They pay me a million dollars-plus in addition to investing $2 million in each picture we make. If fifty million people can see me do a TV spot for free, they won't need to go to the movies. I won't go on the road without the Colonel – I never have done and I never will. And he says he can't do it. His back hurts pretty bad, and he thinks he would break up before a tour was half completed.'

Right on cue, the door swung open and the Colonel was framed against the harsh afternoon light. Ignoring his famous client, he said to me: 'We'll take our coffee in the executive dining suite.'

Outside, I had to run to keep pace.

'Thanks for setting up the meeting with Elvis. I really didn't expect ...'

'Mr Presley?' he drawled. 'I didn't see no Mr Presley.' Slow to appreciate the favour that had been bestowed upon me, I persisted. 'Back there. In the room . . .'

'It must be the sun gettin' to you. I already told you: Mr Presley does *not* talk to reporters.'

Like a maverick bullock the Colonel veered off the lot into the dining complex. We passed through a cafeteria section where extras, stage hands and the lower ranks of the studio hierarchy dined. The Colonel marched on, ignoring the occasional 'Howdy, Colonel.' I received an affectionate greeting from Suzanna Leigh, the British actress filming *Paradise, Hawaiian Style* with Elvis. I returned her wave and wanted to stop, but the Colonel kept walking, and again I had to sprint to catch up. We had entered a medium-range restaurant. Here, there was waitress service.

'Who was that?' asked the Colonel.

'Who was that? You're kidding!' I said, amazed. 'That's Suzanna Leigh, the co-star in the movie you're making here with Elvis. Isn't she?'

With perfect timing, we had arrived at the executive dining room where only producers, directors, studio heads and the most valued stars fraternized. There were checkered tablecloths, crystal water jugs, a *maitre d'* dancing attendance.

'Well, you see where she's eatin'?'

Maybe the sun was getting to me because I drew level and spoke loudly.

'Let's stop playing games, Colonel. Is Elvis going to meet the Beatles or not?'

Various big shots froze, forks in midair, when they heard the Beatles' name. The Colonel, however, knew exactly how to play to his audience.

'You can tell Mr Epstein that Colonel Parker will be delighted to listen to his little proposition.'

After coffee, I visited the closed set of *Paradise, Hawaiian Style* on Stage 5. Elvis was happy to be photographed with me, but insisted that Suzanna Leigh join us. She might be eating with the plebs, but Elvis knew it would help her career if a photograph of them together were published in the British press. It also wouldn't do him any harm in the homeland of the Beatles.

Later that afternoon, I took the Colonel up to the Beatles' rented house at 2850 Benedict Canyon above Beverly Hills. They asked him, yet again, about Elvis's career. 'Elvis is unavailable for personal appearances because of his film commitments,' he explained patiently to the Beatles. 'I've just sent his gold Cadillac on a tour of America. Matter of fact, it's so successful I'm thinking of putting his gold suit on tour.'

As he left, he assured the Beatles that they would meet Elvis, subject to me being able to fix a convenient time and place. This was the best news I had heard on any of my three trips to the States. Things were finally starting to move in the right direction – and quite fast for a change.

The following day, the Colonel and I circled the pool at the Beverly Hills Hotel, and approached Brian Epstein who, clad in swimming trunks and a white towelling robe, straddled a Li-lo outside a cabana. His fresh, babyish face coloured red by the West Coast sun, Brian looked happy and relaxed. The Colonel grasped his outstretched hand and said: 'I'm sure we can work something out.'

Lunch was served poolside. Brian and I ate lobster salad and drank chilled Chablis. 'One of life's little pleasures,' Brian said, mixing his own salad dressing from stoppered bottles of olive oil and vinegar.

The Colonel had chosen chicken, saying: 'I'm mighty partial to chicken. I started out with this little sideshow – dancin' chickens. Now chickens are not by nature Fred Astaire, so how did I make em' dance? Well, you'd dance if you were standing on a hotplate. I'd start each week with seven dancin' chickens and finish with just one.' He flourished a chicken leg. 'A fella's gotta eat!'

The Colonel laughed heartily at his own joke. Then, suddenly serious, he said, 'Let's get down to logistics.'

'As you know, my boys are staying in Benedict Canyon,' began Brian.

'Yeah, I've been there. Could present security problems,' the Colonel decided, automatically ruling it out.

'There are going to be security problems wherever they meet,' Brian replied, colouring visibly. He liked to get his own way as much as the Colonel.

'Mr Presley lives in a secure part of Bel Air.'

'So you insist that *we* visit *you*. Is that right?'

'"Insist" is a strong word. Listen, Brian, you're in *our* country. If Mr Presley were in *your* homeland, *we'd* come to *you*. That's the way of it.'

'You have a point. OK. I've got to go to New York but I'll be back on Friday. What about Friday night?'

The Colonel whipped out a diary and scribbled a note in it. 'Friday night it is. August twenty-seventh.' He snapped the dairy shut and pocketed it. 'Only one stipulation. No publicity – apart from what Mr Hutchins writes in his newspaper after the event.'

'That's going to be tricky, Colonel Parker,' said Brian. 'Fleet Street is here in force. They'll go crazy.'

The Colonel turned to me. 'That's your job. Lay down a false trail. Give the competition the slip.'

I nodded my assent. Of all the stories in my short, though busy, career, this was the one I most wanted to myself.

The Colonel still wasn't finished: 'And another thing. No cameras, no pictures of any kind and no tape-recorders. That agreed?' He offered his hand to the man who loved the Beatles.

'Anything else?' asked Brian, failing to disguise his irritation but shaking the Colonel's hand before it was withdrawn. 'By the way, Colonel, what *is* Mr Presley's address in Bel Air?'

Caught unprepared, the Colonel blustered: 'That will have to remain classified information. I'll send one of my men to pick your boys up.'

'That's ridiculous,' Brian exclaimed.

The Colonel rose abruptly to his feet. 'If that's the way you feel, I'd as soon call the whole damn thing off, only we've shaken on it. Anyway, I'm doing this as a personal favour to my friend Mr Hutchins.'

I jumped up and reassured him: 'I'm sure we'll manage, Colonel. It will be all right on the night.'

Back at 2850 Benedict Canyon, the Beatles received the news from Brian with mixed feelings. They had waited so long that it seemed too good to be true. 'I bet he cancels,' said John. He listened to the account of my audience with the King, and even though I omitted the personal references that Elvis had made about him, he professed to be unimpressed.

'I'm fed up with meeting celebrities,' he said wearily. 'Most of them are disappointing, and I bet he's the same.'

The day after their arrival in LA, the Beatles had attended a party hosted by Capitol Records, which was carpeted wall to wall with some of the most famous people in Hollywood. The guest list included Steve McQueen, Julie Andrews, Richard Chamberlain, James Stewart, Rock Hudson, Gene Kelly, Edward G. Robinson and Jane Fonda. However, once again, the group had been displayed as novelties rather than real people in their own right.

Brian flew off to New York for his business trip and I stuck close to his boys. Neither Ringo nor I could swim and we both tried to learn a few strokes in the pool. John borrowed my camera and took some holiday snaps of Paul wearing Mal's glasses and a nervous Ringo surveying the deep end. We played pool in the games room, Ringo deliberately using the blunt end of the cue. 'This is Ringo time at the table,' he said when someone pointed out his mistake. 'I play my way.' He was starting to become more assertive.

The eve of the long-overdue rendezvous found me driving in the shooting brake along a winding, hilly street in Bel Air with the Colonel and Tom Diskin. We had been touring the salubrious residential district for some time, more or less going round in circles. I now knew the Colonel's guilty secret: he had never actually been to Elvis's home.

'Just carry on up this hill, Mr Diskin,' the Colonel instructed. 'Let's see, Bellagio Road. Every goddam street around here is

Bellagio. It's up here some place. We want Perugia Way. Number 565.'

Consulting a road map of the area, I located Perugia Way at the top of Bellagio overlooking the Bel Air Country Club.

'Ah, yes, the country club,' said the Colonel. 'I remember now.'

Finally, the shooting brake pulled up on the crest of a steep hill outside the high-security gates of 565 Perugia Way. A Rolls-Royce, two Cadillacs and three Harley-Davidson motorcycles were parked in the driveway under a row of palm trees. The courtyard leading up to a panelled front door was lushly planted with petunias, tiny hedges, a profusion of ferns and strips of well-tended lawn. The house, a two-storeyed mansion, was built into the hillside. Most of it was hidden from the roadway by bowed garden walls seven feet high, covered in tropical creepers.

'All right, Mr Diskin,' the Colonel ordered. 'Let's head back to civilization.'

I had hoped to go inside, and said so. The Colonel, however, had a management rule to cover just such an eventuality:

'Never interfere with the client's private life. Mr Presley leads his life and I lead mine. We're strictly business. Friday is business and this is Thursday.' And we drove away to the more familiar territory of Beverly Hills.

'The Colonel is a wily old fox,' Seymour Heller told me later. 'He didn't get too close because he didn't like a lot of the things that Elvis did, drugs or whatever, and he didn't like his friends.'

The house at 565 Perugia Way had once been owned by the Shah of Persia and Rita Hayworth, although not at the same time. It was built around a circular, glass-roofed games room, fifty feet in diameter. A pool table, an illuminated jukebox and California-style furnishings were now visible from the front door. New arrivals to Elvis's home followed a maid across the thick white shag carpet of the foyer, and passed through the living room, where a huge painting of Elvis, Gladys and Vernon outside Graceland dominated one wall above a fireplace. The adjoining den was the King's notorious party room.

'I'm gonna buy a horde of chorus girls and make 'em dance on my bed,' Elvis had promised himself in *Jailhouse Rock*. Now he was living out that fantasy.

At party time, he would sit in the centre of a horseshoe-shaped couch near another fireplace, watching TV. His face was chubbier now, his waistline slightly more rounded, but he was still very handsome. Perhaps a dozen young women would be seated on the couch, six on either side of him. His cousin Gene Smith, Sonny and Red West, and Lamar Fike, an over-fed Southerner whom Elvis called the Great Speckled Bird, would prop up a cocktail bar, ready to cue the laughter that such occasions required.

The girls would be either starlet types with heavily made-up faces and puckered lips or wholesome groupies in jeans. Every one of them would jockey for the best position to catch Elvis's roving eye. He would look around and appear to fix one girl – say, a pert brunette – with a knowing stare. She would instantly smile until she realized that he was looking at the peaches and cream blonde next to her. The smile would vanish. No one would speak unless Elvis spoke to them. Sometimes, something on TV would amuse him, and he would laugh.

However, he was far from amused about the impending arrival of the Beatles. His insecurity came out in several outbursts: he didn't like the movie he was shooting (it was 'the worst yet'), he didn't like the soundtrack ('"Queenie Wahine's Papaya" . . . *yuk!'*), he didn't like the way the Colonel and the studios had transformed him into an 'entertainer' rather than a singer who could also act dramatic roles, like the one he had played in *Flaming Star* ('What's an entertainer? A nice guy that everybody loves, and that ain't me'), and he didn't like the fact that everywhere he went, it was Beatles, Beatles and more Beatles. He complained of having 'a hole deep down that I can't fill no matter what'. Not having had a hit single for more than three years only made matters worse. The Colonel, I discovered later, was having a terrible time controlling him. At one point, it was touch and go whether Elvis would actually open the front door to admit his unwelcome guests.

The Beatles spent their most pleasant day of the tour in a recording studio watching their folk-rocking friends the Byrds record Bob Dylan's latest offering. It was great to watch someone else doing the work. The song they were recording was entitled 'The Times They Are A-Changing'. The King didn't need to hear it – he could feel it with every fibre of his being.

MISSISSIPPI FLASH: A blond Elvis, aged 7, poses proudly with Vernon and Gladys outside the family's two-room shack at Tupelo, Mississippi, in 1942

MEMPHIS MISS: At 15, Elvis the country boy sits on a Memphis sidewalk with his first dancing partner, Betty McMann. (*PICTORIAL PRESS*)

Elvis's birth place at East Tupelo - now Presley Heights - in autumn 1994. (HUTCHINS/THOMPSON)

More than a decade later in the ranch-style house Elvis bought his parents in Audubon Drive, Memphis, the rising star shows his mother some tender loving care.

TWIST OF LENNON: John turns as if to say: 'Here we go again,' as the Beatles touch down in Hong Kong. (*HUTCHINS/THOMPSON*)

Beatles' postcards from the edge.(*HUTCHINS/THOMPSON*)

HELP! Ringo the nonswimmer shows his fear as the Beatles enjoy a dip in the pool at their Los Angeles mansion just before they met Elvis in August 1965.
(*JOHN LOENGARD / LIFE*)

(*Left*) Teenaged Priscilla Beaulieu spins an Elvis disc at her home in Germany. Sgt Presley had returned to the USA. (*RANGE/BETTMANN/UPI*)

Priscilla models for her lover, top British photographer Terry O'Neill, at her home in Beverly Hills after her divorce from Elvis. (*TERRY O'NEILL*)

HIS LATEST FLAME. Elvis and his one-time lover Ann Margret prepare for a duet on the set of Viva Las Vegas in 1963. (*RANGE/BETTMANN/UPI*)

(Above) Looking remarkably like her father, 18-year-old Lisa hugs her mother, Priscilla, by now star of the TV soap Dallas, in Hollywood, 1986. *(RANGE/BETTMANN/UPI)*

(Inset Top) Brian Epstein, their suave but tragic manager. *(PICTORIAL PRESS)*

(Above) PS I LOVE YOU: The Beatles relax during a taped interview in their Plaza Hotel suite during their first visit to America in February 1964. *(BILL EPPRIDGE/LIFE*

TAKIN' CARE OF BUSINESS: Col. Tom Parker and his first wife, Marie.
(*REX FEATURES*).

The Colonel's favourite picture of himself on his showcard souvenir.

(SOME TIME IN NEW YORK CITY: John is reunited with Ringo and his first wife Maureen at an art show in New York in 1971. Phil Spector, the recording genius, is on the right. (PICTORIAL PRESS)

John and his lover May Pang get acquainted with Alice Cooper and a friend called Cindy at a Sgt Pepper party on Broadway in 1974. (STAR FILE / PICTORIAL)

John and Yoko Ono snapped in a Manhattan Street. (PICTORIAL PRESS)

(*Bottom Right*) CAN'T BUY ME LOVE: Fresh faced John fell under the spell of British singer *Alma Coogan* - the girl with the giggle in her voice.

(*Bottom Left*) Alma Coogan, who's sudden death turned John Lennon into a Nowhere Man. (*BOTH PICTORIAL PRESS*)

Hutchins took this unpublished picture of the Beatles rehearsing in a TV studio at the height of their fame in 1964. (*HUTCHINS / THOMPSON*)

EYEWITNESSES: (*Top Left*) Raquel Welch, who shared her Presley secrets with the authors, steps out in 1994 with Terry O'Neill, once the man in Priscilla's life. (*Top Right*) Memphis DJ George Klein; (*Bottom Right*) Graceland Cook, Mary Jenkins.

BEL AIR LAIR: No. 565 Perugia Way, Elvis's rented mansion, where Chris Hutchins set up the famous summit meeting between Elvis and the Beatles on 27 August 1965.

(*Left*) Marianne Gaba, with Elvis, in GI Blues in 1960; and as Marianne Starkman in 1994.

(*HUTCHINS/THOMPSON and D. POOLE*)

GOTTA LOTTA LIVIN' TO DO: Elvis and his buddy Tom Jones rip it up in Las Vegas during party time in 1972.

(*Above Left*) The King in bronze at the top of Beale Street, Memphis. HUTCHINS/THOMPSON) (*Above Right*) The Hilton Hotel, Las Vegas. The Imperial Suite, where Elvis stayed, was below the Hilton sign.

Elvis in his American Eagle jumpsuit on stage in Las Vegas during the last year of his life. (*RANGE/BETTMANN*).

THE JACKSON TWO: Lisa Presley takes her new husband, Michael Jackson, by the hand during a visit to Budapest after their secret wedding in May 1994. (*REUTER*)

CHAPTER THIRTEEN

Elvis Meets the Beatles: Uncensored

FRIDAY NIGHT, 27 August 1965. The bar of the Beverly Hillcrest Hotel was crowded with newshounds in search of a secret. It was already early Saturday morning in London and the big Sunday newspapers would soon be screaming for some action on the Beatle front.

I was drinking alone, keeping the biggest secret of my life carefully under wraps. Don Short, a reporter from the *Daily Mirror,* detached himself from one group and, drink in hand, joined me. Porky Short was a chubby, prematurely balding man with the glow of a relentless *bon vivant.* But he had a wicked news sense and he sensed that something was up.

'I've spoken to Brian,' he said, leaning into the bar to suggest confidentiality. 'Something's going on. He wouldn't tell me what. It's Elvis, isn't it? Elvis meeting the Beatles?'

'Brian's in New York,' I replied. 'Anyway, why ask me? If I knew anything like that, I wouldn't be sitting here, would I?'

'I'm asking you because you're in with Brian and the Colonel. Come on, Chris. We're pals. Remember the times I've helped you?'

'OK, OK. Just keep it to yourself, right? Elvis is meeting the Beatles tonight. But security is tight. I can't get you in. You'll have to find your own way.'

'Just give me the address.'

I levered myself off the bar stool, whipped out a pen and scribbled on the back of my bar check.

'Pick up my tab. If anyone asks, I've gone to the movies.' As I left, I secretly hoped that Porky enjoyed the striptease show at the address I'd written down.

We met Brian Epstein at LAX on his return from New York. As Tom Diskin swung the car, this time a more comfortable station wagon, on to the San Diego Freeway heading north, the Colonel asked Brian: 'Is everything set your end?'

'Well, it was when I left New York,' he replied tetchily.

'Just checkin',' said the Colonel, enjoying himself. Through the windscreen, a street sign read 'SUNSET BLVD'.

'We change cars here,' commanded the Colonel. Everyone piled into a white limousine parked beside the kerb. When we reached Benedict Canyon, we switched cars again, this time into a black limousine with one of the Memphis Mafia at the wheel.

'Sure you weren't followed?' asked the Colonel.

'Not unless they're hiding in the trunk,' the Mafioso answered sourly.

'Go check,' remonstrated the Colonel. 'We can't be too careful.'

The limousine swept past a group of inquisitive fans standing at the five-bar gate outside No. 2850 and into the privacy of the driveway. The Beatles emerged with Neil Aspinall and Mal Evans and piled into the back of another black limousine driven by Alf Bicknell, the British chauffeur who had accompanied them to America. Thoroughly enjoying the intrigue, the Colonel shouted like a wagon master: '*Roll'em!*

The two cars pulled level with the fans camped outside the front gates. There were squeals and screams. Police motorcycle riders pulled into the road behind us, to prevent anyone following. Halfway down Benedict, we veered off to the right and joined Sunset Boulevard near the stone archway into Bel Air. Police cars blocked the roadway, holding up traffic. Red lights flashed and the crackle of police radios sounded in the night. Then the road started to curve and rise steeply. This journey, I thought, had really been uphill all the way.

At ten o'clock that night, I finally entered the doorway of 565 Perugia Way. Elvis and Priscilla were sitting in the centre of the horseshoe couch in the den – the King and his secret bride-to-be cosily at home. He was wearing a red shirt and close-fitting black jerkin, the high Napoleonic collar rising above his sideburns. Priscilla was pure Hollywood starlet: her black bouffant towered above her forehead and she was heavily made up with thick black mascara, midnight blue eyeliner, red blusher and Heartbreak Pink lipstick. She was wearing a figure-hugging, sequined mini-dress, black seamed stockings and black high heels.

The Praetorian Guard – Joe Esposito, Marty Lacker, Billy Smith, Jerry Schilling, Alan Fortas, Sonny West and a couple of men I had not seen before – hovered around the King, casually dressed in slacks, open-necked shirts and sports jackets. The circular games room, bathed in red and blue light, contained their wives, girlfriends and children. Priscilla went and joined them. The sounds of a hit tune, neither Elvis's nor the Beatles's, thundered from the jukebox.

Elvis rose to greet his guests, sun-tanned and outwardly relaxed. Peering round the room like Peter Sellers and putting on an Inspector Clouseau accent to address his reluctant host, John said: 'Oh, zere you are!' The Mersey had finally run into the Mississippi, and already I could see that there were going to be some big waves.

Shooting a quizzical look in Priscilla's direction, Elvis sat down with John and Paul on his right and Ringo and George on his left. There was a sudden silence as the record came to an end. No one spoke. The silence became uncomfortable, and then embarrassing. Everyone looked at Elvis. His nightmare was coming true. Nervously, he picked up the remote control and started changing channels on the big colour TV set.

Throwing the device on to the coffee table, he said: 'If you guys are just gonna sit there and stare at me, I'm goin' to bed. Let's call it a night, right, Cilla? I didn't mean for this to be like the subjects calling on the King. I just thought we'd sit and talk about music and maybe jam a little.'

'That would be great,' enthused Paul, trying to salvage the situation.

'Somebody bring in the guitars,' ordered Elvis.

Electric guitars were produced and plugged into amplifiers scattered around the room, and a white piano was pushed into view. Elvis picked up the bass guitar he had started to learn to play. John and George began tuning up rhythm guitars while Paul sat down at the piano.

'Sorry there's no drum kit for you,' Elvis told Ringo. 'We left that back in Memphis.'

'That's OK,' Ringo replied. 'I'd rather play pool.'

Elvis played a few notes and addressed himself to Paul: 'Still not too good, huh . . . but I'm practising.'

Paul gave him the benefit of some instruction while John played some chords on the guitar he'd picked up.

'Elvis, lad, you're coming along quite well. Keep up the rehearsals and me and Mr Epstein will make you a star,' Paul jibed.

'I hear you guys had a little trouble on the plane ride to Portland,' said Elvis, handling the role of host quite well.

'Yeah, like one of the engines caught fire,' replied George. 'Another time, when we were flying out from Liverpool, the window next to me blew open.'

'I took off from Atlanta once,' recalled Elvis. 'The plane only had two engines and one of 'em failed. Boy, I was really scared. I thought my number was up. We had to remove sharp objects from our pockets and rest our heads on pillows between our knees. When we landed, the pilot was wringing wet with sweat even though it was snowin'.'

'Yeah, we've had some crazy experiences,' said Paul. 'One guy ran on stage, pulled the leads out of the amplifiers and said to me, "One move and you're dead!"'

'It was pretty scarin' sometimes,' said Elvis. 'I remember once in Vancouver, we'd only done a number or two when some of the fans rushed the stage. It was lucky the band and I got off in time – they tipped the whole damn rostrum over.'

'When the fans went for you,' John said, 'you were up there all alone. With us, it's four against everybody and we can draw support from each other.'

Priscilla walked into view and I saw John watch her shapely legs glide across the carpet. In a corner of the games room, the Colonel and Joe Esposito had set up a roulette table. 'Ladeez and genel'men,' the Colonel bawled in his best showman's voice, 'the casino is open for business.'

Brian Epstein hurried across the room to join them. Aspinall and Evans and the members of the Memphis Mafia had moved to the cocktail bar for drinks and tough-guy talk. I was poised near the fireplace between them and the guitar players on the couch. I inspected a model covered wagon, lit from the inside to illuminate the words 'ALL THE WAY WITH LBJ' on top. Priscilla walked over, smiling.

'You've made a big hit,' I told her. 'I can see John likes you.'

'That's his first mistake. Elvis is very jealous.'

'Of you or John?' I asked, only half in jest.

Luckily, she was not required to answer: Sergeant Presley's Lonesome Heartbreak Band was ready to play. In front of a privileged audience of just two dozen people, a billion dollars' worth of talent was lined up to give its one and only performance.

'What's it gonna be?' asked Elvis.

'Let's do one by the other Cilla – Cilla Black,' said Paul, leading into 'You're My World'.

'This beats talking, doesn't it,' said John. He could never resist making some obscure or barbed comment just when things were going well.

The Bel Air All-Stars proved to be pretty good, slipping easily and freely into their individual roles. Elvis's voice rose, richer, deeper and more powerful than the others', his left leg pumping up and down in time to the beat. You could feel the magic and he did it so naturally. Paul, on the piano, joined Elvis in some vocal duets, George worked in some of his neat little riffs and John, even if he were just going through the motions, didn't let the side down. I started to relax a bit and enjoy the piece of music history being enacted before me.

Simultaneously, the roulette game proceeded and Ringo shot pool surrounded by six excited children while the wives and girlfriends watched the jam session with rapt expressions. Each time there was a lull, I slipped off to the bathroom to scribble the notes the Colonel had forbidden but knew perfectly well I would make.

Elvis was getting into the spirit of the evening. 'This is what you guys gave me for my thirtieth birthday,' he said. 'It made me sick.'

He laughed as he led them on bass guitar into 'I Feel Fine'.

'Why have you dropped the old stuff? The rock?' asked John, for once with feeling. 'I loved the old Sun records.'

Elvis squirmed in his seat. This was one line of questioning he had dreaded.

'Listen, just because I'm stuck with some movie soundtracks doesn't mean I can't do rock 'n' roll no more,' he said testily. 'I might just get around to cuttin' a few sides and knockin' you off the top.'

John reverted to his Clouseau accent: 'Zis is ze way it should be . . . Ze small homely gathering wiz a few friends and a leetle muzic.'

He walked over to join me near the fireplace, and it was at this moment that he saw the covered wagon. More particularly, he read the slogan 'ALL THE WAY WITH LBJ', emblazoned across it like some piece of gung-ho graffiti scrawled outside a redneck bar. John frowned. To John, LBJ was a warmonger responsible for the slaughter of innocent civilians in what he regarded as a civil war between the Vietnamese people. John's mood could change in an instant, and that is exactly what happened at Elvis Presley's party that night.

He reacted a little later when he heard Elvis say: 'I'm making movies at a million bucks a time and one of 'em – I won't say which one – took only fifteen days to complete.'

'Well, we've got an hour to spare now,' said the Beatle with the shark-infested mouth. 'Let's make an epic together.'

Elvis looked stunned, but held his tongue. John had been too clever to mention Vietnam outright, knowing that this would only lead to a political argument in which he would be hopelessly outnumbered. His technique in situations like this was to make people look foolish over something they believed in. By putting Elvis down over his movies, he was, I know, also belittling the King's support for the Vietnam war.

In hindsight, I would classify that crack from John as the final insult, the one that started the feud for real. Before that, the disputed territory between Elvis and the Beatles had been about record sales in the marketplace, public acclaim at the box office and headlines in newspapers. Now it would become a highly personal conflict, which had nothing whatever to do with music but everything to do with politics: a stand-off between Elvis, the staunch American patriot, and John, the anti-war protester.

The former tank corps sergeant got up from the couch and went over to Sonny West and Alan Fortas, a former football player known as Hog Ears. Only Elvis and the Memphis Mafia dared call him that.

'Someone ought to talk to the FBI about that sonovabitch,' Elvis said angrily, almost three years' frustration finally boiling over. 'He's stoned out of his mind.'

Fortas's voice boomed across the room: '*Hey, Beatle!*'

Four mop-topped heads swivelled in unison. Assuming that the command was directed at him, John walked over and told Elvis: 'Talking about money, I've got a Rolls-Royce Phantom Five . . . just like the one you've got parked outside.'

By now, everyone was crowding around in a circle of heaving muscles and tight shirts.

'Great party, Elvis,' I said, joining in. 'They told me not to miss the floor show.'

'Happy now? Got what you came for? Filled that little notebook of yours on all those trips to the bathroom?'

When Brian realized that John had talked his way into trouble, he came over, put a protective arm around his shoulder and led him to a quiet corner. But even as the party broke up around 2.00 am, there was a parting shot from John as we bundled each other out of the front door.

'Sanks for ze music, Elvis,' he said, adding sarcastically: 'Long live ze King!'

Still the peacemaker, the Colonel handed each Beatle a boxful of Elvis records. Having noted that Brian was partial to liberal quantities of wine and spirits, he promised to order him a cocktail cabinet.

Not one to be outdone in giving thoughtful and extravagant presents, Brian replied that he would ask Harrods to send the Colonel a Shetland pony to remind him of his days in the circus. Then, to repair the damage with Elvis, he invited the King to Beatleville in Benedict Canyon the following evening.

'Well, I'll see,' stalled Elvis. 'I don't know whether I'll be able to make it or not.'

John turned to some of the Guys who had followed us out into the Bel Air night.

'You're welcome to come *with* or *without* him,' he said pointedly.

As we walked to the car, the Colonel said to me: 'Tell the fans it was a great meeting.'

John laughed and said: 'Tell them the truth – it was a load of rubbish.'

Elvis politely shook hands with chauffeur Alf Bicknell. 'He called me "sir",' said an astonished Alf, who was more to Beatle-style informality. 'Elvis Presley called me "sir"!'

Needless to say, Elvis did not visit the Beatles and he never spoke to John Lennon again. John, however, was soon talking about Elvis in glowing terms, which I knew to be totally at odds with his true feelings.

'There's only one person in the United States of America that we ever wanted to meet – not that he wanted to meet us! And we met him last night,' he said. 'We can't tell you how we felt. We just idolized him so much. The only person we wanted to meet in the USA was Elvis Presley. We can't tell you what a thrill that was.' Privately, John later gave friends a different opinion. 'It was just like meeting Engelbert Humperdink,' he said sourly.

Asked to comment, Paul would only say that Elvis was 'odd'. Yet, coming from the most diplomatic Beatle, that word spoke volumes.

The close encounter in his own home simply added familiarity to Elvis's contempt. For months, he raged against the Beatles in general and John in particular. His drug intake shot up.

Priscilla recalls finding him soon afterwards, stoned in the back garden, gazing down the escarpment to the greens of the Bel Air Country Club, where a sprinkler system was in operation. 'Can you see 'em, Sattnin?' he asked her. 'See what, honey, the water?' 'The angels out there.' 'Angels?'

'I have to go baby. They're calling me. They want to tell me something.'

Elvis started to walk down towards the 'angels' on the lawn and had to be gently led back to the safety of his house.

By autumn, the Colonel knew that Elvis had to say something to his fans about the Beatles. He persuaded him to make the following statement:

> People have said my absence from personal appearances has given the Beatles their big opportunities. I know nothing about that. As for the Beatles, all I can say is – more power to them. I have watched all their television appearances over here. I don't think I should say what I feel about them. It wouldn't be fair to fellow entertainers.

I'll say the Beatles have got what it takes and in great abundance and that they've been given a heck of a vote of confidence. I'm sorry, but I have to be diplomatic and I'm honest about it. They are entertainers like myself and I guess they're as dedicated as the rest of us. Which, in the long run, is all that matters. I wish them luck.

John told me: 'I'm not sure who's the bigger bullsh***er – him or me. The vendetta that had begun at 565 Perugia Way still had a long way to go. There was to be no winner.

CHAPTER FOURTEEN

John, Jesus and Sir Elvis Presley

THE MEETING in Bel Air had proved that the Colonel was a great fixer. He had what Las Vegas called 'juice', casino slang for the right connections. Anyone in show business who had ever crossed swords with him knew that for a fact.

Following their initial skirmishes, Brian frequently called him for help. Sometimes the Colonel offered his advice whether the Englishman had sought it or not. The Colonel was evasive on this point when I asked him who had placed the call, late on the afternoon (Pacific time) of 6 August 1966, during one of the Beatles' darkest hours – Brian Epstein or himself? Not that it really mattered. The distressed tone that was usual in Brian's voice in such situations had been the memorable thing. An avid news-watcher, particularly when a story concerned other entertainers, the Colonel was well aware of the big trouble the Beatles were in.

Five months earlier, John had obliged his journalist friend Maureen Cleave with an interview for London's *Evening Standard,* in which he remarked that the Beatles were 'more popular than Jesus'. The quote had gone virtually unnoticed when the *Standard* published it, but the full interview had just been reprinted in the American magazine *Datebook,* with the seemingly blasphemous one-liner, 'Bigger than Jesus', splashed across the front cover. The Beatles were about to start their third major tour of the US, and John's *faux pas* was flashed across the nation like news of a major catastrophe.

What John had actually said was:

Christianity will go. It will vanish and shrink. I needn't argue about that; I'm right and I will be proved right. We're more popular than Jesus now. I don't know which will go first, rock 'n' roll or Christianity. Jesus was all right but his disciples were thick and ordinary. It's them twisting it that ruins it for me.

Although he was still recovering from glandular fever, Brian had left his sickbed to fly to New York in a desperate attempt to salvage the tour. He had evaded questions fired by journalists awaiting his arrival at Kennedy Airport only by promising to give a full-scale press conference at his hotel, the Sheraton, the following day.

Brian admitted to me later that he had been tense as he discussed with the Colonel the best strategy to employ with the now-hostile media. The older man hardly needed to remind him of the advice he had already given him on several previous occasions: that the Beatles should not give interviews in which they confided their private, innermost thoughts. 'You have to think of the fans, Brian,' he had said. 'The fans don't want their idols mixed up in controversy.'

'Controversy' was an understatement for the situation facing Brian. The pop manager was about to become a Daniel in the lions' den. His intelligence sources provided bleak news from all fronts.

Promoters who had booked the Beatles to appear in stadiums across America were being bombarded with protest calls. Tickets remained unsold; cancellations were rising. The office of Nat Weiss, Epstein's friend and New York lawyer, had received dozens of complaints, mainly from the Bible Belt, warning that John would not go unpunished for his sacrilege. More than thirty radio stations announced that they had banned Beatle records. Even those dubious defenders of the faith, the Klu Klux Klan, were marching to the crackle of Beatle records burning on bonfires.

'Tell the boy to apologize,' advised the Colonel now.

'He refuses to apologize for something he didn't say.'

'What are you planning to do?'

'I'll cancel the tour if necessary.'

'That'll cost you plenty.'

'I've already checked and I've been told it will cost us a million dollars, but I don't care. I'm not going to put the boys' lives at risk even if it costs $10 million. This is developing into a holy war and I'll cancel . . . unless . . .'

'Unless what, Brian?'

During his transatlantic flight, Brian had feverishly examined his options, and he now ran one possibility past the Colonel. It had not escaped Brian's attention that the centre of the most fanatical anti-Beatle activity was Memphis, Elvis's home town and the so-called 'buckle on the Bible Belt'. Even now, Memphis city council was meeting to discuss a possible ban on the group's concert because of the Jesus remark.

Brian now wondered aloud whether Elvis, a devout (if prodigal) Christian, might be prepared to help out. Perhaps he could issue a statement saying that John's quote had been misunderstood, that he had said 'more popular than Jesus', not 'bigger than Jesus', and was really a good chap: a God-fearing Beatle.

By this time, nothing fazed the Colonel. He was used to being asked to lend Elvis's support for one purpose or another. And he was used to saying no. On this occasion, however, he saw an opportunity to test his rival's mettle. It was Epstein's winding-up remark he found irresistible: 'And needless to say, if there is anything *we* could ever do for *you* . . .'

The Colonel must have smiled to himself. He so admired titles and the honours that invariably went with them (so much so that he had bestowed one on himself even before two obliging governors no less, in Tennessee and Louisiana, had seen fit to approve it). He had, for instance, been greatly impressed the previous year to read that the Queen had presented the Beatles with medals at Buckingham Palace. He believed that the Beatles' MBEs had been cleverly engineered through

Brian's contacts in English society, soon after Brian had struck up a close friendship with the Queen's sister.

Now it was the Colonel's turn to wonder aloud. Perhaps somebody could suggest to Her Majesty that an honorary award for Elvis might be in order. It would be Britain's way of showing its appreciation for such a fine, upstanding and much-loved American. If Lennon were to be elevated to St John, why not Sir Elvis Presley? The Snowmen's League was in session and the Colonel was in the chair.

Brian said that he had tried to explain that he really had not had a hand in the Beatles' royal honour.

'These things are worked out between the prime minister and the monarch,' he told the Colonel. 'You just can't negotiate them in the way it might be possible to swing a showbusiness award.'

By now, Brian was convinced that the old showman was playing games with him. He couldn't seriously believe that he could pull strings to get Elvis an honorary knighthood. Or could he? The Colonel had performed the seemingly impossible on so many occasions and now here he was challenging his rival to do the same.

Brian's next call that night was to John Lennon. Whether or not he told him about Parker's proposition is unknown, but *something* shifted the Beatle's previously intransigent position. His most stubborn client agreed to make a conciliatory statement to the press.

'I'm not anti-God, anti-Christ or anti-religion,' John said soon after the Beatles reached Chicago. 'I was not saying we're greater or better. I believe in God, but not as an old man in the sky. I used "Beatles" because it was easier for me to talk about Beatles. I'm sorry I said it really. I apologize if that will make you happy.'

The tour went ahead, only for the Beatles to be unnerved by an anonymous death threat, saying that they would be shot in Memphis. There were some tense moments when firecrackers exploded at the Mid-South Coliseum during the concert, but apart from that, there were no hitches.

With his love of intrigue, the Colonel has never owned up to what he failed to pull off for Elvis, but he acknowledged to me that 'there are many things you know about from knowing us that I can't stop you from writing.'

By the time he was selling Elvis in the mid-Fifties, there was already a secrecy about his *modus operandi* and a mystique about the man himself that many people found infuriating and not altogether edifying. It was tempting to some to dismiss him as nothing more than a carny hustler, a man who dyed sparrows yellow and passed them off to suckers as canaries or who sold foot-long hot-dogs with bits of frankfurter sticking out at either end and none in the middle.

The Colonel played along with this stereotype because it suited his purposes. In fact, it was his own invention, and he was often guilty of spreading these stories himself. Neil Aspinall remembers this classic: 'He told us about an aged circus lion that had lost its teeth. The Colonel had a set of false teeth made up and he put them in the lion's mouth every time it had to go on show. But first, he smeared them with a bit of mustard. The lion was constantly irritated in its mouth and would roar *aaaargh!* as though it was really fierce although it was fifty years old and could hardly move. But the Colonel was such a bullsh***er anyway, he was probably making it up.'

However, many people who heard these stories swallowed them whole and accepted the Colonel on face value. What you saw, they said, was what you got: an overfed, moon-faced huckster who had somehow got lucky and was now revelling in playing the big shot. Big, bluff and boastful, he looked like a man who had just eaten a plate of self-congratulation for lunch.

However, I had come to realize that his public persona was simply a front, a mask to hide the real person. Men of the world such as Frank Sinatra, Sid Bernstein and Henri Lewin, the Hilton Hotel boss, knew this instinctively. 'He was the first man who did not call the star by his full name – just *Elvis*,' Lewin told me. 'You know, Sinatra copied that ten years later. The Colonel was tough. If he had died first, I'm convinced Elvis's career would have ended. The Colonel was the one who made this thing last.'

There was more to the Colonel than met the eye and he went to great lengths to disguise it. Two of his most useful props were the cigar and the hat, both of which gave the impression that he equated power with size. It was noticeable that, as his ability to influence events developed, his cigars grew longer and the brim on his hats increased in width. Over the years, he graduated from small Dutch cigars to large Havanas, and from battered trilbys to stately, ten-gallon Stetsons.

In other ways, he seemed to be incredibly small-minded. The audience of 55,600 people that Sid Bernstein had packed into Shea to see the Beatles in 1965 might have been bigger than any Elvis got until ten years later, but the important thing to the Colonel had been who had the hot-dog concession. The Beatles drew phenomenal crowds, but according to Elvis's manager, it was the detail that made the difference. Raised in the heyday of the carnival, the Colonel had learned a simple truth: if enough nickels and dimes went in the same direction, you counted the profit in millions of dollars. He was a happy man if he could print a million Elvis photographs for a nickel each and sell them for a dime.

'The Colonel was very shrewd – he got money from everywhere, even the photos,' said Sid Bernstein. 'I would see the Colonel stand in the lobby and sell photos. When I worked with him from '72 to '74, he was charging a buck a time.'

For Bernstein, the Colonel was an acquired taste. 'At first I did not like him – I thought he was an egomaniac but quite a good twister, you know,' he said. 'One day he took me to lunch at Plato Reserva, which is a very wonderful Italian restaurant in Little Italy.

'"Sid, you don't like me very much, do you?" said the Colonel.

'"What makes you say that, Colonel?"

'"I can tell."

"'You're right, Colonel."

"'I want you to understand something. Elvis Presley is my client, he is the biggest act in the world, my one job is to protect him and, if that offends anybody, then I am sorry but, understand, I'm just here to take care of my client. I was born to do that and this is my job and I hope I do it as well or maybe better than any man.

Sitting there over the pasta, Bernstein had had a sudden change of heart. 'From that moment on, I respected him,' he said. 'I got to like him and understand him and we became good friends. He was the greatest manager that ever lived.'

The bigger picture tended to confirm this. The Colonel made movie and merchandising deals that brought Elvis $5 or $6 million dollars a year, and when the movie money dried up, he sold him on a Las Vegas tablecloth for another $5 million for just ten months' work spread over five years. And that was before he had shifted a single Elvis mugshot, souvenir programme or statuette.

If Brian Epstein prided himself on knowing what people wanted, the Colonel's genius was in persuading them to buy what they didn't need. As a salesman, he had few equals.

But Brian was a fast learner and he came to appreciate the Colonel's skills and to regard him as something of a mentor, even if he remained a mystery. Brian told me he consulted him on numerous occasions, particularly on matters of security, such as the successful getaway from Dallas airport in the laundry truck. On other occasions, Brian booked rooms for the Beatles in several hotels, just as the Colonel had advised him to do, to throw unwelcome newshounds off the scent. He even considered another of the Colonel's suggestions: to have them lie down on canvas-covered couches to be smuggled in and out of hotels by furniture removers. But these were all tricks of the trade. The Colonel guarded his personal secrets jealously, and for good reason. He had never intended the world to discover that he had been born not Thomas

Andrew Parker in West Virginia, as he had allowed others to believe, but as a Dutchman of humble origins.

Jack Kelly, one of the two Los Angeles private investigators hired by Vernon Presley, had turned up a wealth of material about the Colonel during his enquiries.

'In further checking the Colonel, I have determined that my original information on him was slightly awry,' Kelly told me in one of several written reports. 'The correct spelling of his name is Andreas Wilhelmus von Kujik and he was born on 26 June 1909, at Breda, Holland.'

Two days after the Colonel's birth, his father Adam von Kujik had gone to the Breda town hall to register it, a blacksmith and a shoemaker acting as witnesses. Andreas (later it was shortened to the diminutive Dries) was Maria van Kujik's fifth child and there were to be four more. The man who was destined to manage the biggest star of the 20th century, and to become as wealthy as the American dream would ever allow, had been born to the unpretentious van Kujiks in their apartment over some stables on a modest Breda street called Vlaszak.

Young Dries made a pet goat the star of his own mini-circus, charging friends a small fee for admission. That was before he learned to crack a whip and make huge draught horses trot slowly around the stable yard, turning about on command. Jack Kelly's report picks up the story:

Dries left Holland in 1927 to avoid military service, spent a few months in England, then went to the West Indies. He entered the US in 1928. He sold hotdogs in a carnival [the Royal American, which toured Canada and the US by railroad] until 1931 when he enlisted in the US Army, supposedly serving in Panama for a while.

He was discharged in 1936 with a small pension for a back injury. That same year he wrote home for the last time and told his family that he had legally changed his name to Thomas Andrew Parker.

He next surfaced in 1940 when he was the dogcatcher of the Humane Society of Tampa, Florida. He started booking shows at the weekend into a little theatre in Tampa. It was during this period that he met the country & western singer Eddy Arnold and became friendly with him. In 1945, he convinced Arnold that he could expand his career [which he did] and became his fulltime manager.

The Colonel had first gone to Las Vegas with Arnold in 1944 after doing a deal with the William Morris Agency. That same year he signed Arnold to the RCA record label, and the deal took off with a massive hit, the million-seller 'Bouquet of Roses'.

The Colonel had based himself in Nashville and, after securing Arnold's Vegas and RCA deals, bought a sprawling eleven-room, one-storey house on Gallatin Road in Madison, Tennessee, operating his business from the garage. The Colonel's assistant in those days was the dapper Tom Diskin, who remained with him throughout Elvis's career, just as the Colonel stayed faithful to RCA and the William Morris Agency, subsequently committing Presley to both.

Jack Kelly's report continued:

Through his association with Arnold, he met and became known to all the performers and bookers of country & western, including Hank Snow. Now Snow at that time was one of, if not the biggest country & western star.

In 1954, Parker and Hank Snow formed a company called Jamboree Attractions, which booked touring shows starring country & western performers. This probably is the single most contributing factor for the spread of country & western music throughout the US. Formerly it had been confined to the South and Southwest.

In 1954, Parker was in Texarkana, Texas, scouting for some new acts for his Jamboree Attractions when he first saw Elvis Presley performing. That was all the Colonel needed and the rest is history. Checking with the FBI and Interpol does not reveal any criminal record under either his given or adopted name.

Loyalty was the Colonel's watchword. 'You gotta be loyal to people,' he had once told me. 'When you are loyal to them, they're loyal to you and everybody gets to make a buck or two.'

In 1966, the Colonel had reason to doubt Elvis's loyalty to him, but he acted with great self-control. Elvis had fallen under the influence of Larry Geller, a self-styled 'hair nutritionalist' and spiritualist from New York. Geller, who had started cutting Elvis's hair in 1964, coaxed him into reading such esoteric books as *Through the Eyes of the Masters, The Wisdom of the Overself, Cosmic Consciousness, Cheiro's Book of Numbers* and Paramahansa Yogananda's *The Autobiography of a Yogi*. Elvis lapped up the new knowledge and started to ask questions about the direction his own life was taking.

Geller guided him to the Self-Realization Fellowship Center on Mount Washington in the Hollywood Hills. As the Colonel and the hard core of the Memphis Mafia watched in alarm, Elvis started changing in definable ways, not all of them conducive to the old, free-spending lifestyle that had guaranteed that he would have to work almost constantly to pay the bills. He experimented with marijuana and LSD, saw Stalin's face in some clouds over the desert ('the Anti-Christ'), and heard Jesus's voice in birdsong. He was definitely moving to a higher plane of consciousness.

When Elvis had an accident in the middle of the night at his new home, 10550 Rocca Place in Stone Canyon, the Colonel moved in for the kill.

'He was taking downers that were making him slur quite a bit and, from what I understand, were responsible for him having a fall at home, hitting his head,' said Sonny West. 'He may have even taken the prescribed amount, but he got up to go to the bathroom when he shouldn't have.

'He had in his employ a barber to cut his hair to have him looking nice for the movies, who was also bringing him all kinds of spiritual books.

'At that time, Elvis had those books burned and the guy was dismissed and that was it.'

In fact, Geller was not dismissed, although the spiritual texts that he had encouraged Elvis to read were blown to the four winds in a very occult bonfire. The Colonel also ruled that one of the Guys had to be present whenever Geller cut Elvis's hair. This put an end to the cosy téte-a-tétes that the guru had enjoyed with his employer, and so he quit. However, Elvis invited Geller to join his personal entourage when he started touring again in the Seventies.

His head recovered from both the fall and the mystic mindset, Elvis went on to make *Clambake,* in which he stars as a rich man who trades places with a poor man so that people will accept him for himself. Geller must have found that highly amusing.

Marijuana and LSD also took John Lennon into the depths of torpor after the Beatles gave their final concert at Candlestick Park, San Francisco, on 29 August 1966. He mooched around the grounds of Kenwood with no particular place to go, or lay perfectly still in his red-walled den. However, the end of touring and the pressure on him to write new songs for the next Beatle LP, *Rubber Soul,* only contributed to his depression. In September, his great love, Alma Cogan, had been admitted to Middlesex Hospital, London, and John knew that she was dying. Yet another important person in his life was being taken away from him. Unable to cope with his feelings, John numbed them out.

Alma had been ill throughout 1965 and, after collapsing several times, had undergone surgery for stomach cancer. The man keeping a vigil at her bedside was Brian Morris, the Ad Lib manager to whom she had secretly become engaged. This was the real background to the song that summed up John's view of himself, 'Nowhere Man'. As the weeks passed and Alma's life gradually slipped away, John completely lost his musical muse. 'I'd actually stopped trying to think of something,' he said. 'Nothing would come. I went for a lie-down, having given up. Then I thought of myself as "Nowhere Man sitting in his Nowhere Land". It all came out.' The group recorded the song on Thursday, 21 October, just six days before Alma's death. She was just thirty-four.

Like Elvis, John was on a drug-induced journey through the void of self-obsession. If the two superstars had been on speaking terms, they might have found it productive to compare symptoms and work out the obvious cause of the problem. They were trying to mend a hole with corrosive substances that made it bigger, not smaller.

John's relationship with Cynthia suffered, and he started to ignore Julian. 'As far as I was concerned, the rot began to set in the moment cannabis and LSD seeped their unhealthy way into our lives,' she recalled bitterly.

Finally, John accepted the role of the gormless Private Gripweed in Dick Lester's film *How I Won the War,* which appealed to the Beatle because it was the antithesis of *GI Blues.* It was fortunate that soldier John was merely marking time in the acting profession because, in a properly scripted role, he was so hopeless that he made Elvis look like an Oscar candidate. John decided to seek answers outside the entertainment industry, whose razzle-dazzle and ruthless exploitation had left him disillusioned and emotionally spent. 'I don't believe in the dream anymore,' he said. He needed to find his own spiritual guru and, with the help of George's wife Pattie, he found one.

CHAPTER FIFTEEN

Marriage, Death and Rebirth

FOR HOURS, Elvis concentrated on the lyrics of new Beatle records as they were released, trying to detect any anti-American propaganda or coded messages about drugs. When *Sgt Pepper's Lonely Hearts Club Band* was released in the summer of 1967, he thought he had hit the jackpot.

One of the songs, 'Lucy in the Sky with Diamonds', contained just such a reference – to LSD – in its title. John had actually borrowed the line from his young son Julian, who said it was the theme of a painting he had drawn at nursery school, but to Elvis, *Sgt Pepper* provided positive proof that what he had suspected all along was true. The Beatles, now shaggier than ever with large drooping moustaches, were the bellwethers of America's great unwashed druggie flock.

This was a difficult time for Elvis. The Colonel, it is widely believed, had decided that marriage would be a good career move for him and had arranged a secret wedding ceremony in Las Vegas. Elvis married Priscilla at the Aladdin Hotel on 1 May, squeezing his nuptials and the briefest of honeymoons in between filming scenes for *Clambake*. George Klein, however, believes that it was Elvis's idea all along and that the Colonel did not apply any pressure on him.

'I was one of fourteen people in the room – I was a groomsman,' said George. 'Elvis had called me from California on 4 March to tell me that he was going to get married. There I was, sitting on one of the greatest secrets in show business of all time.

'The weekend of the wedding, I flew out to LA and then to Palm Springs in the Lear Jet that Elvis had chartered. It was me and Elvis, Priscilla, and Joe Esposito and his wife Joanie. We flew from Palm Springs to Vegas and the rest of the wedding party followed in another plane. We got into Vegas late at night, maybe two or three o'clock in the morning, and Elvis and Joe went to the registrar to get the wedding licence. It's open all night long and actually Elvis went down there at 4.00 am so that they wouldn't be crowded. We got about three hours' sleep and they had the wedding about ten o'clock in the morning. After the ceremony, we went downstairs to a reception, where the rest of the party were waiting.

'Elvis got married because he was in love with Priscilla. They had been dating for a long time, and he felt that it was the right time. He also wanted a family. I don't think the Colonel had anything to do with it; that's a misconception.'

The last thing that Elvis wanted as a wedding present was yet another collection of soaraway Beatle hits, but that is precisely what he got: the group's greatest-ever creative masterpiece, a *tour de force* so dazzling in its musical concept and so brilliant in its technical execution that it would revolutionize popular music.

The *Sgt Pepper* album also provided convincing evidence of a subtle change in the Beatles' attitude towards Elvis. It was Paul's idea to feature dozens of celebrities, both living and dead, on the most famous record cover of all time.

'We want all our heroes together here,' he said. 'If we believe this is a very special album for us, we should have a lot of people who are special to us on the sleeve with us.'

Each of the Beatles was asked to submit a list of twelve favourite heroes and heroines from throughout the ages for a tableau to be created by the artist Peter Blake and photographed by Michael Cooper. When the lists were handed in, one obvious name was missing: Elvis Presley.

Stu Sutcliffe was there, along with Bob Dylan and Dion from the pop world, Marilyn Monroe, Mae West and Diana Dors (but not Jayne Mansfield), Tony Curtis, Marlon Brando and Lawrence of Arabia (ironically three of Elvis's own heroes), W. C. Fields,

Marlene Dietrich, Carl Jung, Edgar Allen Poe and Fred Astaire. Oh, and Albert Einstein. Two of John's candidates, Adolf Hitler and Jesus Christ, were ruled ineligible on the grounds of taste.

Elvis noted the omission of his own face as he scoured the line-up searching for incriminating clues. The face that attracted his eagle eye was the bearded, patrician figure of Karl Marx, practically the godhead of Communism, who was standing between Oliver Hardy and H. G. Wells. If anyone had doubted that the Beatles were Reds, here was the proof. In the United States, *Sgt Pepper* sold more than 2.5 million copies in three months and won four Grammy awards, further confirmation in Elvis's eyes that American youth was held in dangerous thrall.

Brian Epstein took the unusual step of holding a special press launch party for *Sgt Pepper* at his London house in Chapel Street, Belgravia, on 19 May 1967. The more I saw of him, the more I understood why the Beatles – and Paul in particular – were concerned about his mental health. We dined frequently at Overton's restaurant in St James's. He would pore over the menu, carefully choosing his dish of the evening and instructing how he wanted his vegetables cooked or his salad prepared. He would then pop a handful of pills, insisting that I join him in what he called 'our little helpers'. The uppers were appetite suppressants, and by the time our food arrived, neither of us wanted to eat. Time after time, the food would be sent back to the kitchen with 'Mr Epstein's compliments to the chef', but never an explanation as to why it had not been touched.

On just such an evening, he explained his absence over a prolonged period: he had been detoxed in an expensive west London treatment centre. 'I've been in the Priory getting over a slight problem,' he confided. 'You see that chap over by the door? He's my bodyguard. He's supposed to protect me from myself, if you've ever heard such nonsense. Anyway, he doesn't let me get any blues, so I hope you are carrying plenty.' Alas, I had a new career of my own to develop and I had sworn off drugs. Brian was furious, but at least he ate his dinner.

Bidding me goodnight, he said: 'I'm off to a party where I know they'll have lots and lots of little goodies. I do hope my shadow doesn't get too tired.'

In the event, that is exactly what did happen. Brian stayed awake for three days and three nights, a feat his bodyguard could not match. He finally dropped from exhaustion at Brian's country house at Kingsley Hill in Sussex. Brian gave him the slip and made his way back to Chapel Street. Inside his house there, he indulged himself until his heart could take no more.

On 27 August 1967, the butler knocked on his bedroom door but failed to get a reply. The door was broken down and Brian was found dead. He was lying on a single bed, dressed in pyjamas, some correspondence he had been reading spread out over a second, unoccupied single bed beside him. Police found seventeen bottles of pills by the beds, two in a briefcase and eight in the bathroom. Death had been caused by bromide poisoning due to 'an incautious self-overdose' of a prescribed drug called Carbrital.

The news reached the Beatles in the Welsh seaside resort of Bangor, where they had gone to be indoctrinated in the art of transcendental meditation. Pattie Harrison had met the Maharishi Mahesh Yogi after a lecture on spiritual regeneration at Caxton Hall and had fallen under his spell. She had told George about the power of Indian mysticism and he had converted the other Beatles, who had become interested enough to go on a spiritual retreat that weekend.

Their lack of public reaction to Brian's death owed as much to the teachings of the Maharishi, who assured them that death was simply part of the process of reincarnation, as it did to the fact that they knew Brian had previously tried twice to commit suicide because of clinical depression.

A message bearing Elvis's name arrived, which expressed 'deepest condolences on the loss of a good friend to you and all of us'. There were no prizes for guessing who had really sent it.

John was grief-stricken, although he appeared blissed out in the company of his giggling guru. Cynical though he might be, he had a very soft spot for Brian, whom he regarded as a protected species. Not only was Brian one of the few people safe from the Lennon lemon acid, John didn't like anyone else putting Brian down and that included the other Beatles.

John – the Liverpool Lip – was the most cutting person I ever met, even with royalty. He didn't like Princess Margaret because of her airs and graces, although he knew that Brian adored her. It had been Margaret who said that 'MBE' stood for 'Mr Brian Epstein'. In response, John changed her name to 'Priceless Margarine'. He told me about a time when he thought he had heard the Queen's sister remark that Beatle fans had inconvenienced her arrival at a cocktail party.

'I said I didn't know why she had bothered to turn up if our bloody fans were a nuisance to her,' he said. 'I didn't say it to her directly, but I'm sure she overheard me. I just hope I hadn't misheard her!'

John had to go along with the Establishment for the sake of the group, "but he would rather have been one of the Stones, whom Andrew Oldham had groomed to be as anarchic as they liked. However, when John and Andrew did get together, weird things started happening.

'The Stones were still dying in the North so I decided to go and see the Beatles, the opposition, playing in Liverpool,' Andrew told me. 'After the show, I had the pleasure of being driven back to London in John's psychedelic Rolls-Royce. I'm not saying we weren't on acid and I'm not saying we were. I was high on the event, anyway, because it was a welcome-home concert after they conquered America. Somehow, we got into hysterics about what would happen if the car windows suddenly shattered. John said, "It would be great – we'd have to wear the bear suits." It would be interesting to analyse that statement to find out what he meant.

'I later tried to buy that Roller from John because I believed it had two sets of windows. I was just so stoned that I hadn't realized that the windows were shut at one stage of the journey and open at another.'

Elvis was beginning to change for the better because of an impending birth. Priscilla had become pregnant soon after the wedding and, with the arrival of his first child approaching, the father-to-be was fired by a new enthusiasm. For the first time since 1957, he abandoned Hollywood schmaltz and went back to his roots in blues and country & western, recording 'Big Boss Man', 'High Heel Sneakers' and 'Guitar Man' during a highly charged session at the RCA studios in Nashville.

Lisa Marie Presley was born in Memphis at 5.01 pm on 1 February 1968. 'Nungen, us has a baby girl,' Elvis lisped to his wife. Had Lisa been a boy, he would have named his son and heir John Baron Presley. But he had never been prouder than when he took mother and baby home, first to Graceland and then to the West Coast to 1174 Hillcrest Drive on the Trousdale Estates in Los Angeles. As soon as Priscilla was fit enough to celebrate, Elvis decided to take her to see Tom Jones, who was playing to packed houses at the Flamingo in Las Vegas.

In 1966, I had left the *NME* to set up my own public relations company, and Tom was my first client. I had contacted his manager Gordon Mills after seeing Tom's picture in a women's magazine, in which he was wearing an apron and washing dishes, with his wife Linda drying up. Mills agreed to meet me for lunch, and I outlined the following strategy: Tom should seldom be available for interviews and photographs; no attention should ever be drawn to his marriage; his sexuality should be projected both on and off stage; we should exploit and even exaggerate his successes so that both fans and promoters would start to think of him in the same light as Presley and Sinatra.

I walked out of the restaurant as Tom's imagemaker for the princely sum of £25 a week, all Tom could afford at the time. I immediately began planning to promote him in America in much the same way as the Colonel had sold Elvis. I had learned a lot from the Colonel during my three trips with the Beatles, and I frequently sought his advice once Tom started to happen in front of American audiences. Women adored the miner's son born Thomas Jones Woodward in Pontypridd, South Wales. They threw their panties, bras and room keys at him, and he didn't always throw them back.

The sudden decision to see Tom on stage was typical of Elvis's competitive nature. He wanted to see for himself what all the fuss was about. One Saturday afternoon in April 1968, Joe Esposito phoned me from LA to request a table in Elvis's name for the midnight show. This had been sold out for weeks, but I arranged for an extra table and chairs to be set up directly in front of the stage. At fifteen minutes to midnight, Elvis and Priscilla walked through the casino to the lounge, having flown to Vegas in a private jet. To make sure they didn't feel lonely, eight companions had tagged along for the ride. No expense was spared when the King took his Queen on a night out.

The lights were still up and the crowd buzzed with excitement at the sight of America's rock royalty. To catch Elvis in a public place was a rarity. To catch him with Priscilla at a rival performer's show was really hitting the jackpot. With a huge jewelled cluster underpinning her stacked raven hair, and clad in an off-the-shoulder black sheath dress, Priscilla did not disappoint them. She looked top-heavy, but stunning.

Tom stepped on stage to a tremendous reception and gave it everything he had. When he did the first up-tempo number, 'Don't Fight It', Elvis slapped the table and rolled his head in time to the beat. Several times during the song, he turned to comment to Priscilla, a broad smile on his face and a long thin cigar clamped between his teeth.

Later in the act, Tom announced: 'Ladies and gentlemen, we have in the audience tonight a man I have admired for many years, Mr Elvis

Presley.' The audience cheered Elvis, who stood up to wave and take a bow. 'OK, that's enough – sit down,' Tom commanded jokingly. When Tom finished with 'Land of a Thousand Dances', the wildest number in his repertoire, Elvis jumped up and led the audience in a standing ovation. After the curtains had closed, I took Elvis and Priscilla backstage to meet Tom, who was soaking wet in his stage suit. Elvis took Tom's hand in both of his and offered his congratulations.

'Say, Tom,' 'he said, 'we should do a show together at either end of the stage with the Beatles backing us up in the middle.'

Tom screwed up his nose at the mention of the Beatles.

'What's wrong with the Jordanaires?' he quipped.

As members of both entourages packed in, the stars moved into a smaller dressing room to escape the crush.

'You've lost a lot of weight,' Tom told Elvis, who was smart in a dark blue yachting jacket and white roll-neck shirt.

'Sure have – I'm on what they call a "drinking man's diet",' replied Elvis. 'You know, I've got some unhappy memories of Vegas. I was at the Frontier in '56 and I died a terrible death. When I came out with those hip movements, man, they just weren't ready for me!' To emphasize the point, he gyrated his pelvis in the famous way that nobody had seen since he had gone into the Army.

'I gotta tell you, though, that that "Green, Green Grass of Home" is really something,' he continued. 'When it was released here, the Guys and I were on the road driving in our mobile home. Man, that song meant so much to us boys from Memphis we just sat there and cried. We called the radio station and asked them to play it again and they did – four times! We just sat there and sobbed our hearts out.'

When it was time to go, Tom and I escorted the Presleys to their long, low, black Cadillac with darkened windows and masses of aerials.

'You see all these aerials?' said Elvis. 'Well, they don't mean a thing – they ain't connected to nothing!'

Back in the charts with 'Guitar Man' and inspired by Tom Jones, Elvis agreed to give his first TV performance since he had appeared on Frank Sinatra's show in 1960. The King was back, snarling.

'Been a long time, I tell you,' he said during an informal jam session in the comeback special for NBC-TV. He took the opportunity to hit back at the Beatles, declaring that they hadn't produced anything he couldn't match. 'Performers today have learned to trick things up with choruses and electronic gimmicks – but the beat is still there,' he said. 'It's still what I call rock 'n' roll.'

Elvis was on a winning streak. He recorded no fewer than thirty-six tracks when he went back into the studio, this time in Memphis, in January 1969. Reaching deep into his soul, he dragged up towering performances for 'In the Ghetto', 'Suspicious Minds' and 'Kentucky Rain'.

Incredibly, Elvis included a couple of Lennon/McCartney numbers, 'Yesterday' and 'Hey Jude', in his repertoire, but nothing that involved 'electronic gimmicks'. When things were going his way, the vendetta seemed to go into remission, although there were also sound commercial reasons for the decision.

Since the previous November, the Colonel had been planning an enterprise that would put Elvis back in the public eye on his own terms. He would perform at the world's largest resort hotel, the new $60 million International in Las Vegas. The men who pulled off the deal were Alex Shoofey, executive vice-president of the International and a long-time friend of the Colonel, and entertainments chief Bill Miller. I had dinner with the Colonel and Alex Shoofey just before they went into a ten-minute huddle to sign a simple two-page contract.

The meeting was held in Shoofey's office at the Flamingo, just a mile from where the International was reaching for the sky on Paradise Road. Elvis turned up at the hotel building site to add his name to the contract while the cameras snapped the historic moment.

Elvis had nearly three months to prepare for his first show in early August, when he would follow Barbra Streisand, who had been booked to open the hotel for its owner Kirk Kerkorian.

'Elvis won't even start thinking about what he's going to sing or wear until we've finished *Change of Habit* [his last movie],' Joe Esposito told me. 'No, he's not nervous. The first two or three nights he'll get butterflies, but Elvis will take it all in his stride.'

Watching Elvis perform live on stage was something I had dreamed about since hearing 'Heartbreak Hotel' for the first time. I didn't realize then just how close I would get to the eye of the hurricane.

CHAPTER SIXTEEN

Supper with Truman Capote

ELVIS SPENT his weekends away from Priscilla at his secluded home in Chino Canyon Road, Palm Springs. Between games of Scrabble, motorbike racing and sex with young girls, he had come under another, more benign, influence.

In the desert resort, he struck up the most bizarre friendship of his life with one of his neighbours. Of all the people whom Elvis had ever encountered either by choice or by accident, he had elected to befriend one who seemed to inhabit an entirely different planet: the writer Truman Capote. Capote of *Breakfast at Tiffany's* and *In Cold Blood,* Capote with the ultra-sophisticated taste, waspish New York wit and camp lisp, Capote the son of an alcoholic mother who had committed suicide. They made an odd couple, the King and his friend Tru-boy.

Only five feet three inches tall, the baby-faced social butterfly was more accustomed to flitting from one society beauty to another, cross-pollinating them all with the latest gossip from the others. But in his company, Elvis was able for the first time to face up to the truth about his own childhood and the mother he had idolized above everything.

His high-pitched voice lowered to a confidential whisper, Capote described his own mother Nina's drinking binges and her endless string of lovers in the southern hotels he had called home before she abandoned him into the care of her cousins in Monroeville, Alabama, at the age of four.

'My mother was a very beautiful girl and only seventeen when I was born. She used to lock me in these rooms all the time, and I developed this fantastic anxiety,' Capote would say. 'I pounded and pounded on the door to get out. That did something to me. I have great fear of being abandoned by some particular friend or lover.'

When he later, in New Orleans, asked a witch to turn him into a girl, she had answered: 'I hear a baby crying.' The image provoked memories from Elvis's own distant past. He remembered Gladys's mournful sobbing and heard a small voice crying in the dark of that cold Mississippi shack: 'What wrong, Mommy?' The spirit of his twin brother Jesse Garon was never far from Elvis and his mother. Gladys drank moonshine to drown her grief that Jesse had died at birth; Elvis cried tears of guilt because he had been the twin to survive. Capote helped him to uncover the root cause of his insecurity.

The writer seemed to understand this intuitively. He was, he admitted, an alcoholic and a drug addict, first with prescribed medication and later vast amounts of cocaine. Asked why he drank and drugged, Capote replied: 'I can tell you in exactly one word: anxiety. I think certain people have a feeling of anxiety. A lot of analysts call it "free-floating anxiety". You know it doesn't mean anything, but it's always there.'

Just as Elvis had done, Capote collected doctors who would supply pills for insomnia, anxiety and copious other ailments, real and imagined. By nature, he loved to isolate himself, scribbling furtively with his pen in a ruled exercise book behind locked doors, his booze and pills close at hand. But perversely, he also craved the spotlight. 'Every single person who's really been close to me in my life has been a recluse,' he said. 'I can't imagine why I'm attracted to them when my attitude is "Let's go to a party."'

Elvis totally identified with that feeling: he was himself a classic case of the loner who needed to be the centre of attention. 'I get lonesome right in the middle of a crowd,' he once said. The way Capote explained it made sense of a lot of the contradictions in his life.

It was indicative of Capote's personality that he should take a shine to both Elvis Presley and his arch-enemy, now known as

John Ono Lennon. 'Elvis was nice, I sort of liked him,' Capote said. 'And I liked John Lennon a lot. He was very intelligent. He was a sensitive, very good-hearted person. I couldn't stand her. The Jap. She was always paranoid. The most unpleasant person that ever was, in my opinion.'

Capote wasn't the only one to take a dislike to Yoko, who had met John at the Indica Gallery in London in November 1966. They kept their affair secret until John sent Cynthia away on holiday in May 1968 and Yoko promptly moved into the marital home. The other Beatles believed her influence over John contributed to the band's break-up, a claim that he hotly denied. It was ironic that it should be John, the Great Beatle Protector, who had introduced a *femme fatale* into the group. Elvis lapped up the gossip from London whenever he saw his friend Truman.

As Elvis's date at the International drew near and the butterflies started to circle, he pleaded with Capote to be there.

'He was going to open this big hotel in Las Vegas,' the writer recalled. 'He was making some sort of comeback. He hadn't appeared in public in a long time and he invited me to come up and see it 'cos I had never seen him. In fact, I really had never heard any of his records either. So he said if I would come up, he would give this dinner party for me. I was more curious as to who in the world he would invite to this dinner party than I was about anything else, so I went with a friend. The one and only time I've ever been to Las Vegas.'

Steeped in Fifth Avenue chic, Capote hated even the thought of Las Vegas. Uncultured people making whoopee in brash casinos offended his aesthetic taste. Nevertheless, Elvis was his friend, and his curiosity had been aroused. He packed his tuxedo, buttoned his cardigan, put a fedora on his large round head and, cigarette holder clamped firmly between his even teeth, took off for Nevada.

The scene that greeted him at the International eclipsed any previous display of vulgarity it had ever been his misfortune to witness. The single world 'ELVIS' covered the hotel's huge marquee, fair warning of what was to come inside. The Colonel had excelled himself. In the lobby, the casino lounge, the restaurants, everywhere, he had Elvis show posters, Elvis Styrofoam hats, Elvis balloons, Elvis hound dogs, Elvis teddy bears and other kitsch Elvis souvenirs. With the management's connivance, he had turned the entire hotel into a tacky Elvis sideshow. His senses reeling, Capote headed for the bar.

Elvis had been so anxious about the reception he would receive at his first live performance since the Fifties that he had invited a host of old friends, including Sam Phillips, to attend the first night. I was there, too.

Anyone who thought Elvis's performance in the NBC special had been a carefully staged one-off for the cameras was to be pleasantly surprised. He put more effort into recruiting his band, led by the guitarist James Burton, rehearsing his two backing groups – the Imperial Quartet and the Sweet Inspirations – and choreographing his own stage moves than for any other performance in his entire career. He had worked so hard that he had shed fifteen pounds in the run-up to opening night, and when I saw him before the show, he was thinner than I had ever seen him, as well as extremely nervous. But, once he got in front of the audience, the butterflies started to fly in formation.

His rock band, backed by the hotel's twenty-five piece orchestra, thundered the defiant 'Baby, I Don't Care' as the gold curtain lifted to reveal the man himself. Priscilla rose from her table near the front of the vast, multi-level showroom and led 2000 people in a standing ovation before her husband had even sung a note. Dressed in a black karate outfit slashed to the waist, he let rip with a very fast and very short version of 'Blue Suede Shoes' before going into 'I Got a Woman'. Then he paused, drank some Gatorade and, looking around the huge amphitheatre decked out with a Roman colonnade, murals of Greek ruins, some Louis XIV waxwork figures and a flight of celestial cherubs, said: 'Good evening, ladies and gentlemen. Welcome to the big, freaky International Hotel, with those weirdo dolls on the walls, and those funky angels on the ceiling . . . and man, you ain't seen nothin' till you've seen a funky angel.'

Elvis, of course, had seen some very funky angels in his time, but drugs did not impair his style that night as they would in the years ahead.

It was a fabulous show with something for everyone. He gave us his new hit singles to show that he meant business. His hair almost Beatle length, he did 'Yesterday' and 'Hey Jude' to show he was just as good as the Liverpool Four. 'Johnny B. Goode' was for Chuck Berry to show he recognized a true master, and 'Mystery Train' was for his own mentor Sam Phillips. He closed with 'What'd I Say?' but came back with 'Can't Help Falling in Love' for Priscilla, as an encore.

After the curtain had gone down to tumultuous applause, Elvis hugged a tearful Colonel and changed hurriedly for a press conference. Asked about his movie career, he said: 'I couldn't dig always playing the guy who'd get into a fight, beat the guy up and in the next shot sing to him.'

Did he regret doing so many soundtrack albums? 'I think so. When you do ten songs in a movie, they can't all be good songs,' he said. 'Anyway, I got tired of singing to turtles. I get more pleasure out of performing to an audience like tonight than any of my film songs have given me.'

Inevitably he was asked about his rivalry with the Beatles. 'I well remember my meeting with the Beatles and have recorded "Hey Jude" for my next album,' he replied. 'They are so interesting and experimental, but I liked them particularly when they used to sing "She was just seventeen, you know what I mean?"'

On that enigmatic note, Elvis adjourned upstairs to entertain Truman Capote at the only dinner party he ever threw for anyone.

'We saw the opening show, and the dinner party was in between shows,' Capote recalled. 'I can't say that I was at all impressed by his performance. So we went to this apartment he had there in the hotel, and the dinner party consisted of about eight young men and one old friend of mine who had flown all the way from Honolulu, mainly because she was a fan of Elvis's. She loved Elvis, and guess who it was? Doris Duke.'

Elvis and Doris had become friends in Hawaii where the heiress, another reclusive figure hiding from the world behind dark glasses, high walls and security guards, had been holed up at her Shangri-la estate. Doris had embraced mystical Eastern religions and, like Elvis, meditated daily and believed in reincarnation. They had become very fond of one another. Tall, slim and middle-aged, Doris was the sole heiress of the tobacco mogul James Buchanan Duke who, in 1925, had left her $80 million. She could be a reckless spender – she had the dubious distinction of having taught her friend Imelda Marcos the art of shopping – but was also so astute financially that her fortune had multiplied to an estimated $1.5 billion.

'So we had this dinner party,' said Truman Capote. 'This table was full of orchids up and down, and everything looked very fancy in a gauche, peculiar way. But the dinner was incredible. It was all kinds of different things, fried pork and fried chicken and fried catfish.'

In honour of his guest, Elvis had ordered the chef to prepare a meal in the southern style. Capote, however, had actually spent most of his life eating French and Italian cuisine in the better restaurants of New York City and wondered what on earth he was eating. His *bon mots* might have been lost on the rugged and be-ringed members of the Memphis Mafia, but no one cared. The King was back where he belonged, and an hour or so in the company of a small, dainty gentleman he obviously admired was a small price to pay.

For once, Elvis was really happy.

Truman Capote was not the only important figure Elvis met in Palm Springs. He buttonholed Vice President Spiro T. Agnew and regaled him with a diatribe against the forces trying to destroy America, *his* America.

Richard Nixon's deputy had come to the desert in late November 1970 to relax in the winter sun. In the event, he was warmed by Elvis's fervour.

Elvis explained that his fears were motivated not only by the murder of the actress Sharon Tate and other ritual killings by the self-styled Manson family, which had stunned America, but also by threats against his own life. He was a wealthy man with the means to protect himself, Priscilla, Lisa Marie and members of his extensive entourage, he told the Vice President. But the time had come for people in the public eye like himself to stand up and be counted. He, for one, was really, willing and able to tackle the problem of violent dissent head-on.

Elvis tried to give Agnew a Colt .357 snub-nosed magnum for his own protection, but the politician explained that, as a public official, he could not accept gifts from citizens. He was, he said, quite happy with the protection already afforded him by the Secret Service.

When Agnew returned to Washington, he mentioned the meeting to White House staffers. Then, embroiled in the problems of the Nixon administration – and an investigation into his own crooked past – he promptly forgot all about it.

Elvis, however, had been deadly serious. He started using the alias 'Colonel John Burrows' to shield his identity while on tour, and collected as many as thirty badges from law enforcement agencies, ranging from the LAPD to the Royal Canadian Mounted Police. He carried at least two guns, one in a shoulder holster and another strapped to his leg. After the Sharon Tate murders, he slept with a gun under his pillow and breakfasted with a gun beside his plate. The Memphis Mafia carried so much hardware that they resembled a SWAT team.

Sharon Tate had been eight months' pregnant when she and four others were murdered at the Beverly Hills home she shared with her husband, film director Roman Polanski. The bodies were mutilated with knives and the word 'PIG' smeared in blood across the front door.

The murders took place on 9 August 1969, just as Elvis was hitting his stride in Las Vegas. The next night, the killers executed supermarket tycoon Leno LaBianca and his wife Rosemary. The words 'HELTER SKELTER' and 'DEATH TO PIGS' were daubed in blood at the LaBianca residence. These vicious, mindless acts inspired enormous fear among the rich and famous of Los Angeles. Elvis ordered security stepped up around his imitation French regency home on Hillcrest Drive. 'It could have been us,' he told Priscilla. 'We're getting outta here.' He put his house on the market and moved his family to more secure premises at 144 Monovale Road, between Bel Air and Beverly Hills.

Almost immediately, details began to emerge of a weird sect called 'The Family', the members of which took LSD and other drugs, practised Satanism and listened to Beatle records. Their leader, a drifter called Charles Manson, who had dubbed himself 'Jesus Christ', recruited young dropouts from the streets and took them to a desert hideout, where they were blooded in crude techniques of assassination. By December, Manson and three young women disciples had been arrested and charged with the murders.

When the Manson trial began in the summer of 1970, it was claimed that the bearded, long-haired hippie had been motivated by the lyrics of 'Helter Skelter', one of the tracks on the Beatles' *White Album*. The prosecution believed there was a definite link between the murders and the Beatles' music. Manson, himself a song writer, proclaimed that the Beatles were prophets who, through the words of 'Helter Skelter', were predicting the outbreak of a race war in the United States. He interpreted the title as meaning 'armageddon'. According to Manson, when Helter Skelter came, the Black Panthers – led by Rocky Raccoon (the name of another track on the *White Album*) – would rise and kill the Piggies (the title of a third track). Added together, the Beatles' songs represented a signal for Manson to start the slaughter.

Asked about the Manson allegations, John replied: 'Well, he's barmy. He's like any other Beatles fan who reads mysticism into it. I don't know what "Helter Skelter" has to do with knifing somebody.'

In fact, it had been Paul McCartney who had penned the words to 'Helter Skelter', about an innocent fairground ride. 'Piggies', which Manson saw as an incitement to murder members of the White Establishment, was actually a George Harrison composition and the line, 'What they need is a damn good whacking', came from something his mother had once said.

But the notion that the Beatles were more dangerous than ever stuck in Elvis's mind. It was at this point that he was personally involved in a double threat of kidnapping and assassination. Inside Elvis, something snapped.

He had only a few more nights to run of his third successful season in Las Vegas when a security officer at the International Hotel received a telephone call. The date was 26 August 1970. The anonymous male caller claimed that criminals known to him were planning to kidnap Elvis and hold him to ransom. The caller said that he had been approached to take part in the conspiracy, but had opted out.

Kidnapping being a Federal offence, the Las Vegas Police Department immediately contacted the FBI. Barely had the agency started to act on the first call when a second one was received the following day when I was visiting the Colonel in his office on the fourth floor of the hotel.

This call came from a man with a southern accent, who advised the Colonel to treat the threat of the kidnapping as a matter of urgency. Not a man to panic, Elvis's manager did just that before regaining his usual sang-froid and guiding me into the casino to chance our luck at craps.

FBI agents were still processing this call when yet another threat arrived. This time, a caller warned that Elvis would be shot on stage. The would-be assassin was named as a woman who had tried unsuccessfully to sue Elvis over the paternity of her child.

The FBI files that I was able to examine twenty years later contain the following report:

> Call was received at twelve noon, stating that this individual who is going to kill Presley has already departed from Los Angeles airport and has apparently made a reservation for the Saturday evening performance of Presley. The potential killer, a woman, is carrying a pistol fitted with silencer.

The files further show that J. Edgar Hoover issued instructions that he should be kept informed about any developments.

Elvis was alternately fearful and furious about the threats. He might have prophesied his own death in a Manson-style slaying, but to be the target of two simultaneous attempts was defying even destiny. When he was told of Hoover's concern for his safety, he calmed down a bit. The great man himself was on the case. He had found a saviour.

Everywhere I went, the hotel seethed with FBI activity. Fans in Elvis T-shirts and clutching one or other of the Colonel's cuddly toys swarmed excitedly through the hotel's corridors bumping into the well-padded shoulders of men in grey suits and snap-brimmed trilbys. I could tell from the beads of sweat on Joe Esposito's brow that he was nervous. When he became fidgety, I knew he was scared. He held himself personally responsible for Elvis's safety, and things were getting out of hand.

Elvis's bodyguards, some of them specially recruited for the new crisis, were given photographic ID cards not only to identify themselves to the hotel staff and members of the public but also to enable them to recognize each other. As they were all armed to the teeth, there was a very real danger that one of the new faces might be shot by mistake for getting too close to Elvis.

Elvis refused to abandon his act, but he went on stage with a gun tucked in the back of his trouser waistband. If anyone fired at him, he intended to shoot back. As Sonny West and Jerry Schilling were stationed nearby to jump in front of Elvis at the slightest sign of trouble, this could have proved fatal. Elvis had issued other orders as well: 'If anyone gets me, kill 'em before the cops move in. I don't want anyone to become famous for shooting Elvis Presley.' All the precautions worked, and Elvis closed in Las Vegas without a scratch. But his aides privately reported that he was using more drugs and his behaviour was more erratic, even on stage.

Fans were sometimes treated to a rambling version of his life story. I dropped in one night and heard this:'. . . Like to tell you a little about myself. I started out . . . in childhood. I started out when I was in high school, went into a record company one day, made a record, and when the record came out, a lot of people liked it and you could hear folks around town saying, "Is he, is he?" and I'm going, "Am I, am I?" . . . *whew!* . . . Elvis deterioratin' at the Showroom Internationale in Las Vegas . . . Where was I? . . . Oh, anyway, made a record, got kinda big in my home town, few people got to know who I was, that's w-u-z, was. See? So I started down in the wuz . . . Aw, shucks, what I mean to tell you is I was playin' around these night clubs, alleys and things. Did that for about a year and a half, then I ran into Colonel Sanders . . . Parker, Parker . . . and he arranged to get me some [Elvis blew his nose] Kleenex . . . he arranged to get me . . . *Whew,* I'm tellin' you . . . shot to hell, this boy can't even finish a sentence straight . . . Anyway, there was a lot of controversy at that time about my movin' around on stage so I . . . cleared my throat again, looked at my watch and ring and the guy said . . . the guy said? . . . the guy said nothin' . . . *I'm* the guy! I'm telling you, you better get this together, boy, or this is gonna be the last time they let you up on a stage . . .'

There was a lot more of the same embarrassing nonsense. It amounted to one thing: Elvis was losing touch with reality. Sometimes he changed or forgot the lyrics of his songs; at other times, he stumbled around the stage or fumbled with the mike. Not once did the audience lose its reverence. Some fans booked in for all sixty-odd shows a month to catch the King for better or worse.

Elvis was actually in physical pain. According to Charlie Hodge, 'Elvis often needed painkillers after his act. As everyone knows, he could be very physical in his performance, with his karate stunts and so on, and he genuinely used to pull a muscle or damage himself. He did have a high pain tolerance. When they discovered he had an eye condition called glaucoma, I went with him to see the doctor. He said it was so bad that he needed to give him a shot right there, but there was no anaesthetist available. So Elvis said, "Do it!" He grabbed the side of the chair and the doctor just gave him a shot right in the white of the eye. It came up like a tennis ball.'

To celebrate the new, live Elvis, RCA released *On Stage: February 1970*, a collection of songs recorded in Las Vegas, in reply to the Beatles' *Let It Be* album, their 13th – and last.

Suddenly, the most famous group in the world was history. The Beatles had been falling to pieces ever since Brian's death, but the official death knell was sounded on 31 December 1970, when Paul McCartney, who had tried to keep the band together, took out a law suit in the High Court to dissolve the partnership.

'I was stoned all the time and I just didn't give a damn,' admitted John, who now looked like a refugee from a hippie commune. 'Idiots rang up and said, "Yoko split the Beatles." She didn't split the Beatles. After Brian died, we collapsed. Paul took over and supposedly led us. But what is leading when we went round in circles? We broke up then. That was the disintegration.'

Both Elvis and John were showing signs of disintegrating themselves. The chains of addiction had been fitted so subtly that neither realized he was enslaved until he tried to walk away. By then, it was too late.

CHAPTER SEVENTEEN

Nixon's Narc, Hoover's Hound

FOR ONE fleeting moment, Elvis might have sought help from the President himself. Instead, he sank deeper into his obsession to bust John Lennon and, in the process, sabotaged his chance to get well.

When I first wrote, in the *Daily Mirror,* about Elvis's visit to Richard Nixon in the Oval Office, eyebrows had been raised until official confirmation of the story was forthcoming. It sounded so absurd that many found it hard to believe. However, papers released from the archives of the Nixon administration and the liberated FBI files show that the truth was even stranger than I had suspected.

It started at Graceland a few days before Christmas 1970, when Elvis adopted the addict's classic posture towards reality. Driven by an uncontrollable craving to 'get out of it', he started arguing with everyone. He rowed with Priscilla over Lisa, Vernon over his manic spending and with the Colonel over the arrangements for his next tour. He was restless, difficult, demanding and unreasonable.

After one particularly savage exchange with the Colonel on the phone, he stormed off into the night, dressed in a dark blue suit and cape, and wearing a pair of dark glasses. He was carrying a silver-topped swordstick in one hand and, in the other, clutched the leather valise that contained his medication. He was also armed with a Colt .45 pistol in a shoulder holster and carried another gun, a World War II Colt .45 in a presentation case.

Elvis drove himself to Memphis airport, where he boarded an American Airlines jet bound for Washington. His original intention had been to escape from the demons pursuing him, and to do that in the company of the two men he trusted most in the world: J. Edgar Hoover and Richard Nixon. They would understand his problems. They would save him. But once he had checked into the Washington Hotel under his alias, Colonel John Burrows, Elvis started to lose his nerve. Alone in his bedroom, the large quantity of drugs he had consumed merely brought on an attack of paranoia. He couldn't sit still. He was in an agony of indecision. It was already dark outside and he was too frightened to make a move.

Wherever he went, whether it was in Memphis, LA, Las Vegas or passing through some tiny country town while on tour, Elvis had always lived like a Tudor monarch, rarely unguarded and never left on his own for more than a few minutes. Now he was lonely and terrified, and the enormity of his decision to do something without the physical presence of the Guys at his side started to terrify him. Unable to stand the four walls a moment longer, he dashed to the airport and grabbed a plane to Los Angeles.

Jerry Schilling had quit Elvis's service following one argument too many, and was now working on a film in Hollywood. He got Elvis's call in the middle of the night. The plan had changed somewhat during the long flight west, and Elvis, swearing Schilling to secrecy, outlined his new mission. He told his startled former aide that he intended to see both Nixon and Hoover to demand that he be made a Federal agent in the fight against the dual menace of street drugs and Communism.

However, there was a hidden agenda, which he kept to himself. By becoming an agent, he could legitimize his own drug usage, which, he continued to fool himself, involved only properly prescribed medication. It would be the perfect cover to protect his addiction.

Schilling agreed to go along with Elvis, with one proviso. He insisted on calling Sonny West at Graceland and having him fly to Washington to meet them. Elvis agreed. He had lost his taste for solitude.

On the early-morning plane to Washington on 21 December, Elvis, polite as ever, struck up a conversation with George Murphy, a Republican Senator from California. They covered Elvis's favourite topics – politics, drugs and the Beatles – and Murphy offered to help. He suggested that Elvis should outline his plans in a personal letter to the President, while he would contact Hoover at the FBI and John Ingersoll, director of the Bureau of Narcotics and Dangerous Drugs, with a view to Elvis working under cover for both agencies.

A helpful stewardess handed Elvis some notepaper headed with the American Airlines logo, and he carefully composed a five-page letter to the President in his own uncertain hand. When the plane landed, he delivered it to a guard at the White House gate. The letter to Nixon, with syntax and punctuation intact, read as follows:

> Dear Mr President,
>
> First I would like to introduce myself. I am Elvis Presley and admire you and Have Great Respect for your office. I talked to Vice President Agnew in Palm Springs 3 weeks ago and expressed my concern for our country. The Drug Culture, the Hippie Elements, the SDS, Black Panthers, etc, do not consider me as their enemy or as they call it the Establishment. I call it America and I Love it. Sir I can and will be of any Service that I can to help the country out. So I wish not to be given a title or an appointed position. I can and will do more good if I were made a Federal Agent at Large, and I will help best by doing it my way through my communications with people of all ages.
>
> First and Foremost I am an entertainer but all I need is the Federal Credentials. I am on the Plane with Sen. George

Murphy and we have been discussing the problems that our Country is faced with. So I am staying at the Washington Hotel Room 505-506-507. I have 2 men who work with me by the name of Jerry Schilling and Sonny West. I am registered under the name of John Burrows, I will be here for as long as it takes to get the credentials of a Federal Agent. I have done an in depth study of Drug Abuse and Communist Brainwashing Techniques and I am right in the middle of the whole thing, where I can and will do the most good. I am Glad to help just so long as it is kept very Private. You can have your staff or whomever call me anytime today tonight or tomorrow. I was nominated this coming year one of America's Most Outstanding young men. That will be in January 19 in My Home Town of Memphis. I am sending you the short autobiography about myself so you can better understand this approach. I would love to meet you just to say hello if you're not too Busy.

Respectfully

Elvis Presley

P.S. I believe that you Sir were one of the Top Ten Outstanding Men of America also. I have a personal gift for you also which I would like to present to you and you can accept it or I will keep it for you until you can take it.

While this letter was silently making its way through the corridors of power, Elvis arranged to visit the Narcotics Bureau, using Senator Murphy's name to gain entrance. Murphy had kept his word and had contacted Ingersoll, but although the director agreed to a visit, he fobbed Elvis off with his deputy, John Finlater. While Finlater told Elvis that he appreciated his concern for the youth of America, he said that he could not issue him with an agent's badge. He was sorry, but it was impossible. The agency simply didn't work that way.

AmericanAirlines

In Flight....

Altitude:

Location:

[handwritten letter]

The final page of the letter that Elvis wrote to
President Nixon on 21 December 1970

Finlater had other reasons for refusing the King's request. He and
his staff knew an addict when they saw one, and Elvis's sweating face,
uncertain speech and unkempt appearance tended to confirm that
prognosis. But it was the dark glasses hiding from close inspection his
eyes with their pinhole-sized pupils that were the real giveaway.

Elvis was devastated. After two sleepless days, he was starting to
come down and his world seemed to be collapsing with him. However,
there was good news from Jerry Schilling, who had stayed at the
Washington Hotel to await a call from the White House. The President's

office had duly come through, requesting Elvis to be at the White House at noon. Elvis was now elated.

Once his letter had arrived and a check call to the Washington Hotel had confirmed that 'Colonel John Burrows' was indeed staying there, it had become a busy morning at the White House, at least for one Dwight L. Chapin, who sent the following memo (see below) to Nixon's chief of staff, H. R. 'Bob' Haldeman.

The internal White House memo that led to Elvis
getting his Federal agent's badge. (*reproduced on the next page*)

MEMORANDUM

THE WHITE HOUSE
WASHINGTON

December 21, 1970

MEMORANDUM FOR MR. H. R. HALDEMAN
FROM: DWIGHT L. CHAPLIN
SUBJECT: Elvis Presley

Attached you will find a letter to the President from Elvis Presley. As you are aware, Presley showed up here this morning and has requested an appointment with the President. He states that he knows the President is very busy, but he would just like to say hello and present the President with a gift.

As you are well aware, Presley was voted one of the ten outstanding young men for next year and this was based upon his work in the field of drugs. The thrust of Presley's letter is that he wants to become a "Federal agent at large" to work against the drug problem by communicating with people of all ages. He says that he is not a member of the establishment and that drug culture types, the hippie elements, the SDS, and that Black Panthers are people with whom he can communicate since he is not part of the establishment.

I suggest that we do the following:

This morning Bud Krogh will have Mr. Presley In and talk to him about drugs and about what Presley can do. Bud will also check to see if there is some kind of an honorary agent at large or credential of some sort that we can provide for Presley. After Bud has met with Presley, It is recommended that we have Bud bring Presley in during the Open Hour to meet briefly with the President. You know that several people have mentioned over the past few months that Presley is very pro the President. He wants to keep everything private and I think we should honor his request.

I have talked to Bud Korgh about this whole matter, and we both think that it would be wrong to push Presley off on the Vice President since it will take very little of the President's time and it can be extremely beneficial for the President to build some rapport with Presley.

In addition, if the President wants to meet with some bright young people outside of the Government, Presley might be a perfect one to start with.

Approve Presley coming in at end of Open Hour _____

Disapprove _____

As the Watergate scandal in which he was involved later revealed, Bob Haldeman was nobody's fool. In the margin next to the advice Chapin offered in his last paragraph, he scribbled: 'You must be kidding,' but he initialled his approval for the visit nevertheless. On his instructions, a second memo was prepared for Nixon to brief him on the meeting, standard procedure for such appointments. The memo included an impromptu list of useful 'talking points'.

A few minutes before Elvis was ushered into his presence, Nixon rapidly scanned the pages with a practised eye before tossing them to one side. He would, he decided, rely on his own political nous – he wasn't called 'Tricky Dicky' for nothing. Manipulating someone like Elvis Presley would be child's play. With an election coming up in 1972, he might just need a few star names on his team.

Egil 'Bud' Krogh took detailed notes of the meeting and, afterwards, wrote yet another, more selective memo:

216

Memorandum for: The President's file

Subject: Meeting with Elvis Presley, Monday, 21 December 1970, 12.30pm

The meeting opened with pictures taken of the President and Elvis Presley.

Presley immediately began showing the President his law enforcement paraphernalia including badges from police departments in California, Colorado and Tennessee. Presley indicated that he had been playing Las Vegas and the President indicated that he was aware of how difficult it is to perform in Las Vegas.

The President mentioned that he thought Presley could reach young people, and that it was important for Presley to retain his credibility. Presley responded that he did his thing by 'just singing' He said that he could not get to the kids if he made a speech on the stage, that he had to reach them in his own way. The President nodded in agreement.

Presley indicated that he thought the Beatles had been a real force for anti-American spirit. The President nodded in agreement and expressed some surprise.

The President then indicated that those who use drugs are also those in the vanguard of anti-American protest. Violence, drug usage, dissent, protest all seem to merge in generally the same group of young people.

Presley indicated to the President in a very emotional manner that he was 'on your side'. Presley kept repeating that he wanted to be helpful, that he wanted to restore some respect for the flag which was being lost. He mentioned that he was just a poor boy from Tennessee who had gotten a lot from his country, which in some way he wanted to repay. He also mentioned that he is studying Communist brainwashing and the drug culture for over ten years. He mentioned that he knew a lot about this and was accepted by the hippies. He said he could go right into a group of young people or hippies and be accepted which he felt could be helpful to him in his drug drive. The President indicated again his concern that Presley retain his credibility.

[Bud Krogh omitted the fact that, at this point, Nixon spoke into his intercom and ordered that a badge of the Bureau of Narcotics and Dangerous Drugs and a set of credentials be prepared for Elvis and delivered to the Oval Office.]

At the conclusion of the meeting, Presley again told the President how much he supported him, and then, in a surprising, spontaneous gesture, put his arm around the President and hugged him. [The 'surprise' was that Elvis actually broke down in tears.] In going out, Presley asked the President if he would see his two associates [Sonny West and Jerry Schilling]. The President agreed and they came over and shook hands with the President briefly. At this meeting, the President thanked them for their efforts and again mentioned his concern for Presley's credibility.

By the time Elvis was being shown to the door, the agent's badge and the appropriate paperwork were waiting in the outer office and Nixon handed them over. The speed with which they had turned up indicated that the Narcotics Bureau's decision to exclude Elvis had already been countermanded before he had even set foot in the Oval Office.

On 31 December, Nixon covered his tracks in a non-committal letter addressed to Graceland:

Dear Mr Presley,
It was a pleasure to meet with you in my office recently, and I want you to know once again how much I appreciate your

thoughtfulness in giving me the commemorative World War II Colt .45 pistol, encased in the handsome wooden chest. You were particularly kind to remember me with this impressive gift, as well as your family photographs, and I am delighted to have them for my collection of special mementos.

With my best wishes to you, Mrs Presley, and to your daughter, Lisa, for a happy and peaceful 1971.

Sincerely, Richard Nixon

Mission accomplished, Elvis had returned to Graceland proudly displaying his new badge. It was the best Christmas present anyone had ever given him.

Elvis might have been happy, but he had no intention of settling down to a peaceful life. On New Year's Eve, the day Nixon dictated his letter and, coincidentally, the day that Paul began the law suit against the other Beatles, Elvis was back in Washington visiting the FBI, where he pursued his vendetta against John Lennon with all the vigour he possessed.

He had arrived mob-handed the day before with William N. Morris, a former sheriff of Shelby County (of which Memphis was a part), and half a dozen of the Guys. Morris contacted the FBI on Elvis's behalf, and Hoover agreed to the group making a special tour of the Bureau, expressing his regrets that he would not be able to meet Elvis in person. Hoover had his doubts but, like Nixon, was prepared to use Elvis to his own advantage. He would not, however, risk any flak, which a public endorsement of Elvis might attract if things went wrong. He wanted Elvis as a spy, not a Federal agent blessed by his own hand.

Hoover, too, had been gunning for John Lennon for some time, without success. He had tried to prosecute John and Yoko under interstate law for transporting obscene material – the cover of their album *Two Virgins,* which showed them in a full-frontal nude pose – but had been advised by his legal office that such a charge would not succeed in court. In London, however, the drug squad had raided the Lennons while they were staying at Ringo's flat in Montagu Square, with the result that John was fined for possessing cannabis.

His antenna tuned to the possibilities that Elvis's co-operation presented, Hoover ordered an administration assistant to prepare a confidential report on the King's FBI visit. This report details adverse comments that Elvis had made about the Beatles to FBI officers in a private conversation after the tour.

4 January 1971.
From: M. A. Jones
Subject: Elvis Presley
William N. Morris
Former Sheriff, Shelby County, Tennessee
Bureau tour 31-12-70

Presley and Morris and six individuals who provide security for Presley visited FBI Headquarters and were afforded a very special tour of our facilities in accordance with plans approved by the Director.

Regrets were expressed to Presley and his party in connection with their request to meet the Director. Presley indicated that he has long been an admirer of Mr Hoover and has read material prepared by the Director including Masters of Deceit, A Study of Communism as well as J. Edgar Hoover on Communism. Presley noted in his opinion no one has ever done as much for his country as has Mr Hoover and that he, Presley, considers the Director the 'greatest living American'. He also spoke favourably of the Bureau.

Despite his rather bizarre personal appearance, Presley seemed a sincere, serious-minded individual who expressed concern over some of the problems confronting our country, particularly those involving young people. In this regard, in private comments made following his tour, he indicated that he, Presley, is the 'living proof that America is the land of opportunity' since he rose from truck driver to prominent entertainer almost overnight. He said that he spends as much time as his schedule permits informally talking to young people and discussing what they consider to be their problems with them.

Presley explained that his long hair and unusual apparel were merely tools of his trade and provided an access to and rapport with many people particularly on college campuses who consider themselves 'anti-Establishment'. Presley said that while he has a limited education, he has been able to command a certain amount of respect and attention from this segment of the population and in an informal way point out the errors of their ways.

He advised that he does not consider himself competent to address large groups but much rather prefers small gatherings in community centers and the like, where he makes himself accessible for talks and discussions regarding the evils of narcotics and other problems of concern to teenagers and other young people.

Following their tour, Presley privately advised that he has volunteered his services to the President in connection with an Agent's badge of the Bureau of Narcotics and Dangerous Drugs. Presley was carrying this badge in his pocket and displayed it.

Presley advised that he wished the Director to be aware that he, Presley, from time to time is approached by individuals and groups in and outside of the entertainment business whose motives and goals he is convinced are not in the best interests of this country and who seek to have him lend his name to their questionable activities. In this regard, he volunteered to make such information available to the Bureau on a confidential basis whenever it came to his attention. He further indicated that he wanted the Director to know that should the Bureau ever have any need of his services in any way that he would be delighted to be of assistance.

Presley indicated that he is of the opinion that the Beatles laid the groundwork for many of the problems we are having with young people by their filthy unkempt appearances and suggestive music while entertaining in this country during the early and middle 1960s. He advised that the Smothers Brothers, Jane Fonda and other persons in the entertainment industry of their ilk have a lot to answer for in the hereafter for the way they have poisoned young minds by disparaging the United States in their public statements and unsavoury activities.

Presley advised that he resides at 3764 Highway 51 South, Memphis, Tennessee, but that he spends a substantial portion of his time in the Beverly Hills, California-Las Vegas, Nevada, areas fulfilling motion picture assignments and singing commitments.

He noted that he can be contacted anytime through his Memphis address and that because of problems he has with people tampering with his mail, such correspondence should be addressed to him under the pseudonym Colonel Jon [sic] Burrows.

Hoover already knew Elvis's address and a great deal more besides. Files had been opened on Elvis when his gyrations on stage had attracted official scrutiny back in the Fifties. These files were packed with information about his permissive lifestyle and personal drug abuse. Informants had branded Elvis a pervert who represented a threat to the moral well-being of young American women. These files had never been closed.

However, Hoover immediately wrote to Elvis thanking him for his 'generous comments concerning the bureau and me' and assuring him that his offer of help would be kept in mind. The same day he alerted every FBI field office to Elvis's pseudonym and telephone numbers should they need to contact him. Then he ordered a review of all FBI files concerning John Lennon. Elvis had planted a seed in Hoover's mind, which was about to grow into rampant poison ivy. To put it bluntly, Hoover the master manipulator planned to set one junkie to catch another.

The legendary FBI chief was, in fact, nothing like the rugged, crime-busting hero of popular acclaim. Elvis would have been devastated to know that his 'greatest living American' had dodged military service during World War I and that he kept an array of women's clothes in his closet, which he liked to wear on social occasions with his homosexual friends.

Through the press and his own grapevine, Elvis had kept track of John's movements since his marriage to Yoko Ono on the Rock of Gibraltar on 20 March 1969. The odd couple had spent their honeymoon staging a 'bed-in for peace' at the Hilton Hotel in Amsterdam, the drug capital of Europe. John and Yoko had posed for pictures sitting up in bed, each holding a single tulip. Signs saying 'hair peace' and 'bed peace' were displayed behind them. Heavily bearded and with his hair touching the shoulders of his neatly buttoned pyjamas, John looked like a cross between the Maharishi and Charles Manson. There was no doubt in Elvis's mind, as he surveyed the evidence, that this odious oddball was dangerous.

Every one of his activities came into the category of 'unsavoury', each a calculated insult to 'the Establishment' that Elvis purported to admire. John had returned his MBE to the Queen, he had held an exhibition of erotic lithographs, which Scotland Yard had raided after complaints of obscenity, and the music he was recording with the Plastic Ono Band was full of avant-garde messages in which words such as 'peace' and 'love' were used to subvert the young.

Most disturbing of all was that John and Yoko had been admitted to the United States. They had travelled to Los Angeles supposedly to undergo 'primal therapy' with Dr Arthur Janov, doubtless a front for other 'questionable activities'. Whatever gossip came Elvis's way about John, no matter how fanciful, he fed into the FBI system.

The attention that John had received from the British constabulary indicated to Elvis that the former Beatle's day of judgment might arrive much sooner than his appointed hour in 'the hereafter'. It was up to him and the FBI to close the case in the United States. The thought pleased him so much that he decided to take direct action as President Nixon's own authorized drugbuster. Colonel John Burrows strapped on his guns and went looking for trouble.

I visited Los Angeles many times during 1971 and moved there the following year. My wife Jan and I rented Ben Gazzara's house in Holmby Hills, a colonial-style mansion that looked like a miniature Graceland. After the grass-and-acid trips of the Sixties, cocaine had become the fashionable drug. 'You have to line up to get a cubicle in Beverly Hills,' one of the *cognoscenti* told me.

Elvis's cronies hung out at the Luau, an Haiwaiian restaurant in Beverly Hills. At other times, I saw them at the Rainbow, a rock club/restaurant on Sunset. Dealers to the stars operated at both venues without the management's knowledge.

When famous entertainers and members of the pop world were inexplicably raided in their homes by the drug squad, the suspicion grew that someone with connections was leaking information to the authorities. It now seems fairly certain that the informer was Elvis, the narcotics agent. Certainly he had the motive and the opportunity.

John Lennon himself was never caught in any incriminating situation in the United States. In fact, the only solid piece of evidence that Hoover had against him was that he had been granted a visa to enter the country after being given a discretionary waiver against a drug conviction in Britain. When he arrived with George Harrison and his wife Pattie Boyd, a full-scale FBI alert went out.

Date: 23 April 1970

Subject: John Lennon, George Harrison, Patricia Harrison

These individuals are affiliated with the Beatles musical group and Lennon will be travelling under the name of Chambers and the Harrisons are using the name Masters. They will remain in Los Angeles for business discussions with Capitol Records and other enterprises. They will travel to New York for further discussions. Waivers were granted by the Immigration and Naturalization Service in view of the ineligibility of these three individuals to enter the US due to their reputations in England as narcotic users.

While Lennon and the Harrisons have shown no propensity to become involved in violent anti-war demonstrations, each recipient [of this memo] should remain alert for any information of such activity on their part or for information indicating they are using narcotics. Submit any pertinent information obtained for immediate dissemination.

The FBI had a star witness to attest to John's drug-taking: the Beatle himself. Around this time, he was talking frankly about his habit. If he had known the hassle that lay ahead, he might have kept his mouth shut. 'I've always needed a drug to survive; the others, too, but I always had more,' he admitted with reckless honesty. 'I always took more pills, more of everything because I'm crazy probably. I must have had a thousand [LSD] trips. I used to just eat it all the time.'

John, George and Pattie came and went without incident, and John applied to re-enter the US again in the summer of 1970, saying he wanted to edit a film and attend a custody hearing in New York over Yoko's daughter by her former husband, Tony Cox. He was granted a visa to enter the US until September and was then given an extension. When Hoover heard that, he exploded. The FBI files show that, from then on, John was targeted like Public Enemy No. 1.

'Every agent should remain alert for any activity on his part of a potentially illegal nature,' one memo ordered. 'Lennon is a heavy user of narcotics . . . this information should be emphasized to local law enforcement agencies with regards to subject being arrested if at all possible on possession-of-narcotics charge,' said another. The Lennons were followed and harassed at every opportunity.

Fortunately, they were not without powerful friends of their own. When deportation proceedings were issued against them at Hoover's instigation, John Lindsay, the Mayor of New York, where they were living, spoke out furiously about the treatment they were receiving. In a strongly worded letter to the Immigration authorities, he said that 'a grave injustice' was being perpetrated:

> The only question which is raised against these people is that they speak with strong, critical voices on major issues of the day.
>
> If this is the motive underlying the unusual and harsh action taken, then it is an attempt to silence the constitutionally protected First Amendment rights of free speech and association, and a denial of the civil liberties of these two people.

Backing John's application for a green card, Lord Harlech, the former British ambassador in Washington and, ironically, a close friend of Princess Margaret, opined: 'When the musical history of our times comes to be written, there is no doubt that the name of John Lennon will be given a most important place in it.'

This was one up to the Walrus, but in Vegas the Hound Dog was barking loudly.

CHAPTER EIGHTEEN

Partytime with Tom Jones

WHENEVER ELVIS met up with Tom Jones in Vegas, it was partytime. He would catch Tom's act at Caesars Palace and the two stars and I would invariably adjourn to the Imperial Suite, where Elvis threw more parties than Nero. Even Tom would concede that, for eight years, Elvis was *the* main event in Vegas.

'We'd get a call to let us know that Elvis was coming in and a security guard from the hotel would go to the airport to pick him up and bring him here,' Jim Vernon, the Hilton's security chief, told me. 'He'd come in through the north service area at the rear of the hotel in one of our stretch black Cadillacs. The elevator from there went right up to the back door of the 30th floor suite. Secrecy was standard practice. We never let anyone know he was coming in, just the people who needed to know.

'Once he was in the hotel, we had more people to cover Elvis than any other entertainer. There were his people and six of us. They'd tell us if they had heard about a threat to his life, but they took care of their business and we handled certain other things. We escorted him from the suite to the stage and stayed with him during each show. We had people on either side of the stage and in the audience to keep the fans away.'

George Ziros, the Hilton's chief chef, remembers when Elvis first played the hotel in 1969. 'He was a tall, slender guy who was always smiling. Before a show, he came down from his suite surrounded by security guards with a towel wrapped around his neck. He was trotting along – not walking – and waving to people. And the people stood up and applauded him because he was really well-liked by everybody.

'He ate his dinner after he finished the second show around 1.00 am. We sent it up from the kitchens, usually Italian food, spaghetti, meatballs, sausage, steaks, chicken or veal. But he had room service as well so he could order anything he wanted. He liked shakes to drink and he never ordered wine, but I have maybe seen him with a beer in his hand, that's all. Later on, he put on weight, but anybody over the age of 40 puts on weight if they don't watch themselves.

'There were always people up there, thirty or forty at a time, and there were always females. The only one I recognized a couple of times was Ann-Margret. The Colonel would mingle with the crowd after the show, perhaps have a drink and maybe a bite to eat, but I only saw him a few times up in the suite. He would talk to members of the party and then he would just disappear.'

In 1971, Elvis had a new employer when Kirk Kerkorian sold the International to Conrad Hilton. 'We renamed it the Hilton Hotel and I was put in charge,' recalls Henri Lewin. 'It was the largest hotel in Las Vegas, with 1500 rooms and it also housed the largest showroom in the country.'

Elvis made history there. It is said that he never played to an empty seat at the Hilton.

'When you have a star who sells out sixty shows in ten minutes, you have a different opinion about the whole game,' said Lewin. 'There was nobody alive at that time who could even come close to Elvis, not Tom Jones, Engelbert Humperdinck, Nat King Cole, Bill Cosby. You name them: nobody ever reached the numbers he did – a total of 2.5 million paying customers.

'He gave two shows each night for twenty-eight days in February and thirty days in August into September, a total of fifty-six and sixty shows a month respectively, for six years. As a hotel company, we didn't care whether the showroom made or lost money. But people who came to see him stayed at the hotel and we were booked solid for the whole month he was there.

'We had to put twenty extra telephone operators on duty just to turn people away. Some people saw the dinner show and the midnight show, two shows in a row, every night for thirty nights.'

ELVIS MEETS THE BEATLES

ELVIS - IN CONCERT - ELVIS

SUMMER FESTIVAL TOUR

In Association With RCA Record Tours / Management Three

TUESDAY	JULY 8	OKLAHOMA CITY, OKLA. *Myriad*	SHOW TIME 8:30 PM
WEDNESDAY	JULY 9	TERRE HAUTE, INDIANA *Hulman Civic University Center*	SHOW TIME 8:30 PM
THURSDAY	JULY 10	CLEVELAND, OHIO *Cleveland Coliseum*	SHOW TIME 8:30 PM
FRIDAY	JULY 11	CHARLESTON, W. VA. *Charleston Civic Center*	SHOW TIME 8:30 PM
SATURDAY SATURDAY	JULY 12 JULY 12	CHARLESTON, W. VA. CHARLESTON, W. VA. *Charleston Civic Center*	SHOW TIME 2:30 PM SHOW TIME 8:30 PM
SUNDAY SUNDAY	JULY 13 JULY 13	NIAGARA FALLS, N. Y. *Niagara Falls Convention Center*	SHOW TIME 2:30 PM SHOW TIME 8:30 PM
MONDAY	JULY 14	SPRINGFIELD, MASS. *Springfield Civic Center*	SHOW TIME 8:30 PM
TUESDAY	JULY 15	SPRINGFIELD, MASS. *Springfield Civic Center*	SHOW TIME 8:30 PM
WEDNESDAY	JULY 16	NEW HAVEN, CONN. *Veterans Memorial Coliseum*	SHOW TIME 8:30 PM
THURSDAY	JULY 17	NEW HAVEN, CONN. *Veterans Memorial Coliseum*	SHOW TIME 8:30 PM
FRIDAY	JULY 18	CLEVELAND, OHIO *Cleveland Coliseum*	SHOW TIME 8:30 PM
SATURDAY SATURDAY	JULY 19 JULY 19	UNIONDALE (NASSAU), N.Y. UNIONDALE (NASSAU), N.Y. *Nassau Veterans Memorial Coliseum*	SHOW TIME 2:30 PM SHOW TIME 8:30 PM
SUNDAY SUNDAY	JULY 20 JULY 20	NORFOLK, VA. NORFOLK, VA. *Norfolk Scope*	SHOW TIME 2:30 PM SHOW TIME 8:30 PM
MONDAY	JULY 21	GREENSBORO, N. C. *Greensboro Coliseum*	SHOW TIME 8:30 PM
TUESDAY	JULY 22	ASHEVILLE, N. C. *Asheville Civic Center*	SHOW TIME 8:30 PM
WEDNESDAY	JULY 23	ASHEVILLE, N. C. *Asheville Civic Center*	SHOW TIME 8:30 PM
THURSDAY	JULY 24	ASHEVILLE, N. C. *Asheville Civic Center*	SHOW TIME 8:30 PM

TOUR SOLD OUT

ENTIRE CONCERT PRODUCTION PRESENTATION
BY
ELVIS

TOUR DIRECTION - THE COLONEL

TOUR SOLD OUT

ELVIS SUMMER FESTIVAL CONCERTS
LAS VEGAS HILTON
AUGUST 18 THRU LABOR DAY 1975

The itinerary for a typical action-packed Elvis tour:
12 cities in just 16 days

On one occasion, Elvis avoided an international incident between the hotel and a group of fanatical fans who had flown in for one show. 'One hundred and sixty girls from a Japanese factory came to Las Vegas just to see Elvis,' said George Ziros. 'Elvis very seldom got sick – once in a while like any other human being – but as the girls were lining up outside the showroom, it was announced that he had been forced to cancel through ill health. The only trouble was that these girls did not speak any English and they were still trying to get in because they didn't want to miss the show. Finally, we got some Japanese interpreters to tell them: "I'm sorry, but Elvis is sick. He can't perform tonight." The girls got so hysterical that some even passed out and others were crying. They were flying back to Japan in the morning and it had been their only chance to see the show.

'Someone told Elvis and he made arrangements with the airlines and the hotel for the girls to stay an extra day. That night, he brought them to the show personally and sat them all in the front row. The girls went crazy, screaming and yelling, when he did his act. It was unbelievable.'

Touched by Midas, Elvis sparkled on stage in one of his hand-crafted, jewel-encrusted jumpsuits like the high priest of a fabulous, futuristic cult. Each suit had a name: the Inca Gold Leaf, the Mad Tiger, the Mexican Sundial, the Prehistoric Bird, the American Eagle and the King of Spades. He wore embroidered capes until an excited fan grabbed hold of one and almost dragged him off the stage. After that, he abandoned the capes in favour of colourful scarves, which he tossed into the audience. Around his waist was a thick belt embossed with heraldic eagles and shields, and dripping with gold chains. Around his neck he wore a gem-studded collar, great gold crucifixes and a Star of David or Hebrew *chai*. Over the years, he fused the pomp of a coronation with the passion of a religious revival. Added to the ceremonial was his own anthem, the medley of 'Dixie', 'All My Trials' and the 'Battle Hymn of the Republic' – known collectively as the 'American Trilogy'.

'I gave him a gold rope to wear around his neck, three pounds of pure gold, and he threw it into the audience one night,' said Henri Lewin, whose business card nowadays gives his job description as 'MILLIONAIRE'. 'I was there and I got the security guards to catch it. I went up to him after the show and said, "You must be out of your mind. I'm a refugee, I came from nothing and I gave you this gift as a friend. If you want to give something valuable away, go buy it and throw your own stuff away." He said, "Give it to me, Mr Lewin, it's mine." I handed it back and he kept it.'

In terms of audience reaction, no other performer ever topped Elvis, according to Elia Verzilli, the Hilton's theatre manager who has worked in the showroom since its first night. 'In the first couple of years, he was more like a teenager, very lively, very playful, very friendly. He gradually changed over the next six years until he was very heavy and subdued. But everybody liked Elvis, no matter what.'

Security chief Jim Vernon's problem was that some of them liked Elvis too much. 'The main thing was to make sure that he got back to his room all right and nobody bothered him while he was up there,' he said. 'When he went up to his suite, one of our guys stayed outside the door around the clock. No one could get out on that floor unless their name was on a master list, which had been furnished to us. People tried, but they never made it.'

The guard was the first person Elvis's party guests saw when they came out of the lift on the 30th floor, but his jurisdiction ended at the suite's front door. Inside, drugs were freely available, and I have it on good authority from more than one source that, despite Tom Jones's warnings, Elvis was on cocaine in the early seventies. When he tried to tempt Tom into taking the drug, he was bluntly turned down. 'One day you'll overdo it with those drugs and none of us will be around to help you,' Tom warned him yet again.

However, there were intimate moments as well. Elvis confided to his friend that he had never recovered from the loss of his mother.

'Mama died trying to be beautiful for me again,' I heard him say during one visit to Tom's dressing room. 'She would be so proud if she could see me now, a married man with a baby. She'd be a grandmother and that would go a long way to making up for the loss of Jesse.'

Elvis had brought Priscilla with him and I introduced her to Jan. While Tom and Elvis chatted, Priscilla and Jan compared baby pictures of our respective daughters, Lisa and Joanne.

'I found it very hard to accept my daddy's new wife,' Elvis said, referring to Vernon's marriage to divorcee Dee Stanley, the mother of three young boys. 'I still can't get used to the idea of having a stepmother.'

As soon as Priscilla left Elvis, a disturbing picture emerged of his new life. One night, Elvis came to Tom's dressing room when the Welsh singer was showering after a show. Elvis used an adjoining cubicle and they carried on a conversation through the glass partition. After a few minutes, ready to get dressed again, Elvis called one of the Memphis Mafia with a yell of '*Red!*'

Red West knew exactly what was required of him. Entering the cubicle, he pulled up Elvis's skintight leather trousers and, while his boss sucked in his belly, laced them up. Afterwards, Tom went into the cubicle and found a handgun Elvis had dropped on the floor. He was genuinely shocked that Elvis needed to carry a weapon. However, the King constantly talked about being a target, and his use of narcotics only heightened the fear. On one occasion, a camera flash flared briefly in a window high up in the Hilton as Elvis was preparing to step into his black-windowed limousine.

'He made us go back in and search the place for that happy snapper,' Red told me. 'Of course, we had to come down and tell him our efforts were in vain and he got pretty mad. Yet five minutes later, he was happily posing for some chick at a gas filling station.'

Jim Vernon said that Elvis 'never really showed it if he was nervous about his safety'. Red and Sonny took care of any troublemakers who tried to gatecrash the Imperial Suite or fanatical fans who tried to mob Elvis down in the lobby. 'They were real protective, but they put up with Elvis's gags,' he said. 'He was a great practical joker who liked to goof around. He loved water fights, either upstairs in the suite or downstairs; he didn't care where it was. He'd get squirt guns and the Boys never knew when he was going to open fire, so they were the ones who wound up getting wet. Elvis was a great guy and a lot of fun to be around. I miss him.'

However, working for Elvis was never easy, as the silver-haired Dr George C. Nichopolous – a.k.a. Dr Nick – found to his cost. 'Dr Nick', remembered Joe Esposito, 'came on the scene around 1967 when he got called out to Elvis's ranch for something. George Klein's wife worked for Nichopolous at the time, and she called him out. They hit it off pretty well, and about a year later, he became Elvis's personal physician when we had started the tours. He started to come along on the tours and look after Elvis's health from then on.

'Elvis just had the feeling that he needed a doctor around for himself and for the entourage and for the show people. I mean, it wasn't just Elvis he cared for. He was just used for the road work. Elvis had other doctors who attended him in Las Vegas and Los Angeles.'

'My nights were just horrible,' the later much maligned doctor told journalist Stanley Booth. 'I would go to bed when he'd go to bed, and then he might sleep two or three hours and wake up, and I'd have to go in and try to get him back to sleep. On a tour, I had very little time when I could go and do anything. If he woke up and I wasn't there, he'd go bananas. It got to the point where I was working eighteen or twenty hours a day, sleeping in cat naps.'

(In 1980, the district attorney-general's office in Memphis ordered two of its officers, Larry Hutchinson and David McGriff, to investigate the doctor concerning his most famous patient's drug usage. They interviewed many of the key figures in Elvis's life, including the Colonel, Joe Esposito, Linda Thompson and Sonny West. A grand jury later indicted Dr Nick on ten counts of illegally prescribing drugs to patients, including Elvis, but he was acquitted on all charges at a jury trial. The DA's investigators tape-recorded their interviews, and copies of those tapes are now in our possession. They are quoted in parts of this book.)

For the time being, however, the party was still in full swing, with Elvis and Tom Jones as the centres of attention. Their friendship seemed to be untouched by the fiercely professional rivalry between our two camps. Elvis joined Tom on stage on many occasions and they would fool around in front of the audience, although they never actually sang together. Tom's road manager Chris Ellis was told to keep the spare microphone hidden in case Elvis ever tried to do a duet. Tom often told me that, if this ever happened, he would not be able to resist the temptation of singing the legend off the stage. Neither star's management wanted to risk a damaging confrontation like that. Tom's remark showed that the mutual admiration society had its limits. He also told me during one of Elvis's performances: 'Look, he's like a big chorus girl up there.'

Nor was Elvis the Tom Jones fan he seemed to be, according to Sonny West. 'We would go to his shows and Elvis always would say something to knock him,' Sonny said in his memoirs. 'Tom wears very tight pants and Elvis would always say, "He sticks a damn sock down his pants." He would comment on Tom's singing, and during a performance, he would sing along with Tom, making out that he could hit the high notes, which he couldn't.'

Elvis was never critical to Tom's face, but he did ask him once: 'Why do you sing the high notes?'

'Why? Because they're in the bloody song,' Tom replied, wondering what point Elvis was making. 'You can't sing it without them.'

'I leave 'em to J. D.,' Elvis explained, referring to J. D. Sumner and the Stamps, his backing group after 1972. 'It's a lot easier that way. The audience sees me with my mouth open in front of the mike and no one knows who's singing what.'

One unpleasant episode gave me a chilling insight into Elvis's temper. In the Imperial Suite, Elvis had sung his favourite number at that time, 'Killing Me Softly with His Song', and he asked Tom if he liked it.

'Yes, very nice,' Tom answered politely.

Elvis interpreted this as a call for an encore and gave his private rendition of the song again . . . and again . . . and again.

'He must have done it about seven times,' Tom groaned later. 'Anyway, he was about to start it once more when Chris Ellis pulled away the stool the pianist was sitting on. Elvis aimed a karate kick at Chris, but missed. Because of the bad atmosphere, we left, and the following day Elvis's doctor told me he had the hump with us.'

Around two in the afternoon, Ellis was asleep in his room at Caesars when the telephone rang. It was Elvis on the line, 'in a menacing mood,' the road manager calls. 'After a couple of minutes shouting at me, Elvis went off the line and his oriental karate instructor came on saying, "Elvis velly mad. You be here 4.30 sharp to apologize on hands and knees,"' said Chris.

'I asked to speak to Sonny and told him, "If Elvis wants me there at 4.30, I'll be there – but I'll bring a couple of Mafia pals with me and they'll come in shooting." Sonny told me that he would tell Elvis that I had come over but couldn't get in because of the security.'

Tom was working in Houston a few days later when he asked me to get Elvis on the phone so they could sort the situation out 'one way or another'. I placed the call to Elvis's hideaway at Palm Springs and the friendship was patched up. But I doubt if it was ever the same again.

When I asked Tom what would have happened if Chris Ellis had been beaten up, the singer replied: 'I'd have gone over there and rammed his f***ing karate belt right down his throat.'

Time and again, Elvis needed to prove that he was the toughest kid on the block. The captain of an airliner preparing for take-off at Las Vegas airport witnessed one such display of macho behaviour. Standing in the path of the aircraft was a dishevelled man holding up an object that glinted in the morning sun. Even from his lofty position on the flight deck, the pilot was able to tell the control tower that he recognized the solitary figure. It was Elvis Presley, a.k.a. Colonel John Burrows.

Elvis had leapt from his stretch limousine, which had forced its way through an airport barrier. The shiny object in his raised hand was his narcotics agent's badge. Elvis was using his authority to hold up the plane because he believed a passenger he wanted to apprehend might be on board.

The hunt had started after a diamond ring and a picture showing Elvis and a girlfriend had disappeared from his bedside. As one of his entourage was due to fly to Memphis that day, Elvis decided that he must be the culprit.

'Elvis jumped in his car and went to the airport with Sonny and Red,' George Klein, Elvis's DJ buddy, told me. 'As they ran to the gate, a plane was about to depart, so Elvis waved his badge and yelled, "Stop that plane, stop that plane!"'

'Through the combination of Elvis Presley, the Federal badge and all the commotion, they stopped the plane and rolled the steps up to the cabin door. Elvis boarded the plane looking for the guy, while Sonny and Red searched the airport lounge. They found the guy reading a newspaper, or rather hiding behind one, and Sonny grabbed him and threw him into the limousine.

'On the way back to the hotel, this guy started using some lines like in an old Hollywood gangster movie: "I guess the gig's up. Yar gonna put me six feet under. Yar gonna wipe me out." Sonny was driving and he almost started laughing, but Elvis was not amused, he was very perturbed. They got back to the hotel and Elvis slapped the guy around pretty good. He had a ring on and it kinda cut his head.'

His right hand heavily bandaged, Elvis told us the story when he came into Tom Jones's dressing room at Caesars that night. 'I didn't want to hurt the guy,' Elvis said, 'but it was the only way.'

Elvis spotted a two-pound box of chocolates, which a fan had sent Tom. Invited to help himself, he did just that. He ate the lot, stuffing chocolates into his mouth with his good hand. Once he started, he couldn't stop. An insatiable craving for sugar is often a sign of heavy cocaine usage.

'The only time I'm aware of Elvis receiving drugs other than from a doctor was when he was using some cocaine,' Sonny West told the DA's investigators. 'As far as I'm concerned, all the other drugs that he took he got from doctors. He did not go out on the streets and buy drugs. He got all the prescriptions he needed from doctors, but he did use some cocaine that he got from a pusher in Nashville.

'When Red found out about that, he went round there and threatened this fella with harm if he got any more coke for Elvis. Red did scare the guy; he was afraid of Red. Elvis found out about it and threatened Red with his job if he didn't leave that guy alone. He said he needed it.'

Elvis also got liquid cocaine from one of several doctors he used, according to Sonny. 'Elvis used that with cottonballs he put into his nostrils,' he said. The King was indeed killing himself softly.

CHAPTER NINETEEN

Vanity Presley Snubs Raquel Welch

BY THE TIME she hit Las Vegas, Raquel Welch was the most upfront lady in show business. Wearing a mini-dress shorter than a British summer, she disembarked from a limousine at the Hilton.

'I was going to play Vegas and I walked into the hotel, where they asked me if I would like to see Elvis's show,' she told me. 'I was with my choreographer and they put us in the celebrity booth. Colonel Parker came over to say hello, and he said to me, "Would you like to see the boy afterwards? OK then, I'll tell him you're coming backstage." I couldn't believe this man was talking about a prince of his profession, the Valentino of our day. "*The boy*"? He'd "*tell* him", not *ask* him? I'm sorry, but this man was talking about his star as if he were white trash.

'Again, I was disappointed when Elvis came on. Again, he looked more like Wayne Newton than Elvis Presley. Somebody had put the lid on all that raw talent and I thought it was the saddest thing. He had this ridiculous outfit on and the hair was sprayed so that not a strand of it moved.

'After the show, I was taken backstage to the dressing room and I had to believe the man before me was Elvis Presley because it was as if the real him wasn't there. There were mirrors all around the room. He started showing me his rings and stuff, and then, when I was talking to him, I realized that he wasn't looking at me but at himself in the mirror behind me.'

However, it was more than vanity that made Elvis catch his own reflection. He lived in terror that he might be losing his looks, and in the company of stunning women like Raquel Welch, he needed to reassure himself. This is why he preferred the heavily macho presence of Red and Sonny West and overtly masculine friends such as Tom Jones.

Sonny had noticed a change in Elvis during 1972, when his weight started to cause problems. 'He had been keeping his weight down since he opened in Vegas in '69 and he looked real good – he never got over 170-175 pounds,' he said. 'Then in 1972 he started putting on some weight and he started withdrawing more. He went on a diet because he was getting ready to go live via satellite to over twenty-five countries around the world in January 1973. He lost weight and he looked good, but the night after the show, he got totally out of it in Hawaii. I'd never seen him like that.

'At one time or another, we all talked about it, Red and myself and Joe, Dave, Lamar, Jerry – all of us talked about it: "Man, what's he doing to himself?" When we saw him in Memphis on several occasions similar to this, we felt he was getting his drugs in Memphis. I also know that there were times when he left Memphis and went to Las Vegas to replenish his supply.'

Elvis flirted with death so often that Sonny came to believe he had divine protection. He had once overdosed in Palm Springs during a night with a young girl and he came close on at least one other occasion in Las Vegas. Doctors were invariably called in to give Elvis a reviving shot whenever he went too far, but Sonny believes that other forces were at work as well.

'Elvis seemed to be able to project to all of us around him that nothing was going to happen to him. After several close calls, it became even more believable that, maybe, this man wasn't going to die of anything but old age. It always seemed like the hand of God lifted him up out of it in the nick of time. There's such a thing as a guardian angel.'

On many occasions, the guardian angel took the human form of Linda Thompson, who was 23 when she became Elvis's girlfriend after Priscilla left.

'In '74 he almost choked to death on an apple core in Las Vegas,' said Sonny. 'He had taken quite a bit of sleeping medication and he went to sleep while eating the apple. The core was in his throat, and Linda reached in and got it out. If she hadn't been there, he probably would have choked to death. He was laying on his back, 'sound asleep, and he probably didn't know he was choking. His mind was telling him he couldn't breathe, but he couldn't do anything about it.'

Linda remembers that night vividly.

'The problem for us was controlling the sleeping medication, making sure that he didn't choke on his food,' she said. 'That was always a problem. On several occasions, he would fall asleep while eating, and we'd have to take the food out of his mouth to stop him choking. Sometimes I had to call the doctor. There were innumerable times when Elvis choked on his food. I could not recall how many times I had to put my fingers in his mouth.

'One time I woke up and he wasn't breathing properly. I called the nurse and she called Dr Nick who had him brought to the hospital. Another time in Las Vegas he choked on his food and he was completely out of it. I called the Las Vegas doctor and he came over and gave him some injections to help. He was out for hours.

'Another time, when we were flying back from Vegas to Memphis, he was taken ill on the plane. He couldn't breathe properly and was admitted to hospital as soon as we landed. The story was that he was suffering from exhaustion.'

For more than two years, up to September 1973, few witnessed Elvis's decline more closely than his valet, 'Hamburger James' Caughley. In his testimony to the DA's investigators, he said: 'I heard about his eccentricities even before I went to work for him. I met someone who had been working with Elvis and had had a blow-out with him and left.

Elvis, I heard, was getting difficult to work for because of his temperament and, to a lesser degree, because of the entourage who were with him. Starting off, it wasn't that bad. The best way I could describe it was like a graph: you had to be around him twenty-four hours to notice it and then you'd see the problem mounting slowly, and the problem was drugs.

'Sure, '71 wasn't too bad, '72 it started to get worse, and the last months I had with Elvis, it was unbelievable. It was still like a graph in as much that there would be highs and lows. Sometimes, when we were back in Memphis, he would stay upstairs twelve days at a time.

'As errand boy, it often fell to me to go get the prescriptions filled; over the time I was with him, I must have brought back hundreds of pills to Graceland. There was Percodan tablets, there'd be codeine, Demerol in pills and in liquid, some amphetamines, occasional Seconal, Valium. There were a lot of throwaway syringes. A lot of times, Elvis would get a lot of stuff from outside Memphis.

'I used to see Dr Nick most days – on the eight different tours I went on, he came with us. I never saw Dr Nick administer anything to Elvis, never once. But they used to disappear into Elvis's private room and you'd notice the change in attitude.

'Most of the time, he'd be taking things himself. One time, on tour, he OD'd badly and I had to send for Nick. It was my personal belief that he had obtained some pills from another doctor. He barely had a pulse. I mean, I was worried. I'd seen him far out before, but never as bad.

'Sometimes he was so far gone that I'd have to sit him up in bed and run a vibrator over his back to get him awake. But this time I couldn't rouse him, so I had to get Nick. Some of the other boys got him into a chair. Nick said he'd see to him, and Joe Esposito closed the door. Nick did seem to care about him and what happened; he used to get mad about the fact that he was getting stuff from other doctors.

'While we were on tour in Vegas, Elvis was quite often careless. He never worried about wealth or possessions. I might pick up a $10,000 ring he'd left lying around, while cleaning up after him, or hanging up his clothes. Whoever was on duty had to watch everything that Elvis did. He just did not care what he did. I used to get mad when I cleaned up the pill bottles and syringes because I'd find bottles with my name on them. He used other people's names to get the drugs in when we were on tour – to protect the name of Elvis Presley.

'Vernon Presley knew what was going on and it worried him. The Colonel knew what was going on only because he had a line from the Guys which kept him informed twenty-four hours a day. On bad days, Elvis would be like a zombie, just sitting in front of the television doing nothing, going nowhere. He was in a sort of twilight stage brought on by these controlled substances. But the ' twilight times grew longer.'

No one, of course, knew Elvis as well as Joe Esposito. 'I knew him for about eight months before we left the Army,' he told the investigators. 'We got out at the same time and he asked me to go back to Memphis with him and work for him, and I stayed until he died.

'When we got out the job he gave me was a sort of general overseeing of his operation. I would take care of all of Elvis's personal business – looking after the money, paying the bills, make sure everything ran smoothly for him. In order of seniority, it was Elvis, then Vernon and then me. I was the overseer of everything involving Elvis throughout my time with him. I took care of everything that did not fall within the province of Colonel Parker. When I first went there, there was only four of us in the entourage – me, Charlie Hodge who joined us from the Army, Sonny West and Elvis's cousin Gene Smith. Over the years, it became necessary to employ more, but when we got back to Memphis [from the Army], it worked out that Elvis was going straight into the movies.

'The first show we did was in Las Vegas in 1969, two shows a night for a month and then we went out on the road straight afterwards – that was September 1969. They were one-nighters and we got into the routine of playing about 100 towns a year. It was during this period that his health began to deteriorate, although I didn't think much about it at the time. Then he started to have severe problems with his colon in the early Seventies, a twisted colon, and was admitted to hospital for a couple of weeks. He also had blood pressure problems, but it was no big deal.'

Joe was convinced that the loss of Priscilla tipped Elvis into a downward spiral: 'To me, everything started, the erratic behaviour, after his divorce. He could never sit still. He'd be flying around different parts of the country.

'He needed those doctors for his vitamin B12 shots, and medication for his throat. He also needed sleep medication when we were on the road. I don't think Elvis was ever hooked on narcotics, never ever. Yes, he took pills. We all did because of the crazy hours. Otherwise we'd never have got any sleep. But he was never what I would term "hooked". I've seen Elvis go thirty days without taking a pill. I had never seen him overdose. Sure I'd seen him pass out. He fell asleep while we were talking or whatever.

'It became a problem sometimes to get him to sleep and we had to give him the medication to knock him out. Afterwards, he might have a problem getting up. Before he went on stage, he'd have shots – I can't say definitely what they contained. When he came off, the doctor would give him a tranquillizer to bring him down because Elvis used to get really hyped up on stage.

'I have never seen him overdose,' Esposito continued to insist, 'never in my life. I don't know where that story came from. The three times we went to hospital, it was for medical problems, not overdosing on drugs, definitely not. I agree the drugs were a problem. Some members of the entourage had spoken to me about it as his intake increased, and it got worse, and I'd tell them there was nothing I could do about it. I tried to help him out, we all did. I talked many times to Dr Nick about it. He said it was a problem because he was getting drugs from other people. He said he was trying to control it by giving him placebos.

'Dr Nick asked us to keep watch and try to keep track of what he was taking. I know Dr Nick called other doctors to see what they were giving him. We even went to see his father about it. But Elvis was a very strong guy, you know. When I spoke to him about it, he'd say he wasn't doing anything wrong. In the end, he'd just tell me, if I didn't like it, to get the hell out. I left a couple of times over personal rows, but came back.

'The three times he went into hospital, as far as I was concerned, was not for drugs. The first time was for his colon problem. The second time, when he was brought back from Louisiana, was for exhaustion, and while he was in hospital, they decided to try and get him off some of the drugs. I was never told he had gone in for an overdose; I got the same story as everyone else – that it was exhaustion.

'I knew Elvis had a drug problem, specially in the last year of his life. It was a problem, we knew that. I still can't say he was addicted. I've seen addicts and they can't go a day without it.

'I don't like to talk about Elvis. When he died I vowed that I would never talk about him and I never have. I have never talked to anyone about Elvis, never said anything bad about him. It's a personal thing. This is the first time anyone has got anything out of me about Elvis, and no one will again.'

The break-up of the Presleys' marriage had been particularly difficult for Diamond Joe because his wife Joan was a close friend of Priscilla. In Los Angeles, however, the former Mrs Elvis Presley was making up for lost time.

CHAPTER TWENTY

Priscilla's Secret Lover

WHEN THE telephone rang on the table beside Priscilla's bed for the third time that night, her lover slipped from her side and crossed the room. Before he closed the bathroom door behind him, he heard her say yet again: 'No, Elvis, Mike's not here. I told you that before.' She was not lying. Her lover this night was not Mike Stone, the karate instructor for whom she had left Elvis, but the British photographer Terry O'Neill.

Terry, who was later to marry Faye Dunaway, had become used to the calls that interrupted his love-making with Priscilla in her four-poster bed beneath the mirrored ceiling. Elvis felt he had a right to call her at all hours of the day and night. He had, after all, provided her with the comfortable house on Summit Drive in Beverly Hills.

Mike, known to some as 'The Animal', was also desperate for a reconciliation with the ex-wife of the man he had instructed in the martial arts. He had been offered the well-paid job after meeting Elvis and Priscilla in Las Vegas, where he was guarding a prominent record producer. Elvis had learned the basics of karate in the Army, and the idea was that Mike would turn him into a real killer, capable of defending himself against any assailant. In truth, he was never fit enough to train and the whole thing became a charade.

'He just wants to learn the movements to make him look good on stage,' Mike told me. 'I was nothing more to him than a choreographer.'

Mike entered Priscilla's life precisely at a time when she had reached breaking point. 'It had got to the stage with Elvis that I was damned if I

249

left him and damned if I didn't,' she said. 'I wanted badly for people to believe in me. I was always on guard, always dressing to please him, always fighting for territory and fighting for what I believed in. You know – traditions, ideals.

'I wasn't brought up to believe in divorce, and when I married, I thought it would be for ever. Everywhere I went, I had women wanting him. Not just wanting him: right in front of me, there were things going on. It was a shock to be confronted with this at such a young age. How to handle it. All the time I was desperate to please. To Elvis, I was like this kid he had raised. He used to refer to himself as "Daddy".'

Just as Elvis demanded that Priscilla dress like a kewpie-doll, his own appearance became even more dandified as the marriage went into injury time. At 37, his hair was dyed so black that it turned blue in the light, his fingers jangled with rings and his clothes were covered with jewels. He wore jackets without lapels over scarlet ruffled shirts with high collars. His eyes were shaded behind wire-rimmed glasses with 'ELVIS' engraved on them. He wore a belt with an ornate silver buckle and carried a cane with a silver, diamond-eyed bulldog's head for a handle. Inside was a gun.

However, the thought of losing Priscilla was as unthinkable to Elvis as would have been the idea of Gladys and Vernon splitting up when he was a child. The child bride had become his emotional support system.

'Elvis was at his happiest when he and Priscilla were together,' said Mary Jenkins, the Graceland cook. 'They would go horseback riding or go-kart rallying or go swimming and lay out by the pool. They would go running upstairs, holding hands, playing with each other. Yeah, he was real happy. He was real active then, but after the separation he just laid around a lot. Sometimes he stayed upstairs in his room for two or three weeks.'

In her autobiography, *Elvis and Me*, Priscilla dismisses the switch of men in her life in a single sentence: 'My relationship with Mike had now developed into an affair.' But she admits that the relationship coincided with the discovery of a new confidence in herself: 'Off came my false eyelashes, the jewels and flashy clothes,' she recalled. 'All devices that I'd depended on for security I now shed. I was seeing myself for the first time.'

Everything changed drastically for Priscilla after she left Elvis in 1972 to set up home with Mike, taking 4-year-old Lisa with her. At first, they shared an apartment at Marina Del Rey while Elvis refused to discuss the financial provision of a separation agreement. In June of that year, he played his first concerts in New York, jamming 80,000 fans into Madison Square Gardens in four nights. Yet just a few weeks later, he signed a penny-pinching, nine-page contract that allowed his wife a miserly $1000 a month plus $500 to support Lisa. Under a much improved deal, he subsequently provided the house on Summit Drive, and Priscilla was allowed to keep the white Mercedes sports car that I saw parked outside on my visits. In those early months, she lived close to the richest people in the world on less money than most of their maids were paid – and it showed.

Priscilla introduced me to Mike Stone, and I took karate instruction from him at her house (an Elvis Presley picture-free zone from what I could see). I paid him $150 a week for six one-hour lessons. He was always pleased to pocket my contribution to their coffers, saying that the money gave him a measure of independence. After karate, we would play tennis on the court at the bottom of the garden while Priscilla prepared a light meal, usually devilled eggs and salad. Mike would pick lemons from a tree in the garden and demonstrate his strength by squeezing them with his bare hands to provide the juice for the lemonade we drank with our food.

Invariably, the conversation would turn to Elvis. My 1975 diary is littered with such entries as: 'February 13, 1pm lesson with Mike at the house, then lunch with him and Priscilla. She told me Elvis would be getting out of the hospital tomorrow and must be feeling better since he'd already beaten Rick Stanley [his step-brother] quite badly on a visit.'

One morning, I turned up at Summit Drive, unaware that Mike had gone to Hawaii for a martial arts tournament. Priscilla invited me to stay for lunch.

She was clearly fearful of both men: Mike for his raw strength and Elvis for his almighty power. Both had made it clear to her that they could take care of themselves. It later came out that Elvis had ordered one of his Boys to hire a hitman to blow Stone's head off. Fortunately, wiser counsel prevailed and he had changed his mind. That morning, Priscilla needed to express her concern about Elvis after receiving an anguished phone call from him, even though he had the devoted Linda Thompson on hand to share his troubles.

'It wasn't always like this,' she said. 'Elvis used to be kind, gentle and always attentive. But things changed long before our wedding day. I should have realized I was marrying an entourage and only had a share in its leader. It had to end.

'Graceland was the worst. It wasn't a home, it was a carnival and I was one of the acts. I had to get out and become a woman in my own right. It wasn't because of Mike. He just happened to be there at the right time and be the right man.'

Our conversation was interrupted by the arrival of Lisa, then aged 7. As I tucked into the food Priscilla had prepared, her daughter sat at the table and started to write a letter, pausing from time to time to ask me how to spell certain words. The letter began: 'Dear Daddy, Yesterday I went to a birthday party . . .' and ended: 'I miss you very much and Mummy sends her love.'

Priscilla had mistakenly believed that becoming a father would change Elvis and make him act more responsibly. Above all, she had prayed that his daughter would help him to stop taking the drugs that controlled his personality, and that, she freely admitted, he had persuaded her to try.

Mother and father had joint custody of Lisa, but it was Elvis who indulged her. When she asked to see a film, he rented the cinema; when she wanted a merry-go-round, he hired the amusement park. Elvis bought her a mink coat and a diamond ring, both of which Priscilla made her return. When Lisa told him on the phone that she had never seen snow, he flew from Memphis to Los Angeles in the Convair 880 jet that bore her name (and the call sign 'Hound Dog I'), picked her up and soared on to Utah so that she could play in the snow for twenty minutes. The trip cost around $30,000, but no price was too high if it made Lisa happy.

'He was always up to something, shooting off firecrackers or guns, driving golf carts or snowmobiles,' she remembered, in an interview for *Life* magazine. 'He'd pull me in a sled and scare me to death. In that long steep driveway that goes up to Graceland, he'd be pulling me up and falling at the same time. He called me Buttonhead or Yisa. He'd never call me Lisa unless he was mad at me.

'One night when I was about 5 or 6 we were watching the TV. I looked up at him and said, "Daddy, Daddy, I don't want you to die." And he just looked down at me and said, "OK, I won't. Don't worry about it." I always felt protective of him.'

At the time Terry O'Neill came into Priscilla's life, Mike Stone had moved out. She had fallen for O'Neill the day he stepped into Bis & Beau, the clothes shop she ran with designer Olivia Bis at 9650 Santa Monica Boulevard. The boutique numbered Cher, Cybill Shepherd and Barbara Eden among its clientele.

'I just walked in there off the street by chance and there she was, looking quite nondescript,' Terry told me, breaking a twenty-year silence about the affair. 'Something had definitely happened between her and Mike Stone, and she and I were instantly attracted to each other.

'She was dressed terribly – I mean, she was wearing the Seventies flower power gear which her shop specialized in. To be honest, she was a bit of a fashion disaster at the time. I hated those big hats she was wearing and the ridiculously flared trousers. Because of the way she dressed I didn't take her to any of the well-known swank restaurants like the Daisy, but to little bars and bistros where nobody recognized her. I told her what I thought: that she was beautiful but that, frankly, she wasn't making the most of herself. No man had ever talked to her like that and it intrigued her.

'But it was a different story at night. Priscilla would spend as much time as an hour dressing seductively for bed which, in her case, was this huge mirrored four-poster job. Even in the special low lighting of her bedroom, she looked nothing less than sensational in her black negligée.'

It had been a black negligée that, as a teenager, Priscilla had worn on more than one occasion to try to entice Elvis into taking her virginity, an act he restrained himself from performing until their wedding night. 'We have to control our desires so they don't control us,' he would tell her when their heavy petting took them to the edge.

Since leaving Elvis, Priscilla had grown up a great deal. 'She was ultra-feminine, very gentle and terribly romantic,' Terry recalls. 'She was certainly no good-time girl. Before me, there had only been Elvis and Mike Stone, which made her a very chaste woman, particularly by the standards of that town and that era.

'Our nights together were always being interrupted by telephone calls from either Elvis or Mike. Although she never told me what they said – and I certainly wasn't going to ask her – I knew they both wanted her back, particularly Elvis, who she said was heartbroken when she left him. But she returned to my arms each time she put the phone down. I didn't see her as Elvis Presley's former wife and I wasn't intimidated by him. I wasn't even frightened of Stone, although I knew his reputation in karate. I can honestly say that I liked Priscilla for herself.

'If she'd gone back to Elvis, she would have been destroyed. Instead, he destroyed himself.'

Terry recalls the end of his affair with Priscilla just two months after it began: 'I went back to England, and that was that as far as I was concerned. However, I gather that she was pretty upset because, temporarily at least, I had swept her off her feet. I saw her some time later at the Troubadour when Elton John was appearing there. I got her moved up to some seats at the front, but I could tell she was not happy with me. She was a lovely, gentle woman and I'm sorry that things had to end the way they did, but I was based in Britain and her life was in California.'

Terry also admitted his fling with Priscilla to his old flame Raquel Welch as the three of us dined at San Lorenzo in London in June 1994. Preferring to turn a diplomatic deaf ear to the lothario's admission, Raquel said that she now included an impression of Elvis in her stage act – and then proceeded to give a private performance. Quite what the other diners in Princess Diana's favourite restaurant made of her rendition of 'Hound Dog', complete with choreographed shoulder movements and the Presley curled lip, we are unlikely ever to know.

CHAPTER TWENTY-ONE

Baby, Let's Play House-Husband

IF ELVIS had failed as a first-time husband, John Lennon wasn't proving much more reliable the second time around. He very nearly lost Yoko Ono when he ran away with May Pang for a 'lost weekend' of sex, drugs and madness that lasted eighteen months.

When I caught up with him in Los Angeles in February 1974, he had been drinking heavily for six months. Ringo had moved into the lower half of the duplex suite that the runaways were occupying at the Beverly Wilshire, and brandy alexanders were the favourite beverage.

'I heard about your trouble,' I said to John. 'Why don't you go back to New York and sort things out?'

'I want to go home, but Yoko won't have me,' he replied miserably. 'It was all a silly misunderstanding. I left New York looking forward to a return to the good old days. Now look at me: drunk and disorderly.'

May Pang, Yoko's Chinese secretary at the Dakota, had originally served as John's sexual playmate in a *ménage a trois* in Apartment 72, but Yoko had soon tired of the arrangement. When John and May decamped to the West Coast, May proceeded to fall in love with him.

'How long did it take before you missed Yoko?' I asked him.

'About four days,' he said. 'I keep calling her but she won't have me back, man. Can you imagine that? She won't have me back. So I get my daily Yoko from a bottle these days.'

At midnight a few weeks later, John went to the Troubadour Club to see the Smothers Brothers, whom in his outburst to the FBI Elvis had coupled with the Beatles as a bad influence on American youth. The Brothers knew John, having appeared as guests on one of his albums.

The former Beatle turned up at the club wearing a tampon taped to his forehead. This was his first mistake. He was too loaded to tell anyone whether he was making a political statement about the role of women in society or a personal one about himself. Either way, women in the audience took offence, but that didn't stop him.

He removed the tampon and kissed May Pang passionately on the lips for the photographers, knowing that Yoko would see the picture in the New York papers. Then he and his carousing companion, the singer Harry Nilsson, started to roar drunkenly to the accompaniment of cutlery rattled against glasses and plates. When the Smothers Brothers came on for their second show, John continued to sing, pausing only briefly to shout: 'Hey, Smothers Brothers, go f*** a cow.' In case anyone had failed to recognize him, he added: 'I'm John Lennon.'

When the Brothers' manager Ken Fritz tried to reason with him, a scuffle broke out and a table was overturned. John threw punches at both Fritz and a cocktail waitress who tried to intervene. With the place in uproar, John was tossed unceremoniously out into the street and told: 'Go home and sleep it off.' Naomi, the injured waitress, said: 'It's not the pain that hurts. It's finding out that one of your idols is a real asshole.'

John moved back to New York with Harry, leaving May to pick up the pieces in LA. They occupied rooms at the Pierre on Fifth Avenue, but although the Dakota was just across Central Park, Yoko was as far away as ever. It was only after John summoned May Pang to his side and the couple moved into a penthouse on Sutton Place at East 52nd Street that Yoko began to relent. Once she decided she wanted John back, she bombarded him with phone calls, stepping up the pressure when she heard that the couple were planning to buy a house together. In late January 1975, she called John over to the Dakota for 'treatment' to help him stop smoking; he stayed the night. When he turned up the next morning, he told a speechless May Pang: 'Yoko has allowed me to come home.' John packed his bags and scampered back inside the blackened walls of the Dakota, where the door banged firmly shut behind him.

'I was like a chicken without a head,' he said when he surfaced four months later. 'I'd be waking up in strange places, or reading about myself in the paper, doing extraordinary things, half of which I'd done and half of which I hadn't done. You can put it down to which night with which bottle.'

John and Yoko now decided to try for a child, although Yoko had already miscarried several times. After visiting an acupuncturist called Dr Hong in San Francisco, Yoko became pregnant. There was a collective sigh of relief when she gave birth to the baby on John's 35th birthday, 9 October 1975. Yoko was so obsessed with numbers that she had insisted on a Caesarean section so that her baby son and John would share the same birthday. John wanted to call the boy 'George Washington United States of America Citizen Lennon', but settled for 'Sean'. 'I feel higher than the Empire State Building,' he said, resolving to forgo his recording career to become a house-husband and look after the infant.

When Elvis and Linda read about John's wild behaviour, they discussed marriage as a way of cementing their own relationship. 'At this time in his life I suppose Elvis was closer to me than anyone,' said Linda. 'At one point we had planned to marry, but not after a while. That was primarily because of his drugs use, but also through his whole lifestyle. There was no way he was going to change.'

As a compromise, Linda suggested that they redecorate Graceland in a style they both liked. Elvis agreed. The blue and white decor, which dated from 1957, was completely replaced. 'The big fifteen-foot-long white sofa, a lot of the lamps and the big coffee table that Elvis used in those rooms from the time he moved in until 1974 – they all went and he brought in the wild red stuff,' said Todd Morgan, the Graceland communications director. 'All through the years, the drapes and carpet had changed colours, but blue and white were pretty standard from the very late Sixties through to the mid-Seventies. It was Hollywoodish elegant.

'The furniture and the drapes from the front rooms – the living room, music room, dining room and foyer – were put into storage and very fadish new stuff was brought in. It was all very trendy – the whim of somebody who had money to throw around. It was during the same period that Ike and Tina Turner had guitar-shaped coffee tables in their house. This was rock 'n' roll funk: red velvet *faux* French provincial furniture, deep red shag carpet and red velvet drapes. It was kinda wild.'

There was ample time for Bill Eubanks, the decorator Elvis had chosen, to exercise his imagination. His client was on the road for six months during 1974 with only short breaks between trips.

'When we were on tour, Elvis carried a little black bag that contained his medication,' recalls Linda. 'He never went anywhere without it. There were times when he was ready to go on stage and he was still down from sleeping medication, and he would virtually be asleep through his performance. He'd come off hardly knowing he had been on stage and say he was only just waking up. Other times, he was too up on Dexedrine or whatever so that he was too highly strung, giggling on stage and being silly, sometimes being hostile. It was a big worry.'

Whenever they escaped home to Graceland, Elvis would eagerly check out Eubanks' latest improvements, especially the pool room, the TV room and the 'jungle room' in the basement. He was delighted with the changes. 'Elvis spent, spent, spent and Vernon never got over the fear that tomorrow, it might all be gone,' said Todd. 'When he told him money was running low, Elvis would say, "Oh Daddy, I'll just do a tour or do a movie. Don't worry about it."

'So it was a constant problem, but Elvis and his dad were good friends. Certainly he was closer to his mother when he was growing up, but those close to Elvis saw the deepening relationship between him and his father through the years. Vernon was very honest and Elvis trusted him completely. He knew that, as long as his daddy was there running the show at home, every dime would be accounted for because Vernon was known to be tight with a buck.'

Eubanks had swathed the ceiling and walls of the pool room with miles of batik-like fabric, which was gathered and pleated to form an indoor tent fit for a sheikh. Correctly sensing the mood at Graceland, the decorator called it 'Elvis's emotional bomb shelter'.

'In the TV room, Elvis wanted to retain the three TVs he'd put in after hearing that LBJ had three sets sitting side by side so that he could watch all three networks at once,' said Todd. 'He was an admirer of Muhammad Ali and watched his fights, and he loved *Monty Python*, Peter Sellers and the *Ed Sullivan Show*.'

The TV room was perfect for entertaining. Under its mirrored ceiling was a yellow-padded Naugahyde bar and soda fountain with matching barstools. A yellow-and-white 'TCB' lightning bolt on one wall reminded guests where they were. There was a stereo system and a jukebox that was wired for sound throughout the house. One hundred 45s could be loaded into the jukebox, and Elvis's collection included offerings by Tom Jones, Bill Black's Combo, Patti Page, Dean Martin, Buddy Holly and Ray Charles.

The 'jungle room' or den adjoining the kitchen was the largest room in the house. Elvis bought the furniture at Donald's Furniture Store because it reminded him of Hawaii. Monkeys and parts of other wild animals were worked into the chairs, and there was a Tiki god and a waterfall cascading down one wall.

'Elvis added the jungle room on to the house and it became the gathering place,' said Todd. 'It was big and roomy and it looked like a typical suburban American family room for a number of years except for the waterfall, er, which was kinda trendy. All this stuff was a short-lived fad around this area. Well, it reminded him of Hawaii and he was just having fun one day. It's just my opinion that it doesn't really represent his taste as much as his sense of humour. He was having a good time.

'Elvis recorded an album-and-a-half in here. RCA brought the portable equipment and moved the furniture out or around, and shag pile carpeting was already on the ceiling. It was a kinda fadish thing, but it helped the acoustics and they hung blankets and quilts on the walls. Musicians and singers would come in and they'd bring in a piano. Elvis would come out of the kitchen and stand on the landing. He used that studio trick of changing the colour of the light bulbs to match the mood of the song they were recording. They would jam all night.

'They recorded the album *From Elvis Presley Boulevard, Memphis, Tennessee* and six songs from the *Moody Blue* album. That was the last album before his death and included his last single 'Way Down', which was in the charts at the time of his death.'

Some afternoons, Elvis would eat his breakfast in the jungle room at a coffee table made of polished cypress, while staring at the waterfall. Still stoned, he found that the trickling rainbow colours soothed his mind.

'Elvis was very sensitive about his medication and we talked about it from time to time,' said Linda. 'He said he suffered from insomnia from when he was a child. Then, when he became a star, there was so much going on, so much pressure, that he had taken medication to help him keep going or to sleep.

'I talked to Dr Nick about it and I talked to Joe Esposito. I remember Dr Nick telling me that, frankly, I was not the kind of girl who should be around – I was straight. He advised me to leave. He said no one could ever change Elvis, and he was right – one person cannot change another.

'Over the years I was with him, he had all kinds of different drugs. He was very well versed in their effects and their ingredients and would look them up in the *PDR – The Physician's Desk Reference*.

'Elvis would often complain of being in pain. He'd say he was in pain all over, or he had pulled a hamstring on stage. But I always assumed it was a very convenient pain because he enjoyed the effects of the painkilling medication.

'Elvis was a pillaholic. He also injected a lot; sometimes I had to help him inject. He had a psychological dependence. He thought he could not get up or keep going or go to sleep without medication. It is probably true that sometimes his generosity was drug enhanced. He was generous to a fault anyway, but I think it was possible some people took advantage when they saw what kind of state he was in. I look back now and think, "My God, how did I tolerate all that was going on?" But eventually, of course, I could not and had to leave.'

Reckless generosity was often a means of relieving Elvis's guilt over his bad behaviour. His moods could be vile, sometimes violent, as the Graceland cook Mary Jenkins recalls: 'One day Elvis called downstairs for his dinner, or his breakfast – it was late, but it was still breakfast to him – and the phone didn't ring,' she said. 'We were all sitting there in the kitchen, all the Boys and the kitchen help, but nobody heard the phone ring. Suddenly, Elvis was at the top of the stairs shouting, "Hey, where is everybody?" And we all spoke about the same time, "Nobody called down here – the phone hasn't rung." Elvis said, "I been callin' and callin' and it has rung." And we said, "Hey, it didn't ring." And he said, "Well it will ring!" He came downstairs with his pyjamas on and he picked up a chair and took the phone off the wall and beat it into just little pieces.'

Another of those who suffered was Jerry Schilling, who had accompanied Elvis to the White House and on many other escapades. 'I noticed a sustained change [in Elvis] in the last three years of his life,' said Jerry. 'He wasn't having fun any more, except on stage. I suppose at the root was the medication, but of course, when he started cancelling tours, it sort of focused on the growing health problem. A couple of times in Las Vegas, he was unable to go on and it was attributed to his health. He had an enlarged liver, a twisted colon and high blood pressure. The eye condition glaucoma caused a lot of problems.

'It was like a man who was basically healthy all his life, and in a very short period of time, everything started happening to him. He was either going twenty-four hours a day or he was a recluse. It all started to catch up with him. He took amphetamines to get him up for the show, so he could do what he could do ten years ago, and then to counteract the amphetamines he would take barbiturates afterwards. When he was working night after night on tour, he would build up these immunities and require more and more [drugs]. He would look up the *PDR* and try to discover stronger stuff.'

But as fast as Elvis increased his intake, his addictive illness made him crave even higher doses. In January 1975 around the time of his fortieth birthday, he was smuggled into hospital at four o'clock in the morning. In June, he was back again for two days. In August, he went in after completing only three nights of a two-week booking at the Hilton.

'In the hospital, they actually had to give him medication because he had stayed awake for almost four days,' said Jerry Schilling. 'He really was doing better. He had been in hospital for two weeks. It was a very hard thing for Elvis to let his pride go. He was working with a psychiatrist, and it was a very big statement for him to make.'

At least Elvis had the satisfaction of knowing that he had beaten one Beatle record. On that New Year's Eve, he had played to the biggest audience of his life when 60,000 people turned out to see him at Pontiac, Michigan. He had topped the Beatles' multitude at Shea Stadium by a few hundred – but split his pants in the process.

CHAPTER TWENTY-TWO

Sinatra gets Frank with Elvis

NO MATTER who ruled the pop realm, Francis Albert Sinatra was the undisputed emperor of New York, New York. Around midnight on Sunday, 24 August 1975, a merrier-than-usual Tom Jones insisted that we scour Manhattan for Ol' Blue Eyes. Tom had just closed a record-breaking week at a theatre in Westchester and wanted to celebrate with the man he regarded as his mentor.

When we reached Jilly's, Sinatra's regular haunt, we were told that Frank and Jilly were dining at Jimmy Weston's. When we arrived there, a particularly sober Sinatra greeted Tom, Tom's son Mark and me with the words: 'Hey, I just spoke to Elvis in hospital.' As waiters dived in with chairs to accommodate us, Sinatra shook his head sadly. 'He's too young to die,' he said.

Sinatra and Presley had had their differences in the past, but it wasn't in the older man's nature to kick a fellow entertainer when he was down. Frank told us about his phone call.

'When I asked to be put through to Elvis Presley, the girl said, "Who's calling?" and I said, "Frank Sinatra." I fully expected her to say, "Oh, yeah, and I'm the Queen of England" or some such dumb line. But she must have recognized my voice because, a few seconds later, Elvis came on.

'He didn't sound too good. I thought I'd cheer him up by inviting him to join a stars' syndicate to buy our own hotel in Vegas. I told him that, with the three of us there, they could fire a cannon down the Strip and not hit anyone. But I have to say that Elvis didn't seem to care. I guess he's depressed. I told him he's got to look after himself and quit fooling around. He's too young to die, and I told him so.'

If Frank Sinatra was worried about Elvis, Vernon Presley was doubly so. He resolved to trace Elvis's drug suppliers by hiring private eye John O'Grady, a retired LAPD police sergeant, and Jack Kelly, former regional director of the Federal Bureau of Narcotics.

'Vernon had asked me specifically if I could get into Nichopolous's bag, to see what was there,' O'Grady told the DA's men. 'I never did manage to do that. The only time I spoke to Elvis about getting off medication was in 1975, and the response was, "Absolutely not, you sonovabitch."

'I could see the debilitating activity [while I watched] the show. He had a peculiar walking gait, he would ramble, he would tell stories that didn't make sense. He would call me in the middle of the night many times and I do not regret these calls. He called me one night and said he had just buried Jesse there in Memphis. It was meaningless. His brain would wander; he would repeat things a thousand times. He would call perhaps at four in the morning and just ramble for forty or fifty minutes. It was a condition brought on by the narcotics. By 1974, he was in a bad way; it was obvious. From then on to when he died, he was not Elvis Presley. He was a human being under the influence of drugs.

'In 1974, when he was performing in Las Vegas, a hotel employee had found a narcotic needle in Elvis's bed and had turned it in. It was the strangest thing. I was sitting there at the performance, and Elvis got up on the stage in front of everyone and told the entire staff off. They were rotten bastards and should never use narcotics. I watched the show and then went backstage and his aide Lamar Fike said it was ridiculous. Elvis was out there with a 190-degree blood pressure, right now. I couldn't understand why the doctors had let him work. Another thing was his sweating. I've looked at people coming down from drugs and they're covered with perspiration, but I had never seen anyone sweat like that.

He would lose seven or eight pounds in a performance. He was such a strong character that he came through it, but I could never understand how any doctor at that point could allow him to work.

'I kept in touch with Joe Esposito to enquire what Elvis's state was because I was mortally afraid that some young narcotics officer would knock Elvis off. Of all the cases I've worked on, hundreds of them, I have never seen so many drugs prescribed for one person ever before, and I have been involved in drugs enforcement for thirty-two years.'

Elvis was too sick to heed Sinatra's well-meaning advice. He reacted to his problems by purging the ranks of the Memphis Mafia. He ordered Vernon to fire his close friends Red and Sonny West, and another bodyguard, Dave Hebler. The Wests, he decided, were too rough in the strong-arm methods they applied to troublemakers and eager fans, while Hebler was accused of spreading dissent. Elvis recruited Linda's brother, Sam Thompson, as bodyguard and Dick Grob was promoted to security.

'I left the sheriff's department around the middle of June 1976 to go and work for Elvis Presley,' Sam told the DA's investigators. 'He explained my duties would be as a personal bodyguard. Primarily I was concerned with the security of the entourage and Elvis himself while we were on tour. He paid me $350 week and he paid all expenses. Most of the travel was on his private planes.

'Not long after I went to work for him, the relationship between him and my sister became estranged and they separated. Then he began going with this very young girl, Ginger Alden. There seemed to be a strain in keeping up that relationship, which is natural with an older man and a young girl. So I think his personality changes might have been in part due to some emotional stress, plus travelling and working like he did.

'I was with Elvis for twenty months and kept a schedule of all fourteen tours during that period. The tours were headed, for example, "Tour Number Nine under the direction of Colonel Tom Parker". He would go and set up the tours and then hand the schedule to Joe Esposito.

'Usually there were about one hundred people who travelled with Elvis, and there would be other ground staff brought in by Colonel Parker. We had an identification system whereby everyone had a laminated badge with their picture and name, which permitted them entry to, say, backstage areas. There were different coloured passes for each tour, to control the flow of people into the area where Elvis would be.

'When I first went to work for him, it seemed to me – and perhaps I had stars in my eyes – that all the shows were good and he always looked well. But the closer I got to the man, the more time I spent with him, I began to realize that some shows were a lot better than others and some were terrible.

'I saw how much weight he was putting on, and at different times, his mood would be altered drastically in a matter of hours. He would be extremely excitable, hopped-up and erratic, and a few hours later, he would be completely lethargic and almost unable to budge out of the chair or bed. Having been involved in law enforcement, I felt that the man was taking a lot of medication and I didn't feel that it was a stable situation.

'We felt that Elvis was highly irrational. He always carried weapons with him. I'm not going as far as to say we were in fear of our lives, but we did feel that some due caution needed to be taken. I would not have put it down entirely to the drugs. They obviously led to the personality changes, but there were also things about the age of the man.

'We talk about the male menopause when a man reaches 40. Elvis was a superstar, and the fact was that his hair was going grey and he was putting on weight. Image was everything to a man like Elvis. He had no peers. No one in show business had done what he had done. The King of Rock 'n' Roll was going grey, getting a little heavy, a few bags under the eyes. Like most entertainers, his ego was very big.'

One of Elvis's drug suppliers who was frequently named in the DA's enquiry was Dr Max Shapiro, a slight middle-aged man wearing thick glasses and a slippery hairpiece. Shapiro preferred patients to call him 'Dr Max', but his nickname among the Hollywood swingers was 'Dr Feelgood'. When I interviewed him in 1978, he described Elvis as 'a close personal friend for more than twenty years'. It was Shapiro who had taught Elvis about the effects of various drugs and had even given him a copy of *The Physician's Desk Reference,* which had become his medical bible. But there was a touching personal side to the relationship.

'He arranged my wedding to my wife Suzanne,' Shapiro told me. 'He had asked me to go to his home in Palm Springs on 13 January 1977. I asked him if I could take Suzanne along, and he said certainly. He knew we were planning to marry, although she was only 19. In fact, I had taken out a licence that was valid for a year and had it with me on that trip. Elvis talked to me about Suzanne and said she was a wonderful girl and would make a wonderful wife. Then he said, "You know, Max, I've rarely been a best man – can I be yours?" I said we would like that very much. He said, "Well then, let's have the wedding tonight – Ginger would like to be the maid of honour."

'He called in a jeweller to supply a special ring and sent his private plane to Los Angeles to collect a minister. It was two or three in the morning when we were married, and the four of us stayed up until dawn talking about religion. He was deeply religious. He gave us some religious books as wedding presents. He had already given me a Mercedes on a previous occasion, but I had to sell that to pay for my divorce.

'I watched the decline in his health with great sadness. I suppose I first realized Elvis had a heart problem about three years before he died. His hands were badly swollen and there were other symptoms of heart trouble. I warned him and he was very concerned. A few months before he died, I told him I was working on an artificial heart that would have saved him.

'The apparatus is actually a pump powered by the same kind of batteries as a pacemaker, which will step in and either augment a patient's heartbeat or replace the work of the heart if the latter gives out. It is made of silicone and Teflon, and other metals are used in a small electric motor. It will not be rejected because it works on a belt outside the body with tubes going into the groin. I had successfully implanted one in a dog at the University of Wisconsin at Milwaukee and I was convinced that it would work on a human being.

'Elvis asked me to prepare three as quickly as I could – one for himself, one for his father and the third for a member of Ginger Alden's family. I was still working on the first one when he died.

'The stories that I gave him prescriptions for anything he wanted are totally untrue. I only ever prescribed cocaine for him once. He was doing a night-time recording session and was in great pain with toothache. I did surgery on a third molar and gave him cocaine to ease the pain. He went on with the session and made one of his biggest hits of the latter years that night. Elvis was happy; everybody was happy.'

However, the paternal Henri Lewin was far from happy about Elvis's condition. He feared the worst during the final Elvis season at the Hilton. 'I saw him shortly before he died, and he was so loaded up that his eyes were puffed and only half open,' he said. 'I didn't think he was going to die, but he lived a sick type of life. He was just a person who was totally in the world of fantasy. He never had a real life. He was not given the opportunity to have a real relationship with anybody. If he made a mistake, nobody told him.

'When he bought a new car, I remember he said, "I never want to own another red car. I only want black cars," and everybody in the room agreed that black was the best. Somebody bought him a cake and he took a piece and he said, "It tastes like s**t," and everybody said, "It's s**t," and they laughed. He didn't like the way a shirt was ironed, so he sent out for four new ones. How can you go on in life when everybody agrees that everything you say and do is right?'

Seymour Heller recalls enquiring after Elvis's health when he saw the Colonel at the Vegas tables. 'I asked, "How's Elvis?" He replied,

"He's in a hospital in Memphis." "How long is he going to be there?" "Up till next week when we go on a tour."

'I was upset about that. I thought, He's your No. 1 client, one of the biggest guns in the world, and you're here gambling for dollars while he's in hospital. I thought, if I were Elvis's manager I'd be standing by his bedside. Elvis Presley was not a regular type commodity. He was a special kid.'

The Colonel undoubtedly agreed with that, but he knew better than anyone else that he had lost his power over Elvis. All he could do was hope that his prayers were answered.

CHAPTER TWENTY-THREE

The Final Hours At Graceland

MARY JENKINS knew something strange was happening the last time she saw Elvis alive. He was sitting in the dark – and more than anything else on earth, Elvis feared the dark. In his childhood, Gladys had kept an oil lamp burning throughout the night, and he had never been able to relax without a light of some kind in the room. This is the real reason why the TV sets were kept permanently switched on in his bedroom.

When Mary recalls that night, the memory of Elvis and Ginger Alden huddled in that totally dark room is the first thing that springs to mind. Her eyes glisten briefly behind large gold-rimmed spectacles, but the smile rarely fades from her face. A grandmother and devout churchgoer, she wears the Elvis colours of pink and black, and his picture is boldly imprinted on the back of her black leather jacket.

Mary had worked at Graceland since Elvis's 28th birthday on 8 January 1963, and she was completely relaxed about his curious nocturnal routine. After so many years, the summons to go upstairs held no surprise for her, but what she found in the early hours of Tuesday, 16 August 1977 surprised her a great deal.

'Mr P called me on the phone at two o'clock in the morning and asked me to come upstairs and straighten up his room,' she told me at her home in Memphis. 'The maid hadn't got there, so I went up to make his bed. There was no one in the room, so I thought Elvis and Ginger were downstairs on the porch. I was going to fill his water bottles up and the icemaker was in Lisa's room. Lisa was in Memphis, but she was over at her grandfather's house.

'I just pushed the door open and turned the light on and there they were, sitting up in there, and he never sat up in a room without a TV on, yet the TV was off.

'Elvis got up and turned the light off, and I said, "Oh my goodness, y'all in here playing Lovey Joe and I done interrupt everything." He said, "No, May-we, it's nothing like that – all I want to do is rest. I just want to rest."

'I said, "You not going to eat anything for me tonight?" and he said, "No." Well, he hadn't eaten that Sunday night or that Monday, and I said, "I know you're going to eat something for me tonight," and he said, "No, I'm not hungry. I just want to rest."

'I said, "OK then, if you not going to eat anything, I am gonna go and I will see you in the morning. Night, night." He said, "Night night, May-we" – he called me May-we. So when I went to go out the door, I said, "I will see y'all in the morning'." And he said, "OK."'

Mary knew that Elvis was due to leave on another exhausting tour at 1.00 am the following night, and she could understand his reluctance to eat. He was overweight, grotesquely so at 250 pounds, and his voice was shot from drugs. But an 11th hour plea of illness to give him time to recover was out of the question. The Colonel and the advance party were already in place at Portland, Maine, for the sold-out opening concert of the twelve-day tour, and every ticket had been snapped up at Utica (New York), Hartford (Connecticut), Lexington (Kentucky) and several other venues. Most important, the tour was due to end among the home-town faithful at the Mid-South Coliseum in Memphis. He just couldn't back out.

But no matter how much the fans adored him or forgave his ramblings, Elvis knew that his touring days were drawing to a close. The trappings had become more vivid than the performance, and only the American flair for theatre kept the show on the road. His apotheosis into a spiritual icon might be complete, but only his exalted status saved him from being ridiculed as the King of Rock 'n' Roly-Poly.

There was also the additional dread that he would be appearing in public for the first time since the publication, on 1 August, of *Elvis: What Happened?*, the memoirs of the three sacked bodyguards. The shame of Sonny's and Red's allegations about his crazy behaviour was like a dagger in his heart. Yet he couldn't cancel; he needed the money. No-show meant no dough, and Elvis was spending as lavishly as ever.

As Mary Jenkins headed home, she knew from Elvis's solemn demeanour that he and Ginger had been having an argument. It was no secret at Graceland that the 20-year-old Priscilla lookalike had refused to accompany him on the tour. Without a beautiful young woman at his beck and call, Elvis felt old and ugly.

'He liked his girlfriend to go with him,' Mary said. 'Any time Elvis said to Linda, "The Boys are gonna start packing, you start packing," she would go right on and start packing, and when they got ready, she was ready. She went and stayed as long as he stayed, but this child didn't want to go.

'That's what I thought they were arguing about that night. I just thought he was angry. I didn't know he was going to die.

'I believe if he and Linda had been together, he would be living today because she took care of him. She wouldn't go to sleep, she wouldn't close her eyes, until she knew he was asleep. She really did take care of him. And so did Priscilla: she did the same thing.'

When Sam Thompson was questioned by the DA's men about his relationship with Ginger, he admitted that there had been friction between them. 'My sister and Elvis had broken up and she was the new girl on the scene,' he said. 'It was a love triangle thing. I know that all the members of the group resented Ginger being in that situation. Nobody felt that she was really taking care of Elvis in terms of his medication.'

In truth, Ginger found Elvis's drug-taking so bewildering that she had no chance of trying to control it. This was one of the reasons that he had chosen her from the other available candidates. She knew nothing about drugs. 'She was so young,' commented Mary Jenkins.

However, the romance had been anything but tranquil since Elvis's old DJ friend George Klein had brought Ginger to Graceland for the first time in November 1976. Elvis had been immediately smitten. Despite her name, Ginger's wavy hair was dyed jet black like Priscilla's. She was tall and shapely with very kissable lips. The only strike against her was that she was a Paul McCartney fan, but Elvis was prepared to overlook that. He called her Gingerbread.

From the outset, Ginger failed to fall in with the King's very explicit demands. She preferred to live at home with her mother in the family's modest wooden ranch-style house rather than move into Graceland. 'Whatever people say, I wasn't just a girlfriend,' she said. 'I didn't live at Graceland, and Elvis respected me for that. He respected me for my religious beliefs, my sincerity, myself.'

According to Ginger, the courtship led to a proposal of marriage on 26 January 1977, in the bathroom where he was to die. Elvis was an eight according to *Cheiro's Book of Numbers,* and he had checked the date first to make sure it was auspicious. Two plus six equalled eight, so that was all right.

'He loved to surprise me,' said Ginger. 'He called me in, got down on his knees and proposed. I shook and cried and promised him we'd be man and wife. Then he gave me the engagement ring and we just held each other tight and close, but very tenderly. We held hands and prayed.'

Although Ginger wore Elvis's $50,000 gold and diamond ring, their progress towards the altar was decidedly unorthodox. Elvis had several dalliances with other women including Alicia Kirwin, another raven-haired beauty. Born in Memphis, the 20-year-old was a cashier at the United American Bank.

'I knew George Klein since I was about 18, and in April 1977, he called me up out of the blue and asked me if I would like to meet Elvis,' said Alicia. 'It was a spur-of-the-moment call. He said Elvis and Ginger

Alden had had a fight and Elvis was upset. He said he just wanted me to go up there and talk to him.

'I agreed and I went up to Graceland in my car around 10.00 pm and I met Jo Smith, Billy's wife. She was a real good friend of mine. I met Elvis's daughter, Lisa Marie, and we talked. Then Jo took me up to the sitting room, which was full of people. They were talking about a forthcoming tour. Elvis was in the centre. Later on, he and I talked. I had never met him before. We just talked about what I did for a living and so on. It was very relaxed and comfortable. He seemed to be in very good spirits. His physical appearance surprised me. He was very heavy. His voice was slow, but not slurred. I didn't see any kind of medication.

'The room was crowded, the phone was ringing a lot, there were papers everywhere: it was hectic. We talked about Ginger in between times after I'd been there a while. He said he'd had an argument with Ginger and he didn't think he was going to see her any more.

'I left after about two hours. About two days later, I got home from work and my roommate told me someone had called and left a telephone number. It was Elvis and he wanted me to come over. Several hours later, I went over to Graceland.

'I was late, so I was shown into the kitchen, and he kept me waiting for about an hour before I was shown upstairs. In the meantime, I was talking to the maids. Upstairs, I was taken into his daughter's room where Elvis was sitting. Lisa Marie had left that day and he was despondent. He just sat there, drinking iced water. He introduced me to Tish Henley, who I learned was his nurse. He had just given her a bracelet and she showed it to me. It was obviously very expensive. She stayed the whole time I was in the bedroom.

'David Stanley also came in, and then one of Ginger's sisters came in. She was obnoxious. She wanted to know what I was doing there. She was very inquisitive. I talked with Elvis for about an hour, and we went for a stroll around the grounds. I left around 11.30 pm. He was calm and natural, no different from the time I met him before. He showed me some of his cars.

'The next day I received another telephone call, and he asked me if I'd come over. I said I already had a date and he was a bit angry about that and he hung up on me. Then about two seconds later, he called back and said, "What about tomorrow?" He asked me if I could get a few days off work. He said he wanted to take me to Las Vegas in his plane.

'So I got permission from my work and I called back. We fixed a date for the following Wednesday and I drove over to Graceland that evening. We took off for the airport with Jo and Billy Smith, Charlie Hodge and Dick Grob. We went to the airport at about 11.00 pm and flew out on one of the smaller planes. We didn't take any luggage except that one of them carried Elvis's little leather bag. I fell asleep on the plane and I didn't wake up until we were there.

'We had a car to the Hilton Hotel, and that night I stayed with Elvis for the first time. There were a few bottles of pills beside his bed. I assumed they were sleeping pills. He told me they were mostly muscle-relaxing pills. He told me if I couldn't sleep, he could solve it. It was the middle of the night by then and I just fell straight to sleep.

'Elvis woke me for breakfast. He was in good spirits. He never went out of the room, just watched television and smoked cigars. We talked quite a bit. I noticed everybody just bowed to his wishes. They laughed when he laughed and got him everything he needed, even a glass of water.

'Then he announced we were leaving and we took off for Palm Springs, where we stayed until Sunday. It was much the same procedure. He stayed in the house and he had one visitor – it could have been a doctor. That was after Elvis got very upset. He had called his father who was angry because we weren't supposed to be there. He hadn't told his father or Tom Parker we were going to Las Vegas. He had said we were going to Nashville. Vernon was real mad. We stayed until Sunday and went back to Memphis.

'I next heard from him while he was on tour. He called me several times, but in June, I told Billy Smith I did not want to see Elvis any more. It was just too much. I couldn't handle it because he was Elvis Presley. I had never been used to this kind of thing, staying up all hours of the night and all. Elvis called me back a few hours later and wanted me to go over, and I went. He said he was very depressed, and he said he wished he could go out on a Saturday night like other people. We just talked and talked, and then I went home at about three in the morning. He didn't want me to leave, but I left anyway. He was ready to go to sleep and wanted to make sure there was someone close by.'

'I next heard from him a few weeks later. He called me in the middle of the night; it must have been about 3.00 am. He was terribly depressed and asked me to go up to Graceland. I said I had to go to work the next morning, but he persisted. I stayed for a few hours. He just looked so sad. Then he fell asleep. He had taken some medication, sleeping pills, though I hadn't seen him take a lot. I left for work around 8.00 am and that was the last time I saw him.'

Ginger had waited for this moment for three months. She had once turned up at Graceland while Alicia was there, but Elvis had refused to see her. She telephoned frequently, but Elvis wouldn't take the calls. She was getting the Presley freeze-out. However, as soon as Alicia had left for the last time, her virtue having been in no danger from Elvis, Gingerbread was back.

(Alicia had found the Elvis experience so unsettling that she quit her bank job in Memphis and returned to Las Vegas, where she trained as a croupier. She died of a drug overdose a few years later.)

According to Ginger, the thing uppermost in the King's mind as they sat on Lisa's white-furred, hamburger-shaped bed in the dark, early hours of 16 August was their impending marriage. 'He said he was going to introduce me at his concert in Memphis,' she said. 'He told me to look real special. We were going to be married at Christmas.' However, Elvis had other ideas, according to members of the Memphis Mafia and Mary Jenkins.

'It really surprised me,' Mary said. 'He told me that he would not marry anybody unless it was Priscilla. Linda had wanted to get married and have children, but he didn't want that. He told me, "If I ever marry again, it will be to my baby's mother."'

'Now Priscilla came to Graceland two years before he died. She had been to New York, had a lay-over here and she came out to the house and stayed there until she was going to get her plane. But she stayed upstairs with him so long that the plane was gone when she got there, and she had to come back. We started laughing. We said, "You wanted that plane to leave," and she laughed. I really believe that they talked about remarrying that day.'

Mary, who was very fond of Priscilla, knew that Elvis's ex-wife had more influence over the King than anyone else. Elvis and Priscilla had spoken on the phone that Monday evening, 15 August, about Lisa's return to Los Angeles. Priscilla was angry with Elvis for delaying their daughter's departure, so it was a tense conversation. But at least they were still on speaking terms. Mary lived in hope that a reunion might curb some of Elvis's wilder excesses. As the Graceland cook, she knew about his self-destructive eating habits better than anyone else.

'He usually started dieting about two weeks before he'd go back on tour,' she said. 'He would stay upstairs, he wouldn't come down for days and he wouldn't call for anything to eat. He would just drink liquids to try and get some of that weight off.'

Tonight the last thing on Elvis's mind was food. By midnight, he had developed a sudden toothache.

Sam Thompson was drinking coffee, playing cards and talking to the maids in the kitchen. 'I was supposed to take Lisa Marie back to her mother in Los Angeles,' he said. 'Priscilla was very upset because Elvis had been keeping her back until he began the next tour.

'Elvis came downstairs all dressed and ready to go somewhere about midnight. He said he was going to see his dentist, Dr Lester Hofman. Billy Smith, Ginger Alden and Charlie Hodge were with him, and they got into the black Stutz Blackhawk and they left. I was still there playing cards in the kitchen when they came back a couple of hours later.

'They all went upstairs to Elvis's suite, and a few minutes later, Elvis came on the telephone and told me to take Lisa back the following day. I was to take her to Priscilla's house, then I was to fly to Portland, Maine, where the tour began. I telephoned American Airlines and made the reservations. I knew I was going to have a long day, so I went home. I believe that David Stanley was the personal aide on duty.'

After Sam departed, Elvis, Ginger, Billy Smith and his wife Jo went to the racquetball court for some exercise. They didn't play for long. Elvis whacked his leg with his racquet and he retired hurt to the piano, where he played 'Unchained Melody' and tested his voice.

Mary Jenkins recalls: 'I was told that, when he came back into the house, Vera Wood the maid said to him, "Mr P, you look like somebody who wants to eat," but he still said, "No, I just wanna rest." And he went on upstairs.

'In the morning about eight o'clock, he calls up his Aunt Delta and tells her to bring him some water. She takes it up, then she says, "Now, hon, you wanna be woke up when Lisa leaves?" But he said, "Aunt Delta, I don't wanna be woke up for nothin'." And she said, "Don't you wanna see ya baby?" He said, "Yeah, you can wake me up for that, but nothin' else." And she said, "I'll wake you up when she's ready to leave. I'll let nobody bother you until then."

'And nobody was going to try and wake him up or anything because Ginger was up there with him. She said that he got up and went in the bathroom to read.'

Five thousand miles away, the roving ambassadors for the Cosmic Kingdom of Nutopia were in the Japanese resort of Karuizawa on a goodwill mission. But John Lennon could find no peace of mind among

Yoko's kith and kin. If anything, he appeared to be closer to his appointed hour with the hereafter than was his great rival. Strung out on drugs, he had been in a trance since the beginning of August. In his own words, he suffered 'a living death' during which he stayed in bed most of the day, either refusing to talk to anyone or unable to do so. He ate no food and became virtually anorexic. The strain of socializing with Yoko's friends and relatives, few of whom spoke any English, had plunged him into a catatonic state.

Each one of his personalities came to visit him like spirits inhabiting an empty temple. The abandoned child gave way to the juvenile bully, the extrovert rock star disappeared in favour of the stoned philosopher. 'I began to see all these different parts of me,' John told a friend when he was able to describe the sensation. 'But I can't be all these people all the time.' The frightening thing was that whatever phase he was in became dominant to the exclusion of all the others. Thus he had no balance, no stability, no sanity.

'I have no device, no magic, to keep an easy flow from one part of my personality to another,' he said. 'I need that because the secret is to change.' For Elvis, the chance to change was slipping away for ever in the loneliness of his plushly carpeted bathroom.

The afternoon of 16 August was sweltering, even in the shade of the spreading Graceland oak trees. Down at the Music Gates, Uncle Vester Presley watched the ninety-degree heat shimmy in waves along the black strip of Elvis Presley Boulevard. Several times that day he had invited groups of sightseers to accompany him up to the house to take pictures of its famous facade. The old boy liked these little guided tours: they broke the monotony of his long stint in the gatehouse. Some of the visitors snapped pictures of the bathroom window above the columned portico and the blackened glass of the room to the right, which, Vester informed them, was his nephew's bedroom. The tourists shouldered their cameras and walked back down the hill to the Music Gates, totally oblivious to the drama that was being enacted upstairs.

At 1.30 pm, Ginger Alden had awoken from a deep sleep in the double king-size bed in that very room, where the temperature never dropped below a bracing sixty-five degrees Farenheit. Finding herself alone, she had dressed, applied her make-up and made two phone calls. Then she went looking for Elvis. She tapped on the bathroom door and called: 'Elvis?' There was no reply. '*Elvis*?' It was 2.00 pm. 'Ginger just went into the bathroom and found him laying there,' said Mary Jenkins. Dressed only in gold pyjama pants, Elvis was crouched in the foetal position on the floor. The book he had been reading, *Sex and Psychic Energy*, was nearby.

'I thought at first he might have hit his head because he had fallen out of his black lounging chair and his face was buried in the carpet,' said Ginger. 'I slapped him a few times, and it was like he breathed once when I turned his head. One of his eyes was just blood red and I couldn't move him. I didn't want to think he was dead. God wouldn't want to take him so soon.'

Ginger raced out of the bedroom and shouted for help. 'She called downstairs, and Al [Strada] was the only one there at the time,' said Mary. 'But Joe [Esposito] came in right behind and they sent him straight on upstairs.'

'When Joe turned Elvis's head over, I think he knew he was dead,' said Ginger. 'It seemed like hours while we waited for the ambulance.'

The division of the Memphis Fire Department that was stationed one-and-a-half miles away at 2147 Elvis Presley Boulevard received the emergency call at 2.30 pm. Three minutes later, an ambulance with paramedics Charlie Crosby and Ulysses S. Jones Jr on board was screaming towards Graceland. 'As soon as I heard the siren, I opened the gates so they wouldn't have to stop,' said Uncle Vester, who had been alerted by one of the Guys at the house. 'They didn't even slow down.' Leaving some of its paintwork on one of the gates, the ambulance sped up the hill and jerked to a halt between the two stone lions outside the front door. It took five men to carry Elvis downstairs after the medics also failed to get any response. Summoned by a frantic call from Joe Esposito, George Nichopolous arrived in his gold-green Mercedes just in time to jump into the back of the ambulance with Elvis. As the vehicle hurtled in the direction of Baptist Memorial Hospital on Madison Avenue, the physician tried to revive his stricken patient, exhorting him: 'Come on, Presley, breathe. Breathe for me.' At 2.56 pm, Elvis was stretchered into the hospital's emergency room. Staff who witnessed his arrival knew from one glimpse of his blackened, immobile face that he was already beyond human help. At 3.30 pm, Dr Nichopolous officially pronounced Elvis Presley dead, and the hospital announced the news to the world half an hour later. The grief was spontaneous.

'My father came over in Linda's car to take me to Graceland,' said Sam Thompson. 'As I got to the gates, David Stanley came roaring down the driveway in his Datsun 240Z. He stopped and said, "Have you heard the news – Elvis is dead." He just roared out of the gates and that was the last time I saw David Stanley until the day of the funeral.

'I drove on up and there was a Fire Department ambulance at the front door. I drove round to the back and went in, and I saw Vernon with Nick beside him. I got there just in time to hear Nick break the news to Vernon, to actually confirm that Elvis had died. Vernon began to moan and cry very loudly. A large group of people were there and it was like a madhouse. The two ambulance attendants were in the dining room, just sitting there. I was told later that they had brought Dr Nick back from the morgue. Then I got a phone call from Dick Grob, who was at the morgue, and he said, "Well, it finally happened."'

Mary Jenkins remembers the precise moment she got the call. 'My niece Barbara Moseley was working at the hospital and she called me at three o'clock in the afternoon and asked me if I had heard the news,' she said. 'I was looking at my soap opera, *Edge of Night,* and it just went off and I got up to put dinner on, and when I passed the telephone, it rang.

'I said, "What news?" I thought she meant just gossip or something, and she said, "Elvis just died." "Girl, hush, Elvis ain't dead – he's not sick or anything," I says, "It's his daddy, 'cos his daddy is sick." She said, "No, Mary, it *is* Elvis Presley who's dead." I said, "I don't believe it – they haven't even called me." And I said, "I know exactly what I am going to do, I am going to get on the phone and call." So I got on the telephone and the yardman, Tommy Henley, answered the phone. He was the husband of Elvis's nurse, Tish Henley. You could hear him hollerin' at the top of his voice, and I said, "Tell me, is it true?" and he said, "Yes, Mary, it's true, it's true."

'I just hung the phone up and roared, and jumped into some clothes and called a cab to go down there. When I got in, I told the driver, "I want to go to Graceland, Elvis has just died," and I was shaking like a leaf on a tree, and he said, "You mean to tell me that Elvis is dead?" and I said, "He's dead." So we went on and it took us two-and-a-half hours to get just a little better than a block to the gate. Cars were parked all over the streets and they were standing up on cars. It was terrible . . .

'Well, I couldn't get up to the house in the cab so I had to walk up the hill, and when I got there, I went in the back door. I pushed the door in, and Mr Vernon looked at me and he hollered just as loud as he could: "Mary, our Elvis has gone, our Elvis has gone!" All of them were just howling, and his old grandmother just had to lay down. I never went through nothing like this, never have. We were very, very close, Elvis and me.'

Janelle McComb, Elvis's former neighbour, was at her house in Tupelo when the telephone rang. 'The caller said, "Mrs McComb, Elvis is dead." Well, I thought it was a dupe so I hung the phone down. I was always getting crank calls. I went into the living room and the phone rang again and this time I could hear screaming in the background, and they said, "Mrs McComb, Elvis is really dead . . . Can you hear me?" I don't even remember who it was; I just sat down on the floor. My husband came home from work and I was devastated. I could not believe it. I had to get packed, and it was after dark before I left for Graceland.

'When I got there, it was as if Elvis Presley had merely left the building. His presence, his lust for living, his kindness, his generosity to friends, his infectious smile still remained. These precious memories were in my heart.'

After a post-mortem examination, Elvis's body was brought to Graceland, where Larry Geller made up his face and trimmed his hair for the last time, as a favour to Vernon. The body was placed in an unsealed coffin behind the stained-glass peacock windows of the music room. Thousands came to pay homage.

'The night before the funeral, I walked over and touched his face,' said Janelle. 'I thought of all the things he had sung, going back to that small boy singing "Amazing Grace" in church, and all I could say was, "Farewell, my friend."' Elvis was buried at the Forest Hill Cemetery just five months short of his 43rd birthday. Memphis sold out of flowers.

George Klein carries a faded piece of paper in his jacket pocket to prove that Elvis died from natural causes. It reads:

25 October 1977. Office of the Shelby County Medical Examiner, Dr Jerry Francisco:

The cause of death has been ascribed to hypertensive heart disease with coronary artery heart disease as a contributing factor. There is no evidence that medication present in the body of Elvis Presley caused or made any significant contribution to his death. There was an extensive search for illicit drugs and they were not found to be present.

'And that is the legal eagle right there, signed "Jerry Francisco, Shelby County Medical Examiner",' says George, pointing to the seal.

No one who loved Elvis wanted to believe that drugs had killed him either accidentally or deliberately, but it is beyond doubt that he was a victim of his kamikaze lifestyle. The illness of addiction wanted him dead, and it had succeeded.

Raquel Welch took a realistic Hollywood view. 'When I heard he'd died, I was in a rehearsal room in Los Angeles preparing my own show for Vegas,' she said. 'I remember feeling really sad because he was such a big part of all our lives. Then I remember thinking that I wasn't surprised; it seemed as though a big part of him had already died when we met that last time in Vegas.

'It also seemed as though his public had got what they might have wished – America loves dead heroes and they will be happier with a heart-throb who died at 42 than an old man who became weak and bald and all those things that go with old age.'

John Lennon felt no sadness or remorse. A long-time believer in reincarnation, to him Elvis had simply moved on to a higher state of being. But the death did prompt him to take a close look at his own confused personae. On 24 August, he sat down at a typewriter in his Japanese retreat and began writing himself a letter. In thirteen days, he covered just three single-spaced pages. The result – a personal inventory – is like a surreal freefall through time and space. His mind jumps from Yoko to guilt, from loneliness to alienation, from *deja vu* to the future, from his early inspiration to his lost muse, but it signs off with a cursory farewell to Elvis. 'He died the day he went into the Army' was the punchline of John's epitaph. Secretly, he had longed to write those words since the day he saw *GI Blues*.

The 'Ballad of John and Elvis' might have finished its run, but for millions of followers, many still unborn on 16 August 1977, Elvis didn't die the day he went into the Army and nor did he die alone in his bathroom at Graceland. In the final analysis, he was too big a personality and too important in people's lives to be allowed to pass away like any other mere mortal.

The yearning for Elvis to live up to the anagram of his name, 'Lives', has produced a mass of myth-making. Devout followers point to signs and symbols at the time of his death to prove that he was not like other men. On the night he died, the lights in the Meditation Garden suddenly went out, and an angel appeared in the clouds over Graceland. One fan came home to find that her collection of Elvis records had mysteriously melted. That same evening, a couple discovered that the Elvis statue in their den had inexplicably broken apart.

Stacy Horowitz, a 23-year-old Las Vegas cigarette girl, is a typical 'Elvis Lives' believer. 'I was seven years old and watching cartoons on TV at my home in Fort Lauderdale, Florida, when my mother told me Elvis was dead,' she told me. 'My mother is a big fan. She has a pillow with Elvis's face on it and Elvis plates with a gold trim. She was very upset about the news, but I truly believe that he's still alive – he's out there somewhere. I *know* he's out there. He was in too much trouble from drugs, so he covered up his identity and just disappeared.'

CHAPTER TWENTY-FOUR

Farewell, Elvis Beatle

WHEN JOHN LENNON surveyed the Nutopian Embassy inside Apartment 72 at the Dakota, he was aware that, whatever else it might be, it was no Valhalla-on-the-Hudson. He and Yoko had reversed the sexual poles of *yin* and *yang*, and the result was that he had been well and truly emasculated.

Purged of the sin of his eighteen-month 'lost weekend' with May Pang, he had been happy to accept the part of house-husband, a role that placed him in a subordinate position to the fiercely ambitious and cash-conscious Yoko. Although he suffered the agonies of a flawed perfectionist, he found life easier to bear when he was not in charge. Having virtually abdicated her role as John's lover, Yoko had carved another niche for herself: he called her 'Mother'.

They had moved into the Dakota – the Colditz-style castle that John had seen from a distance on his first day in New York City – in 1973. Behind its portals, he enjoyed a semblance of normality and liked to give friends the impression that he had rejoined the human race, faults and all. Walking down a West Side street in 1978, he bumped into Henri Henriod, a Swiss-born roadie-turned-entrepreneur he had known since his early rock days in Hamburg. The first thing Henri noticed was the smart, businesslike three-piece suit that John was wearing and his neat haircut.

'Why didn't you give us a ring to say you were here?' John asked.

'I don't have your phone number.'

'I'm in the book,' John said with as much satisfaction as if he had just scored another hit single. Despite the fact that he had been obliged to use an alias, he was thrilled to be 'in the book' like any other New Yorker.

Henri asked him about Sean.

'He's incredible – and I should know, I'm his mum,' John replied.

'You certainly have changed,' said Henri.

'Well, of course I have. You know what it was like: the pressures, the threats. All that's gone now. Just look at me – out on my own!'

They walked unnoticed towards an art shop that John wanted to visit, two old friends chatting on a Manhattan sidewalk.

'We're buying a big farm in the West – at least I think it is,' said John. 'Yoko takes care of all the buying and selling. I just though it would be nice to raise Sean on one of those ranches like we used to see in the Elvis movies. Funny. Yoko still calls me "Elvis Beatle" if I start drifting back into the old behaviour. She spent ages convincing me that I was John Lennon and not a Beatle or an Elvis clone. Whenever I slip back, she just calls me "Elvis Beatle", and it snaps me out of the nightmare.'

This excursion on to the streets of New York proved, however, to be an increasingly rare outing. As that year passed, John stayed for longer and longer periods inside his apartment. The Dakota became his Graceland, and, like Elvis, he chose to spend much of his time inside the permanent night of his shuttered bedroom, where the giant TV screen that helped compensate for his short-sightedness was rarely switched off. Taut as a bowstring behind closed doors and darkened windows, he resented the time that Yoko devoted to other pursuits, even if some of them were aimed at multiplying what was left of his Beatle fortune. John was obsessed with a different kind of numbers game: the business of adding up figures in his life and discovering that they came to the highest number: nine. The Dakota obliged since it was situated on the corner of Central Park West and 72nd Street: seven plus two equalling nine. The apartment was No. 72, another nine.

The mansion block was circled by a moat and surrounded on three sides by a high black iron fence, which at regular intervals sprouted the head of an ominous Neptune flanked by pairs of sea-dragons. The cavernous entrance was guarded by a doorman in a bronze sentry box inside a black wrought-iron gate, over which an Indian head was carved in stone, and circled by the digits 1-8-8-1, numbers that, John noted, made eighteen or twice nine. He firmly believed that providence had brought him to the Dakota, and its connotations of the grotesque suited his mood.

The date of Elvis's demise had not escaped the notice of the numerologist in John: 16/8/1+9+7+7, or sixteen (two eights), one eight and twenty-four, which was three eights. If sixteen and eight were added to 1977, they made 2001, the popular title of Richard Strauss's classical composition *Thus Spake Zarathustra*, which Elvis had always used to announce his presence on stage.

John remembered Jayne Mansfield's tarot reader and shuddered as he recalled the man's prediction. He was already hooked on the divinations of Yoko's collection of astrologers, psychics, soothsayers, sorcerers and clairvoyants, without whom she was incapable of making a journey or a business decision. John believed in astrology so deeply that he would never venture far from home if Mercury were retrograde.

Like Elvis, he had become obsessed with Jesus and the idea that he, John, was a messianic figure. After his run-in with fundamental Christianity in 1966, he had gone through a phase of actually believing that he was a reincarnation of Christ and that it was his mission to spread love and peace on earth. Yoko's practitioners in the supernatural arts had cured him of that obsession, and he now happily described himself as a 'born-again pagan'. It was so much easier. He was greatly relieved to discover during one regression that he wasn't Christ at all, but a member of Egyptian royalty.

Early in 1979, she shaved off his beard. Preoccupied with his weight, the once-podgy Beatle dieted until he weighed less than 140 pounds.

Unlike Elvis, John didn't have to go out and earn a living. He slept on a mattress between a bedhead and a footboard made from church pews. He restricted himself to a macrobiotic diet of brown rice and vegetables, but drank coffee as well as tea. He smoked Gitanes *filtres* and marijuana and, like Howard Hughes, became obsessed with personal cleanliness. He bathed at least a dozen times a day and constantly washed his hands, but not because he feared bacteria. The washing was symbolic of discarding one disturbed personality as yet another surfaced inside his mind. His familiar granny glasses had long since given way to plastic spectacles with blue-tinted lenses.

John knew he was paranoid, but he regarded the condition as a virtue and described it to others as a 'heightened state of awareness'. Strangely, it did not compel him to pay much attention to his own protection, although he employed a full-time bodyguard for Sean.

With so much time on his hands, John became an avid reader. He bought books on religion, psychic phenomena, the occult and death, took large numbers of magazines and all the supermarket checkout tabloids from which he devoured every line of gossip on the rich and famous. There were some trips out of the city to look at (and occasionally buy) large houses that had seen better days. These included Cannon Hill, a wooden mansion on Long Island's North Shore with a magnificent view over Cold Spring Harbor. The Lennons had also invested in a farm in upstate New York, but hardly ever ventured there.

In March 1979, Yoko decided that John would benefit from a break in Florida. From the socialite Brownie McClean they rented El Solano, a large ocean-front mansion in West Palm Beach, and Julian Lennon was summoned from England to spend his 16th birthday with his father. There, on the first night, a restless John made tea in the kitchen for his aide Frederic Seaman, and told him of at least one reason why he was grateful for his wife's powers and mystic connections: 'When the Nixon government was trying to deport me, the reason they couldn't pull it off was because Yoko knew beforehand every move they were going to make in court. Her psychics told us what the government lawyers were planning to do, so we were always one step ahead. We simply outmanoeuvred the other side since Yoko could anticipate their every move, you see. They never knew what hit 'em.' Even a voodoo priestess had been brought in to cast a spell on the judge, John added.

It was during another holiday, in the summer of 1980 in Bermuda, that John decided he could return to music and write a new LP – his first for more than five years. Searching for a title, he wandered through the island's botanical gardens and came upon a label naming a plant 'Double Fantasy'. His search was over. The muse returned to him, and one by one the songs fell from his pen. Lennon's last great musical venture had begun.

At the piano of a rented island house, he crafted the music and lyrics for 'Watching the Wheels', explaining to Fred Seaman that the trick was to make the mind go blank – a prerequisite for receiving input from 'a higher power'. Yoko's absence only fired him to complete his last great collection. 'Paul never stopped working,' he recalled. 'We'd finish one album and I'd go off and get stoned and forget about writing new stuff, but he'd start working on new material right away, and as soon as he had enough songs, he'd want to begin recording again. I would have to scramble to come up with some songs of my own. I wrote some of my best songs under that kind of pressure.'

John returned to New York on 29 July and began assembling musicians to record his new works, instructing Yoko to negotiate a contract with the best available record company. As enthusiastic to get into the studio as he had been two decades earlier, he declared: 'It looks like I'm going to be 40 and life begins at 40, so they promise. And I believe it, too. I feel fine and I'm very excited. It's like, you know, hitting 21, like "Wow! What's going to happen next?"'

Double Fantasy was completed at breakneck speed and signed to David Geffen's fledgling label, Geffen Records. John and Yoko began giving interviews to promote the album. On 6 December 1980, John gave his last interview, and talked about the freedom he had discovered with the demise of Beatlemania: 'I would be walking around tense like, waiting for somebody to say something, or jump on me, and it took me two years to unwind. I can go right out this door now and go into a restaurant. You know how great that is? Or go to the movies?' However, the album, which featured John and Yoko on alternate tracks, was widely panned, the New York *Daily News* berating 'John's flabby, sentimental bit of vampish Elvis-isms'.

At 10.50 on the night of 8 December, the Ono Lennons pulled up in a limousine outside the Dakota after visiting a recording studio. The usual crowd of fans had gathered around the entrance to catch a glimpse of their hero or perhaps exchange a few words with him. John had had a haircut that day, short at the front with curls tied at the back, was clean-shaven and still slim but visibly older, peering through his glasses.

He had previously stopped signing autographs because, he joked, he had read somewhere that Robert Redford always refused such requests. But earlier that day, he had signed a copy of *Double Fantasy* for a chubby, bespectacled young man who didn't look as though he had a lot going for him. Now, as John passed him, the same young man, Mark Chapman, pumped five shots into his body. John staggered but kept going, unaware that he had been shot.

'It was so sudden . . . so sudden,' said Yoko. 'I didn't realize at the time that John had been hit. He kept walking. Then he fell and I saw the blood.'

When I heard the full story, I remembered John's aversion to autograph hunters from our trips to the US in the Sixties when Beatlemania rolled the King. And I thought of another thing: If Elvis had succeeded in having him banned from the United States, John Lennon would still be alive today.

As friends, fans and family descended on New York and mounted a pavement vigil outside the Dakota, Yoko announced that there would be no funeral for John but that, later in the week, she would set a time for prayers to be offered for his soul. Ringo and his new wife Barbara Bach were among those who visited Apartment 72 to pay their last respects. John's remains were taken in a body bag from the morgue to the Frank E. Campbell funeral chapel on Madison Avenue. (Eerily, Elvis's body had lain in the hospital morgue on Madison Avenue, Memphis.)

Two nights after the assassination, Doug MacDougall, the ex-FBI agent who was Sean's bodyguard, arrived at Yoko's office suite in the Dakota and placed a gift-wrapped box on a desk. 'What's that?' Fred Seaman asked. 'That,' replied Doug, 'was once the greatest rock musician in the world.' That afternoon he had picked up John's body from the funeral parlour and driven it to the Ferncliff Mortuary where he watched as it was placed in the oven. Two hours too late, Yoko had phoned to try to hold up the cremation, stating that Sean wanted to take a last look at his daddy.

I remembered John's prediction that he would die on a day with a nine in it two months after his birthday. Although he had been shot in New York before midnight on 8 October, it was already the 9th in his hometown of Liverpool, so I guess he got it right after all.

'John is a winner, Crispy Hutch,' the young Brian Epstein used to tell me during one of our 'we'll conquer the world' lunches in the days before the Mersey ran into the Mississippi. But the way destiny had played the cards, there *were* no winners.

CHAPTER TWENTY-FIVE

At The Colonel's Secret Shrine

INCONSPICUOUS AMONG the Lincolns, Cadillacs and stretch limousines, a small, plum-coloured Buick pulled neatly into the outside lane of the glass *porte-cochere* at the Las Vegas Hilton.

Behind the wheel was the vivacious 50-something former Miss Loanne Miller, once assistant to the hotel's publicity chief, Nick Naff. At her side was her husband of two years, Colonel Tom Parker, now in his 85th year. It was exactly noon on Columbus Day, Monday, 11 October 1993, and the Parkers were right on time for our appointment at the famous Elvis landmark.

'You be seated on the valet-parking boys' bench opposite the hotel entrance,' the Colonel had instructed me. 'Tell 'em you're expecting your uncle, the Colonel. Don't tell anyone where you're going, Chris, and on no account give anyone my address or telephone number.'

In the telephone call to my room at the Hilton three hours earlier, he had been as curt as he was specific. He knew better than anyone that no thorough investigation of the Elvis story would be complete without a close inspection of his own role in it.

Killing time before we met, I went up to the 30th floor, where the Imperial Suite was being torn apart to make way for three 'sky villas' suited to the more modern tastes of high rollers. A plaque commemorating the Elvis years at the Hilton had already been torn down and the place was as musty as a mausoleum.

I walked down the three curved steps into the sunken living-room, which had been the great partyroom when Elvis was in residence. The floor was bare and my footsteps echoed. The fireplace was still intact, flanked by bookshelves, which included at least one Elvis-owned titled: a paperback edition of *The Autobiography of a Yogi*. There was a Steinway grand piano awaiting removal, an unstocked bar and some old newspapers. The four bedrooms, six bathrooms, sauna, dining room, kitchen and pantry had also been abandoned. Elvis's bed on its raised dais resembled a pharaoh's sarcophagus that had been well and truly plundered. This was where he had acted out his sexual fantasies until drugs had ended the performance some time before he died.

The suite had the faded feel of an old movie set on a redundant back lot. The symbol had lost its substance, and an inconvenient piece of history was being swept on to the scrap heap.

From the patio, there was a view of the Las Vegas Country Club golf course, the greens neat and well-watered. It was a hot, clear day, and the mountain rim showed up on the cratered lunar horizon. Elvis might be long gone, but the Colonel was very much alive and we were having lunch.

The lift that took me down to the ground floor was packed with casino types eager for action. My own first visit to Las Vegas had been with the Beatles in 1964. Five years later, in this same hotel, the Colonel had taught me how to shoot craps. I remembered that night as I walked across the pink-and-gold-flowered carpet of the casino lounge, bigger now and brighter since chandeliers of the finest Austrian Strauss crystal had been installed. Carly Simon was singing 'You're So Vain' above the crash of coins. Row upon row of slot machines made an almost melodic, pipe organ sound as they spun. Cocktail waitresses in black tutus and Keno girls peddling $100,000 promises were continuously on the move.

Bells rang, change clanged and an avalanche of coins clattered out of a chrome mouth into the plastic bucket of a mute punter. Arms moved automatically up and down, brain and limbs programmed by a form of hypnosis. It was depressing just watching the 'grinds', as low rollers are called.

In a fenced-off area stood the $25-a-spin Double Diamond slots that the Colonel still liked to play. The supervisor, guarding the entrance to exclude the idly curious, was tight-lipped about him, but one regular told me: 'He sometimes feeds four machines at a time.' The Colonel's presence still created a buzz.

In the centre of the lounge, a scoreboard announced that the jackpot for the Fabulous Fifties was $1,180,935 and rising. Gambling machines using the latest state-of-the-art technology had names like Megabucks, Quartermania and Motherlode. At the craps table, the action was a little quieter.

It was here that the Colonel had painstakingly directed my gambling and enabled me to make a modest $300 profit in one two-hour session. Convinced that the sum would have been much larger if he had not forbidden me to raise the small stakes, I waited until he had gone to bed before gambling at my own pace. In twenty minutes, I had lost $3000.

'I met the Colonel the first day I arrived in Las Vegas in 1971,' recalled Henri Lewin. 'He arrived at 8.00 pm sharp, as he had promised, to discuss some points about Elvis's contract with me and my colleagues. We shook hands with the Colonel and took over the contract. The Colonel is a very good man: a handshake is all you need because he never goes back on his word. He knew what he wanted, he knew his product and he had things which other managers never thought about.

'For instance, he was interested in the prices we charged for dinner in the Showroom. He told me that the people who came to see Elvis couldn't afford to spend twenty-five or thirty dollars on a dinner. Make it twelve, he said, and we did.'

The Showroom was now billing *Starlight Express,* but right on cue, as I crossed the lobby at 11.45 and approached the bronze Elvis statue in the lobby, the King's voice could be heard singing 'Burning Love'. I moved through the brass revolving doors and out on to the concourse.

Shimmering above me, the Hilton rose like the three-feathered flight of a silver arrow embedded in the desert sand. Below the rooftop HILTON sign, the ghosts in the Imperial Suite played to an empty house. Elvis was gone, but the Colonel was about to make his entrance.

Mrs Parker II pulled the Buick away from the hotel, heading down Paradise Road. The Colonel sat next to her in the front passenger seat, safety belt buckled over his paunch. He neither cast a glance back at the hotel that had been the scene of his greatest managerial triumph, nor did he turn to take a closer look at me, yet he was able to venture: 'You haven't changed much.'

That was the Colonel, always pretending to have eyes in the back of his head when he had really stolen a glance in the rear-view mirror. I had known him for close to thirty years and had long since learned to respect the ritual dance that accompanied each and every one of our numerous meetings.

A half-hearted attempt to return the compliment was greeted by the response: 'For a man going on 85, I'm in reasonable shape. I'm up at five every morning to do my bendovers – managed twenty this morning, so this is a good day for me physically.'

The restaurant he had selected for lunch specialized in turkey dishes, and he paused to point with his stick to one of the huge birds roasting juicily on a spit in a large mock fireplace. He recalled 'the desert rat' he had told me I was eating midway during the first meal we had ever shared in his office at Paramount.

'I couldn't tell you what it was before you ate it or you would not have enjoyed it,' he said, savouring the moment. 'As a matter of fact, you liked it so much I was sorry I told you it was desert rat because you didn't like the sound of that at all. But you know what it really was, don't you?'

'No. I've always assumed it was desert rat.'

The Colonel laughed heartily. 'It was quail, one of the finest delicacies. They just happen to look like desert rats without the long tail.'

He always had to have his little joke, and to his way of thinking it was rarely funny unless it shocked the victim. Elvis had once warned me: 'Beware of that ol' man – he can be mean.'

It was in retaliation for such humour that Presley occasionally changed the lyrics of 'Are You Lonesome Tonight?' and, instead of 'Do you gaze at your doorstep and picture me there?', sang: 'Do you gaze at your bald head and wish you had hair?' Elvis convulsed in laughter each time he did it. It was one joke the Colonel never seemed to enjoy.

Leaning heavily on the arm of his second bride, the Colonel made his way to the round table she had reserved for our uncertain reunion. 'That woman is more a nursemaid to him than a wife,' had commented one who regularly observed the Parkers on their Vegas outings. My mind slipped back to my meeting with the first Mrs Parker at the apartment they occupied in the Westwood suburb of Los Angeles.

Like the Colonel's maternal grandmother, she was named Marie, although he called her 'Miz Ree' – so that it sounded like 'misery'. The dark-haired daughter of a Spanish-American war hero, Marie Mott had already been married twice and was the mother of a 10-year-old son by the time she encountered Thomas Andrew Barker. They met early in 1935 at the South Florida State Fair, where she worked on the Havatampa cigar stand. Elvis was so fond of Marie that he called his daughter Lisa Marie after her. It was because of Marie Parker that the famous Elvis scarf tradition had begun.

'Early in his career, the Colonel took a scarf from his wife's neck and put it around Elvis, saying, "Now you're ready. Go on stage and sing your heart out,"' Henri Lewin told me. 'During the performance, Elvis used the scarf to wipe his face and then he threw it into the audience. The scarf ritual started from there.'

For the last years of her life, Marie was stricken with cancer and was virtually comatose. The Colonel funded round-the-clock nursing for her at their house in Palm Springs until she died from a heart attack in November 1986. His gratitude to her clearly matched his love.

I studied the Colonel across the table as Mrs Parker II fussed over him. As always, he was dressed for comfort rather than effect. He wore navy blue serge slacks and an open-neck blue shirt with a fine white stripe in it. Just in case any newcomer to town might fail to recognize his famous figure, 'THE COLONEL' was embroidered on the breast pocket, clipped to which was his ever-ready pen. He was still very much a player.

In appearance, though, time and tide had actually corroded much of that familiar, well-paunched, heavy-jowled physique. Disfiguring liver spots had aged his skin even beyond his eighty-four summers – the backs of his hands were almost black with them – and the flesh hung in folds at his throat. His shoulder, broken years earlier when it was crushed by a revolving door in Los Angeles, was still giving him trouble.

'Here's a tip for you,' he said. 'If you're ever injured in an accident, don't move until the ambulance arrives. Lie still. I made the mistake of getting up and dragging myself off to see a doctor, and that allowed the building's insurers to maintain that I'd injured my arm some place else.'

When he removed his off-white Stetson hat – 'a present from George Strait, the country singer, it would have cost me $100 to buy' – it was to reveal a bald head made unsightly by wisps of white hair.

'Let's get this straight,' he told me following a cursory glance at the menu. 'I don't intend giving you any information about Elvis or about me that you haven't already come by through knowing us over the years. But I will guide you. I've already been offered a $2 million advance for my story against $4 for each copy they sell of the book plus the rights to a major motion picture based on it.' The expression of disbelief that must have registered on my face did not escape his attention: 'And if I were to expire before completing it, Mrs Parker here has all the information to finish it,' he added.

Knowing the Colonel as I did and the games he played, I doubted that even Marie (his book-keeper as well as his wife) knew many of the secrets of his highly confidential relationship with Elvis. The arrival of a waitress other than the one who usually served him disconcerted him for a moment, but he rattled off his order. He liked everything to be familiar – people, places, things.

I asked him about the Elvis display in the Hilton lobby, which included a poem he had written in honour of his star. 'Those people over there know nothing,' he stormed. 'I don't know why you're bothering talking to them. They can't even get the display right. You see that fancy white suit in the glass case next to Elvis's statue? The inscription says he wore it on the first night of his first engagement there. That's nonsense – he never wore anything that decorative until two or three years into his contract at the Hilton. I wrote to the president of the hotel about that.'

He paused.

'By the way, I also called him to tell him you were arriving. Are they looking after you?'

His tone gave me reason to interpret 'looking after you' as 'keeping a close eye on you'.

The Colonel plunged an inquisitorial spoon into the bowl of turkey soup that the unfamiliar waitress had placed before him. 'Where's the turkey?' he demanded. 'I usually get more meat in my soup than this.'

The girl smiled sweetly and began to walk away, but the Colonel was not letting her off that lightly. 'You won't get much of a tip,' he called after her, ignoring the looks of disdain from other diners.

This was his less acceptable side. But that was the nature of the real Colonel Parker, the man who counted the pieces of turkey meat in his soup to make sure he wasn't short-changed. I realized that I had been as guilty as anyone of taking him at face value. The real man had successfully eluded me as well.

Mrs Parker II did her best to lighten the mood with small talk as she wiped drops of greasy soup from her husband's shirt. Then, from a phial she carried in her handbag, she produced three capsules.

'Time for your vitamins, Colonel,' she said. Even Loanne did not call him Tom.

At this point, I knew that the truth I wanted to establish to my own satisfaction was a simple one. Had the Colonel ever loved Elvis? I had watched the two men fall into each other's arms after Elvis's comeback performance in 1969, and I had seen the Colonel's eyes glisten. But were they tears of love?

The first promise the Colonel ever made to Elvis was that he would take his million dollars' worth of talent and turn it into a million dollars. In fact, he had turned it into $1.5 billion. Now it was the Memphis Mafia who were coining it and the Colonel did not like that one little bit.

'I don't approve of those guys who worked for Elvis making money out of their stories about him,' he said, conveniently forgetting his own $2 million offer. 'One of his boys came to me and told me he'd been offered $100,000 for his story. I said, "Be sure to write about Elvis bailing you out when they were going to take your house away. And be sure to tell 'em it was Elvis who paid the doctor's bills when your wife was sick." But they never write that stuff. That's not what they think people want to read about him, right?'

His sole client had been dead for more than sixteen years, and yet he worked day and night to preserve the image of 'Elvis & the Colonel'. Most of the dollars that the Elvis industry still generated now went direct to the Presley estate after some highly public litigation instigated by Priscilla had prised it free of the Colonel's experienced and, some said, voracious grasp. One lawsuit claimed that he had defrauded the Presley estate out of $5 million. Rebutting the charges, he had counter-sued. He had informed me at the time: 'I'm no cheat. These charges are unfair to me and Elvis. I highly respected Elvis Presley, and I have made every effort to honour his name and preserve his memory with dignity. These unjust charges not only attack my name and reputation, they are an insult to the memory of Elvis and his father, Vernon. Just as I did with Elvis and Vernon when they were alive, I have always dealt fairly and openly with the executors.'

But in the twilight of his life, the Colonel was keen to talk about money. I jotted down on a paper place mat the stream of figures that came pouring out from his cerebral computer. There was the $50,000 he boasted about getting Ed Sullivan to part with for Elvis's three appearances. 'The standard fee then was just $750. He offered $1500 for Elvis, but I held out for five weeks until he came up with the $50,000. I told Brian Epstein he should have got me to negotiate the money for the Beatles' appearances on *Sullivan* – I'd have got them a lot more.'

While the waitress, still under threat of an abysmal tip, served his turkey fillet and side salad, the Colonel continued in full cry about the deals he had squeezed and the sums he had handed over to charity. 'I've kept a list of every dime I have given away. For example, every year I paid $125 to one cause so they could send a kid to summer camp. Well, on my 80th birthday, I gave 'em $10,000 so they could send eighty boys.

'I've been offered $50,000 to do a lecture tour of Australia, but I'm not ready to go yet,' added the man who had taken several minutes to negotiate the few steps from his car to the restaurant table. 'Right now, sitting talking to you, I could be getting $12,500 for giving a talk somewhere in this country. The offers keep coming in, but I'm too busy working for Barron Hilton. I fix the hotel's radio spots just like I used to when Elvis was singing there.

'I've been loyal to the people I've done business with. RCA gave me a plaque to commemorate our fifty-seven years together, I've been with Hill & Range and the William Morris Agency for fifty years as well. People these days are just too fickle – look at the way they're trying to destroy Michael Jackson. He's a good boy. He came over to see me and have some pictures taken just the other week when he was in Vegas. I feel sorry about what has been happening to the kid – it would never have happened if I'd been managing him. You never saw Elvis in a mess like that.'

The food came and went, and Loanne Parker paid for the meal, conveniently forgetting to undertip the waitress who had dared to serve the Colonel a bowl of soup light on turkey meat. As we left the restaurant, Nevada's most famous yet reclusive resident announced: 'Now I'm going to take you back to the house and show you a few things nobody gets to see.'

I wasn't sure who was more surprised – me or Mrs Parker II. I had repeatedly been reminded during lunch that he would do nothing to enlighten me on the subject of Elvis or the secrets of his own life. Loanne, however, was truly astonished. Raising one eyebrow, she declared: 'You *are* honoured – the Colonel hardly ever takes anyone inside our home. We're very private. It's our refuge. The last one he let in was Bill Clinton's mother, Mrs Virginia Kelley, and he thought twice about that!'

We drove in silence past the forest of neon hotel signs, which glared brighter than the afternoon sun. Marquees proclaimed *Starlight Express* at the Hilton, Engelbert Humperdinck at Bally's and the imminent opening of such new palaces as the Luxor, an enormous black-glass pyramid of Egyptian splendour, Kirk Kerkorian's MGM Grand Hotel (which Barbra Streisand would open, twenty-two years after she had opened the International for the same tycoon) and the Treasure Island hotel/theme park complex. The city was gambling billions on its future.

They were made for each other, Las Vegas and the Colonel. 'You're having lunch with *the* Colonel?' or 'You know the *Colonel?*' were common reactions among Las Vegans. The subject of how well the Colonel looked after his own money was a matter of some debate. An inveterate gambler, he was said by many to have handed much of his personal fortune over to the casino operators as fast as Elvis could earn it. One who knew him well, Liberace's former manager Seymour Heller, says he believes the Colonel lost a million a year on the tables.

'Every time he wanted a rack of chips, he got $25,000 worth at a time,' said Heller. 'He always played roulette. They had to set up a private table for him, and you dared not talk to him – no matter how much he liked you – while he was gambling. You cannot win at roulette if you play all the numbers and he played all the numbers. He put down a big stack on some and just a few chips on others. If he hit the big stack, then he made a lot of money. He had to get something back, but he lost an average of a million dollars a year there.'

As we drove on, I asked the Colonel what keepsakes of Elvis he treasured most. Neatly anticipating that he might yet again break his self-imposed code of silence, Loanne interjected: 'Oh, I think your memories are the most precious, don't you, Colonel?' Ignoring his wife's remark, Parker replied: 'His personal letters. He wrote me a lot of letters, you know, warm and understanding letters. All handwritten. I keep 'em at the house with the rest of my memorabilia. I sold a lot of the stuff to Graceland for their exhibition, but I hung on to the letters and a few other things. You'll see.'

It was a curious statement. I had heard the tape on which the Colonel had given evidence to the district attorney's investigators, which told a different story. 'While he was in the service, there was very little contact with him,' he had said. 'He called three or four times, long distance. I never got any letters. Elvis was not in the habit of writing letters. I got a thank-you note from him one time, but that was all he ever wrote in twenty years.'

Our conversation turned to Elvis's early TV appearances. I asked the Colonel how he felt about the time that Ed Sullivan had filmed him from the waist up.

'Naw, that was a publicity stunt Sullivan himself dreamed up,' came the surprising answer, the first indication that the old man was beginning to let his guard down. 'I can tell you now that nobody really wanted to censor Elvis, but those stories in the papers got the show bigger ratings than it had ever had. Sullivan used Elvis, but it didn't do us no harm.'

Having given another man credit for what was one of the most successful publicity stunts in the crucial early stages of Elvis's career, I wondered aloud if the Colonel had suggested that Elvis dress in a tuxedo for the Frank Sinatra show in 1960.

'No, that was the Sinatra people's idea,' he replied. 'They came to me and said, "How do you feel about Elvis wearing a tux?" and I said, "Well, that'll cost you an extra hundred bucks for each one of us." They asked why and I told 'em, " 'Cos we don't have tuxedos and that's how much they cost." They went for it – still got mine at the house, and the shiny black shoes they paid for to go with it.'

The one idea he did take credit for was the very one Elvis was known to have hated: singing 'Hound Dog' to a real canine on the *Steve Allen Show*. 'And they paid for the top hat and tails,' he said.

As Loanne swung the Buick into a small private estate, a guard in the gatehouse raised the barrier and saluted the Colonel ' as though he were a five-star general. The impressive entrance to the compound was deceptive: a local realtor said later that the larger homes ranged in value between $350,000 and $450,000, a far cry from Beverly Hills' prices, and the Parkers did not have one of the larger houses. Mrs Parker pressed a button to open an electronic door and nosed the Buick inside. The Colonel was anything but abashed by his unpretentious abode.

'You ever see a garage as clean as this?' he demanded. It was carpeted, too. 'It's nice here, isn't it? Private. But cold in the wintertime.'

We stepped on to a modest porch and through the front door into a hallway that was lined with framed pictures, many of which I had first seen on his walls at Paramount. There were pictures of Elvis and of the Colonel with famous friends including one of Elvis's manager with Frank Sinatra and Spencer Tracy. One by one, he read out the glowing testimonials. Both of his favourite female singers, Dolly Parton and Barbra Streisand, had paid pen-and-ink homage to this man, who now stood waving his walking stick at their likenesses as if it were a baton pointing out the areas to be taken on a battlefield plan.

'Somewhere here, I've got a letter from Maurice Chevalier in his own handwriting, saying, "If there were more colonels like you, Colonel, we wouldn't need no wars."' He found one from Elvis. 'Here, read this one out,' he commanded. It was a cable humbly extolling Elvis's thanks to his manager for 'the loyalty you have shown to me and my family', expressing his implicit trust and promising to stay with him 'through thick and through thin'. Yet another pledged Elvis's services to Colonel Thomas Parker 'in all matters'. This one was signed by Vernon and Gladys Presley.

The Colonel had explained his early dealings with Elvis on the investigators' tape: 'As a manager and promoter, I tried to get him in motion pictures, record contracts, tours and personal appearances. For a while, we had a contract when he was underage. Then for a while we went without a contract – we went on a handshake. And then, when I had to sign for Elvis and so on, we made a new contract.

'My percentage fluctuated. It started out at 25 per cent, some deals I created were 50 per cent – some deals were separate. They varied between those two figures. We did our own promotion, the tours and so on. Back in 1955, I was booking shows, and Elvis had a manager who called me to see if I could use Elvis on some dates. We played Memphis and I met Elvis backstage. Then his father called me up and said they wanted to make a new record contract for Elvis. At the time, he was with Sam Phillips at Sun Records. From 1955 to 1960, I was in a contractual agreement to promote Elvis in all fields.'

We had paused briefly in the Parkers' wholesome parlour when the Colonel announced: And now you are going where precious few have been allowed to tread.' The look of astonishment returned to Loanne's face, and she made herself scarce while I was led into a den: the Colonel's secret shrine.

The room resembled an Aladdin's cave crammed from wall to wall and stacked from ceiling to floor with bright, gaudy artefacts. There were numerous clocks loudly keeping time, a myriad souvenirs from the Colonel's circus days and at least a score of brass and ceramic elephants mutely contemplating me. Everything had been carefully dusted and neatly positioned.

This was why the Colonel was obsessed about security. He had gathered the most treasured possessions of his entire career into one irreplaceable collection. From a hand-carved swivel armchair, he could focus on any object of his choosing and quietly reminisce about the past glory it symbolized. To lose this to a thief would break his great sentimental heart. Instantly the showman, the Colonel pointed to two huge glass spheres on his desk.

'Biggest crystal balls in the world,' he growled. 'I've been offered $20,000 for 'em.' Another presentation piece – a china circus montage – would, he said, have fetched $100,000 if he had accepted the offer. Many more framed pictures were carefully grouped to make identification easier. In one area, he kept autographed pictures of the US Presidents he had known: Lyndon B. Johnson, Jimmy Carter, Ronald Reagan, George Bush and Bill Clinton, although surprising, in view of the part he had played in Elvis's drug-busting activities, there was no sign of Richard Nixon.

'Have you ever seen so many pictures of Presidents?' the Colonel demanded, impressed by his own trophies. Pride of place in the group was occupied by a black and white photograph of the Colonel and Eddy Arnold with President Harry S. Truman.

'I flew with Mr Truman in a helicopter to Mr Johnson's ranch when he was entertaining the President of Mexico to dinner,' he explained. 'Eddy Arnold had been invited, and he asked me if I would go with him. The guy in charge of the helicopter in Austin said, "Colonel Parker, your bus will be here in an hour." I said, "I don't have a bus. I understood I was going in the helicopter." Eddy Arnold was to entertain there, so I remained seated on the couch until the guy came back and said, "I was mistaken – you're going on the helicopter with President Truman." I'd been a friend of Mr Johnson ever since he ran for Congress because we went out in Texas to entertain for his campaign.'

Speaking of political winners, the Colonel drew my attention to a signed photograph of Margaret Thatcher. 'Somebody came here from

Mrs Thatcher's office to see me and I gave him a signed picture of myself to take back to the Prime Minister,' he said. 'She returned the compliment to me. But I never use Mrs Thatcher in any of my stories because it's private and it wouldn't be fair. There's a certain protocol involved.'

There was a picture of the Colonel with Andy Gibb, the tragic Bee Gee brother killed by drugs, and with Joe Esposito and Frank Sinatra. While I examined an exquisite model snowman carved in gold, he produced from the drawer of his desk a boxed cigar bearing his name and handed it to me.

'It's my last one, but I shan't be needing it. Woke up one morning and saw an ad in the paper. It said if you sent this guy $98 he would stop you smoking. I thought, "Here's a good way to stop smoking," so I gave it up there and then and saved myself $98 into the bargain.'

Seated in his swivel chair, he pointed his stick again – this time at the cupboard behind me. 'Open it up and take a look inside,' he said. A massive file detailed every dollar that he had ever donated to charity: a round-up in the preface showed a total of $447,000 with a further figure detailing 'expenses absorbed'. Then he pointed to a large tin box. It was crammed with copies of telegrams sent by 'Elvis and the Colonel'.

'There's nearly 4000 in there. That's how I kept Elvis's name alive while he was in Germany,' he said. 'I sent famous people wires on their birthdays, their wedding days, their tour openings. When Elvis got home, he would keep coming to me with a big grin on his face saying that people were thanking him for the cables he had sent them. "Gee, Colonel," he'd say, "I don't remember wiring those people." That's when I showed him that box you're holding.'

'Do you miss him?' I asked, not a question anyone had ever been able to pose to the Colonel before, let alone get an answer. He considered his reply.

'Frankly, no,' he said finally. 'There's no point missing what you haven't got. Elvis is dead and buried, but there's still his business to take care of, and if I waste time mourning what has passed, there's plenty of people ready to come in and cut the ground from under our feet.'

He had described his working relationship with Elvis to the investigators: 'We had a respect for each other, but we were never close socially. I was around as often as I could. In the early days, I spent about 50 per cent of my time with him. And when he moved into motion pictures, I was spending all my time with him.'

I pressed on. Was Elvis the son he never had?

Leaning forward and speaking in hushed tones, the old man replied: 'I have to be honest and tell you, I can't say yes to that one either. I never looked upon him as a son, but he was the *success* I always wanted. You know, although we were together a lot of years, we never got too close. That's the easiest way to bust up a good partnership. He had his friends and I had mine. I looked after my money and he took care of his – I never tried to advise him on what to do with it, I just made sure we got paid every dime we were entitled to. I couldn't have done that if I'd been out there worrying what he was up to and what time he was getting home at night.

'Managers who operate that way and party with their artists don't stay managers for too long. On the other hand, Elvis knew if he had a problem he could call me any hour of the day or night. There would be times when he'd be home in Memphis, perhaps at two in the morning, and he'd go into a room where he could be in private and call me to talk something over. I had promised him I'd always be there for him, and I was.'

Henri Lewin agrees with that. 'The Colonel is a strong, very capable man and he never took advantage of anything,' he said. 'If Elvis didn't have the Colonel, Elvis would have given away 100 per cent before he had received it. He needed a man like that.'

I asked the Colonel about one of the most controversial areas of his partnership with Elvis. Did he sweet-talk Vernon and Gladys into signing that first contract? The reply was louder: 'Of course Vernon signed the contract for him because Elvis was under-age, but, you know, I never handled Elvis's money A lot of people who don't know about our arrangements have looked at me in a critical light and asked, "Whatever happened to Elvis's money?" Vernon was his business manager and *he* made his investments.'

Remembering Vernon's early conviction for forgery, I asked as delicately as I could: 'Was he qualified to do so?'

'Well, I guess he knew enough to back off when something didn't look too good. But Elvis trusted Vernon, and Vernon trusted me – he said some very nice things about me on TV and radio. Then as soon as Elvis died, he wrote me a letter asking me to stay on and handle everything. When Vernon himself died a year later, Priscilla wrote me a similar letter, so I stayed on.'

'What was Gladys really like?'

The Colonel paused and gazed at a picture of Elvis on his desk before replying. 'Gladys was a very worried woman, she worried a lot,' he said not unkindly. 'She was very anxious for her boy, and she didn't really want to know about Elvis the star. He was her son, and when he was on the road, even though he was bringing a lot of money home, she worried about him. She couldn't handle his fame. If she spotted a reporter approaching the house, she would run inside and lock the door.

'I have to say that Gladys Presley was not a well woman, and I suppose I was never comfortable around her. But I was managing Elvis, not his parents.'

On the DA's tapes, the Colonel had answered questions about Elvis's health. 'The first time I noticed any change in him was when Elvis went home one time from Vegas in 1974, and he was home about a month,' he had said. 'He came to my house and he looked terrible. I told him he didn't look well. That's when Elvis told me to stay out of his personal life. He said "No disrespect, Colonel, but I know what I'm doing. Stay out of my personal life."

'I'd say that I first noticed his drugs in the late Sixties, not that it specially concerned me. When we were making the movies, he was always good, he was on time, learned his lines and completed the job. Then he went home. What he did when he got there, I don't know because I did not go down to Memphis that often. When I really got concerned was that time in 1974 when he came to my house: he'd gained too much weight. Now, I spoke out, but I couldn't get involved. There were a couple of complaints sometimes when he didn't do a show too good. I was aware he was treated by physicians in Las Vegas and Palm Springs, but I had no personal experience of his visits.

'Sonny West told me one time that he was getting prescriptions in other people's names, but I didn't know about that. Dr Nick was often in the dressing room before a performance. There were always people around [Elvis]. He'd be hyped up and anxious about the show. I never saw Elvis being given drugs, though I know that Dr Nick has said he prepared medications for Elvis before he went on stage and when he came off.

'Let's face it, Dr Nick was there for some reason or he wouldn't have been there. I don't know how you'd judge the overall reaction. You know every performer has good days and bad. He had some bad days, other times he was outstanding. The only time I ever saw him sick while he was on stage was in Vegas one night, when he went off stage for about a minute, then came back and finished his show. He only ever cancelled once – in 1974 in Louisiana when he couldn't go on. A local doctor was called and pronounced him sick and he was flown back to Memphis and admitted to hospital. I was already in the next town and had to cancel the rest of the tour. That was the only time.

'I never heard of him being admitted to hospital for an overdose of drugs. True enough, I was concerned some times, but I couldn't talk to him about it. I never saw drugs. I never saw any member of the entourage in a bad way. I never saw them stumbling or falling about. They may have when they were not working. If they were stumbling, I'd have noticed it. They were all concerned, I'm sure. It's a sad situation. I had no control over him. That was Elvis's choice.'

In 1977, I had asked the Colonel why he had refused to express his grief to a sorrowing world. 'If I shed a tear after Elvis died, nobody saw it,' he told me. 'If some people had as much as seen my eyes glaze, they'd have been busy trying to get their hands into our pockets. And I couldn't have had that. No, sir! My partners – Elvis and Vernon – wouldn't have liked that one little bit. Elvis is still with us in spirit, and I won't let up for a minute while he's still around. Elvis would turn over in his grave if I retired.'

His views altered somewhat in the intervening years, especially after writers and film-makers began taking a critical look at his relationship with Elvis. In 1991, he commented, 'Everyone seems to think I was a tyrant to Elvis. I don't know why – maybe he painted that picture himself. He was difficult from the start. He always thought of himself as a superman and I had a helluva job controlling him.' This sounded much more like the real story as I understood it.

When the plum-coloured Buick deposited me back at the Hilton, the Colonel was still calling the shots. 'What you gotta do is go to Memphis and talk to the people who really loved Elvis,' he directed. 'Go there in January for the birthday celebrations. Find out where the fans are staying near Graceland, and put a sign on the hotel noticeboard saying that you're holding a soda pop-and-cookies party for them. They're the ones who know the real Elvis.'

Soda pop and cookies. Nickel mugshots sold for a dime. Fake canaries, phoney hotdogs and toothless lions. Perhaps he was, after all, just a hustler who had got lucky, but I seriously doubted it. However much he might deny it, the Colonel had really loved Elvis Presley, but not always for the right reasons. His last words made me recall a promise made on the doorstep of 565 Perugia Way the night Elvis had met the Beatles thirty years ago.

'You know, I never did get that Shetland pony from Brian,' he said. With a wave in the direction of the phantoms lining the ramparts, the old magician was gone, and the Snowmen's League was once again in recess.

After Lisa Presley (she has dropped the 'Marie') married Michael Jackson in the Dominican Republic in May 1994, I rang the Colonel for his reaction. He replied curtly: 'Some lady stopped me and said, "What do you think about the marriage?" I said, "Somebody got married in your family?" She said, "Aw, you know what I'm talking about." So I said, "No, I don't. Goodbye."

'That isn't my affair – that belongs to the Presley family. Sure, Michael has been to see me because I've known him a long time. But I don't get involved in other people's business. I'm like the bull, you know – I don't know nothing. I only know about Elvis and the Colonel.'

DIANA'S NIGHTMARE
THE FAMILY

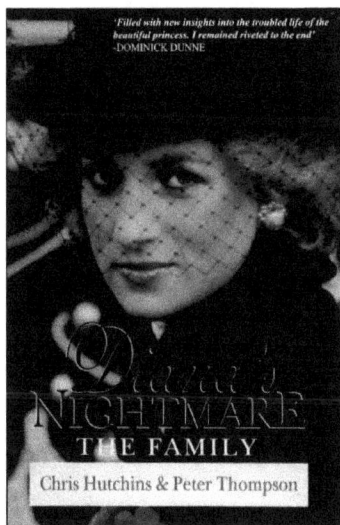

CHRIS HUTCHINS & PETER THOMPSON

EVEN BEFORE Lady Diana Spencer married into the most revered family on earth, she had her suspicions that the kith and kin of Prince Charles were not all they seemed-to-be. No sooner had she become the Princess of Wales and moved into Kensington Palace than her fears were confirmed: the House of Windsor constituted a flawed dynasty. She found herself trapped in a world of scandal, deceit and treachery. *Diana's Nightmare* reveals the previously untold secrets Diana discovered about her royal relatives. This book exposes how intensely Charles and Camilla Parker Bowles contrived to exclude her, it reveals the Queen was angry and bitter at her family's indiscretions, how the Queen Mother's indifference was matched only by Prince Philip's blind range over Diana's determination to find her own path, what really went on between the Duke and Duchess of York and how Prince Edward witnessed Diana's tantrums at Balmoral . . . Diana's own secret life.

And much, much more . . .

HARRY
THE PEOPLE'S PRINCE

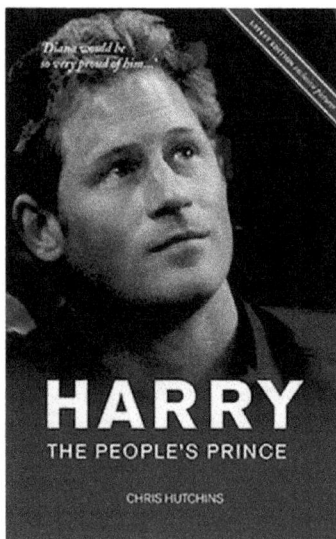

CHRIS HUTCHINS

PRINCE HARRY is the most interesting – indeed the most exciting - member of the Royal Family and this no-holds-barred biography tells his story for the first time. Son of the late Princess Diana – the most famous woman on Earth – and Prince Charles, the next king, and brother of William, the king after that, he is determined to live by his mantra: 'I am what I am'. From a childhood overshadowed by his parents' troubled marriage and scarred by the tragic death of his mother, to his brilliant public performances at the Queen's Diamond Jubilee celebrations, the London Olympics and his brother's wedding, this book charts the remarkable journey of a young man with an extraordinary destiny. It also reveals details of his extraordinary love life, telling for the first time what caused his affair with Cressida Bonas to collapse. The author has enjoyed unparalleled access to a wide variety of people whose lives Harry has touched: senior aides, humble members of palace staff, aristocrats, bodyguards, school friends, comrades-in-arms . . . and old flames. They piece together the tale of a young man who admirably has created a life so different from the one set out for him by what he describes as 'an accident of birth'.

'Warm-hearted. Brave. But at times recklessly impulsive. A new biography gives a fascinating psychological insight into the forces that shaped Harry, the playboy Prince.'
Daily Mail.

ABRAMOVICH

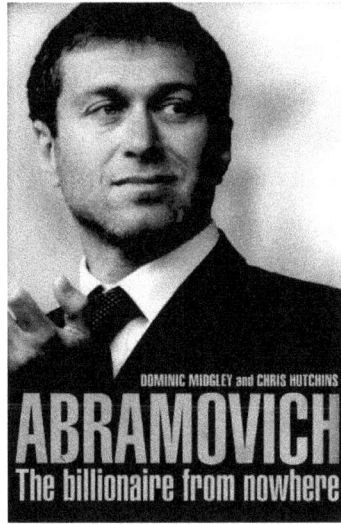

DOMINIC MIDGLEY and CHRIS HUTCHINS

ABRAMOVICH
The billionaire from nowhere

DOMINIC MIDGLEY AND CHRIS HUTCHINS

'AN INCREDIBLE STORY' – *Mail on Sunday*; 'Well researched and fluently written' – *The Times*; 'Draws a picture of a man of immense ruthlessness, nerve and charm . . . offers a Vanity Fair of Russian oligarchy' – *The Spectator*; A superb insight into the Chelsea boss . . . a must read for both football fans and business tycoons' – *Sunday Business Post*; 'A well-researched investigation into the life and times of Chelsea's owner' – *World Soccer*; 'The first sustained effort to uncover the making of Chelsea's oligarch' – *Guardian*'; 'Authors Dominic Midgley and Chris Hutchins go to commendable lengths to tell the story' – *Sunday Times*; 'Where this book sets itself apart is in its quest to discover Abramovich's true identity. Interviews with his childhood friends, neighbours and teachers in Russia offer an original perspective on the man while access to the informed such as Boris Berezovsky, his one-time mentor, provides a picture of a canny dealmaker and consummate politician' – *The Times*'; 'Most fascinating account . . . should be read by anyone not just with an interest in sport but also in business and in politics' – *Press and Journal*.

FERGIE CONFIDENTIAL

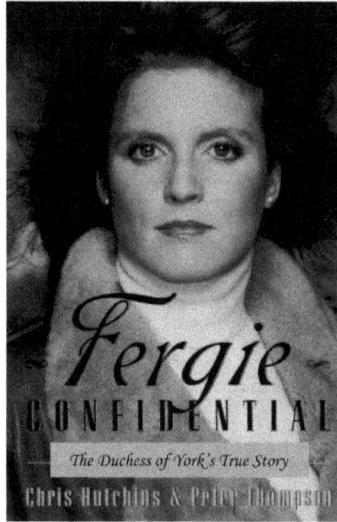

CHRIS HUTCHINS & PETER THOMPSON

IT SEEMS that almost every week Sarah Ferguson - the Duchess of York, known to one and all as Fergie - makes headlines with her efforts to re-brand herself and explain her troubles. There are the weight-loss problems, the ongoing differences with the Royal Family and her financial difficulties. But how did it all start? It seemed like a fairy-tale come true when Sarah married the Queen's favourite son, Prince Andrew, and became one of the best-known women in the world. She was feted wherever she went – and she went everywhere. But the Duchess's world was to come crashing down in spectacular fashion.

We all heard the rumours, now here's a book that sets out the facts about all the scandals. Finally, the explosive truth from two experts – CHRIS HUTCHINS, the writer who broke the palace-rocking story of Fergie's risqué liaison with handsome Texan Steve Wyatt, and PETER THOMPSON, a former editor of London's *Daily Mirror*, the paper that ran the sexy St. Tropez stories of Fergie and her "financial advisor" Johnny Bryan. The book also details her often-tempestuous relationship with Princess Diana and how both women decided to end their marriages.

ATHINA:
THE LAST ONASSIS

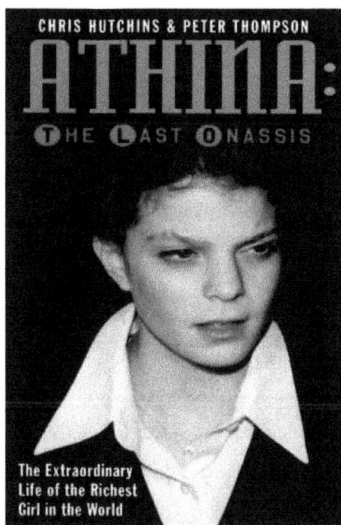

CHRIS HUTCHINS & PETER THOMPSON

BY WAY of light relief as Greece continues to stand face-to-face with financial meltdown, it is well worth visiting the story of Athina Onassis Roussel, who became the richest little girl in the world when she inherited unimaginable wealth from her heiress mother, Christina Onassis. This compelling book explores the legend of Athina's grandfather, the shipping magnate Aristotle Onassis, and examines the legacy that became Athina's extraordinary birthright as The Last Onassis. No 20th-century saga features more great names than that of the Onassis dynasty; the Kennedys - including JFK and his widow Jacqueline, who became Onassis's second wife - the opera diva Maria Callas who longed to be the third; and Prince Rainier and Princess Grace, with whom he fought a celebrated feud for control of Monte Carlo. The cast list is endless: the Hollywood stars Elizabeth Taylor, Richard Burton, Marilyn Monroe and Greta Garbo, the politicians Sir Winston Churchill and Richard Nixon, the tycoons Stavros Niarchos and Howard Hughes and the FBI chief J. Edgar Hoover.

ELVIS A PERSONAL MEMOIR

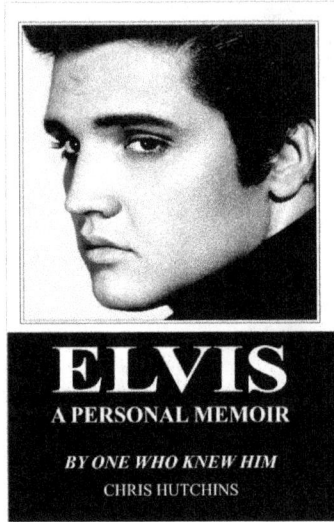

CHRIS HUTCHINS

ELVIS PRESLEY and the author Chris Hutchins got to know each other through a common mentor – Colonel Tom Parker. The man who managed the King of rock 'n roll treated the writer as a confidant. And that's what makes this book unique. Right from the earliest pages, the Colonel reveals his true feeling about Elvis and the unusual relationship they had. In one of the many letters he wrote to Hutchins he explains for the first time why it wasn't his fault that Elvis never travelled to perform outside the United States. Moving as freely within the Presley circle as he was able to, the author came into close contact not only with Elvis himself but also his family, friends and staff: everybody from Elvis's wife Priscilla, daughter Lisa, father Vernon, tour manager and closest companion Joe Esposito, show business buddies like Tom Jones – even his cook Mary Jenkins knew and talked to Chris Hutchins who even took the Beatles to party at his home. That's what makes this book A Personal Memoir.

THE BEATLES
MESSAGES FROM JOHN, PAUL, GEORGE AND RINGO

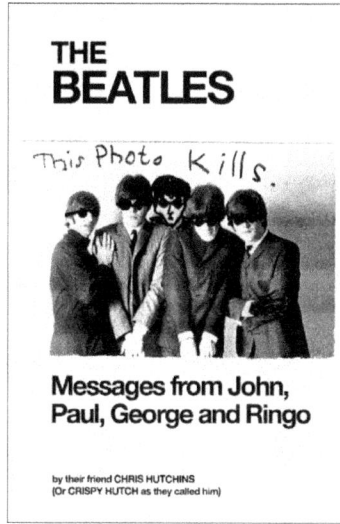

CHRIS HUTCHINS

THIS IS the inside story of the Beatles by a writer who knew them from the Hamburg days and was with them through the height of Beatlemania. He relates the secrets of their lives on the road and at home, and tells the full story of the night he took them to party with Elvis Presley and its astonishing consequences. John's secret shrine to a Beatle who died; the night Bob Dylan came to call; the Hollywood siren John mixed a most unusual cocktail for. It's John, Paul, George and Ringo as you have never read about them before ...

GOLDSMITH

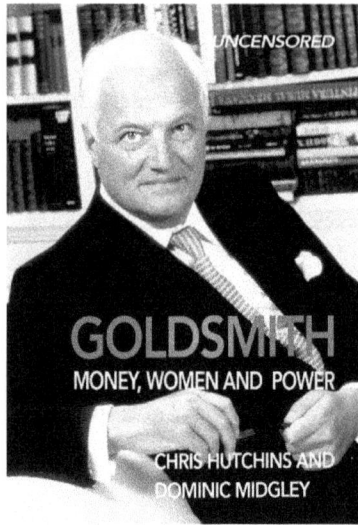

CHRIS HUTCHINS & DOMINIC MIDGLEY

THE INSIDE story of Sir James Goldsmith's elopement with the teenage daughter of a Bolivian multi-millionaire . . . The incongruous friendship between his second wife and his last mistress . . . The daring business deals that made him a billionaire . . . How Richard Branson pushed him into his own swimming pool and was told he was no longer a welcome guest . . . Lady Annabel Goldsmith's fascinating relationship with Princess Diana . . . The sad tale of the eldest son living in Central America . . . The niece who made her name in soft porn films . . . The full story of his £20-million push for political power . . . And an Indian doctor's account of how he tried in vain to help Goldsmith in his battle against cancer.

MR CONFIDENTIAL

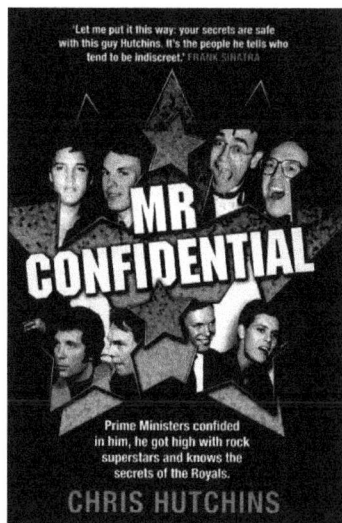

'Let me put it this way: your secrets are safe with this guy Hutchins. It's the people he tells who tend to be indiscreet.' FRANK SINATRA

MR CONFIDENTIAL

Prime Ministers confided in him, he got high with rock superstars and knows the secrets of the Royals.

CHRIS HUTCHINS

CHRIS HUTCHINS

ELVIS PRESLEY, Princess Diana, Elton John, the Beatles, Tom Jones, Fergie Duchess of York, Richard Branson – they all figure in this extraordinary book of revelations. Previously untold stories of royals, celebrities and the occasional politician are all relayed in this rich and unrivalled mix of anecdotes by the master.

Chris Hutchins is a journalist and author. For more than a decade his *Confidential* column chronicled the lives of the rich and famous and was featured in three national newspapers. Think of a moment in popular culture in the last three decades and the chances are that Hutchins either covered it or got caught up in it.

At one time he also operated the UK's most successful music PR company, shaping the careers and sharing the lives of Tom Jones, the Bee Gees, Eric Clapton and many other international stars. As a writer on the *New Musical Express,* he toured the world with the Beatles and took them to meet Elvis Presley who became his friend.

THE WHO BEFORE THE WHO

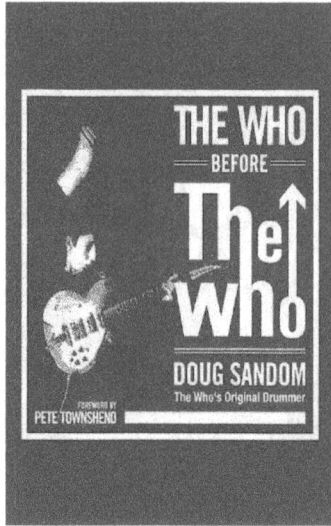

DOUG SANDOM

DOUG SANDOM'S part in the making of the most exciting rock band in the world can never be underestimated. He joined The Who – then known as The Detours – as their drummer in 1962 after an unexpected meeting with Roger Daltrey on a west London street. It was a time when fires were being lit under the music scene worldwide, everything had to change and The Detours had a long way to go to become revolutionary leaders in their field.

Having finally decided to write his memoirs, Doug Sandom chronicles each stage of the band's transition right up to his, Roger Daltrey's, Pete Townshend's and John Entwistle's emergence from their chrysalis as The Who. It is a punchy tale of gritty determination and ever-burning passion for music. As Pete Townshend writes in his moving Foreword, 'Doug Sandom's work with our band gave me the confidence to drive the band as a writer and creative thinker . . . '

DIANA ON THE EDGE

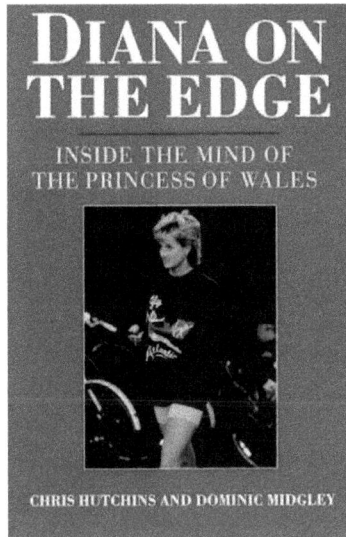

CHRIS HUTCHINS AND DOMINIC MIDGLEY

THIS IS THE BOOK which caused something of a sensation when it was first published since it delved into the mind of the Princess of Wales, one of the most controversial women on earth, during the latter years of her life.

Ostracised by the Royal Family after the breakdown of her marriage to Britain's next monarch, detached from her friends and tainted by stories of her romantic adventures, she was being pushed to the very limits of her endurance. Drawing on high-level sources – some of whom had never spoken before – and a team of distinguished specialists, this book examines her troubled mind. It probes the dark secrets at the root of her bulimia, the childhood traumas that cast a dark shadow over her adult love life, the pressures placed on her by the Palace hierarchy, the obsession with bodily perfection and the angry scenes she seemed unable to avoid. What drove Diana to the brink?

It's all told here.

www.ingramcontent.com/pod-product-compliance
Lightning Source LLC
Chambersburg PA
CBHW051906090426

42811CB00003B/479